FACTS STRANGER THAN FICTION

They say lightning never strikes twice. But it did in the case of Roy Cleveland Sullivan. He was struck by lightning seven times in his life and survived every time.

Eleven-year-old surfer Nick Christides was swept out to sea, and for the next four hours, he drifted helplessly in shark-infested waters. But he was saved by a friendly dolphin that circled him, and fended off would-be attackers until a rescue plane spotted him.

Defense Department physicist Robert Sarbacher has revealed the "most highly classified secret in the United States." The American government possesses the remains of crashed extraterrestrial ships and the bodies of alien beings.

CHARLES BERLITZ'S
WORLD OF STRANGE PHENOMENA
will make a world of difference in the way you think.

Also by Charles Berlitz:

ATLANTIS: The Eighth Continent*

NATIVE TONGUES

DOOMSDAY 1999 A.D.

THE PHILADELPHIA EXPERIMENT
(with Wm. Moore)*

WITHOUT A TRACE*

THE BERMUDA TRIANGLE

MYSTERIES FROM FORGOTTEN WORLDS

THE MYSTERY OF ATLANTIS

DIVE (revision)

THE LOST SHIP OF NOAH*

* Published by Fawcett Books

CHARLES BERLITZ'S WORLD OF STRANGE PHENOMENA

Charles Berlitz

FAWCETT CREST • NEW YORK

A Fawcett Crest Book
Published by Ballantine Books
 Published in the United States by Ballantine Books, a division of Random House, Inc., New York, and simultaneously in Canada by Random House of Canada Limited, Toronto.

Library of Congress Catalog Card Number: 88-17297

ISBN 0-449-21825-2

This edition published by arrangement with Wynwood Press

Manufactured in the United States of America

First Ballantine Books Edition: February 1990

Beneath the tides of time and space—
strange fish are swimming!

Contents

Foreword

The fascination that mystery exerts on the human mind has been the reason for the extension of our knowledge of the world around us and the development of modern science. Our continuing desire to solve the mysteries of space has pushed us toward exploration of our solar system, the stars and planets of our universe, and then to the other universes beyond.

During the last five hundred years we have nearly exhausted our exploration of the world's geographic mysteries. We have mapped or photographed most of the earth's surface, and, since the 1940s, have been able to record the approximate position of the mountains, gulfs, plains, and abysses on the sea bottom. Hunters and zoologists have alternately exterminated or catalogued most of the world's animal life, although the depths of the sea may have reserved some surprises. Modern and ancient man have been exhaustively studied and classified. Even remote and uncivilized populations have been made familiar to everyone via television, which itself only a few centuries ago would have been considered a breathtaking manifestation of magic.

In a world of computers, robots, guided missiles, space travel, manipulative genetics, and the first steps in the artificial creation of life, one wonders if there are any further mysteries to be solved, or, considering the dangers of the atomic age and the development of scientific warfare, whether there will be time to discover further secrets of the universe—before mankind is destroyed.

Certainly much still remains clouded in mystery. Even today, at the apogee of our scientific expertise, the mysteries of space, time, coincidence, paranormal manifestations, and exceptions to what we consider natural law remain elusive. As our search for the unknown has progressed, our formerly separate concepts of science and the paranormal have begun to merge. We now classify a whole range of paranormal potentialities.

The power of the human mind, for one thing, is proving to be much more powerful than previously thought. Quasi-physical manifestations of the mind now being extensively studied include telepathy, teleportation, telekinesis, and the ability to see what is happening in far places and in other times.

Ghosts are paranormal phenomena that have overstepped the boundaries of fiction and are making their way into serious scientific studies. What are ghosts? The Indians of the Amazon and the natives of New Guinea have no difficulty accepting the visual actuality of ghosts when they see films of tribesmen who they know have died. It is difficult to explain to them that the movie camera has reproduced scenes from the past. To them it is much more simple: The camera has captured the departed spirit. To ourselves, we can explain the camera; but how can we explain the multitude of "haunted" places—houses, castles, battlefields, and ships—so often reported in our modern scientific world? Do there exist residues of personalities or events that can be captured and reconstructed?

Thought transference through telepathy is on the verge of becoming an accepted theory. It is believed that animals, within the pack or herd, employ this ability for warnings and hunting, and it is probable that human beings made use of this faculty as well before they became civilized. Even now, cloaked in our veneer of civilization, we often experience moments of unlearned prescience, which seem to indicate that we possess some powers of telepathy. The power to foresee future events, however, is still a mystery, one that may be linked to the final secrets of space and time.

Are all future prophecies simply lucky guesses? Jules Verne, in writing of a trip to the moon by rocket 150 years before such an event happened, imagined and then described the length and shape of the rocket accurately. His fictional rocket missed the arrival time of the real rocket by only fourteen minutes.

Verne's prediction may have been just a lucky guess, but as

far as prescience in prophecy is concerned it is extremely difficult to discredit Nostradamus, who, during his lifetime in the sixteenth century, accurately foretold the duration of the not-yet-existent British Empire, details of the French Revolution two hundred years before it happened, the two World Wars of modern times, complete with air raids and city evacuations and a German Führer with the slightly garbled name of "Hister." Nostradamus foretold earthquakes on the west coast of the New World and even some of the most recent events in Libya and Iran.

We have no acceptable explanation for the accuracy of detailed prophecies from the far past. Time, as we understand it, is a road from the past to the future through the present. But perhaps it is a two-way street, a theory of some who believe that time, like space, may be circular.

Perhaps the most striking example of prophecy comes from ancient India, from descriptions in the *Mahabarata* and other records composed thousands of years ago. These books described projectiles that would burst with the force and heat of "ten thousand suns," obliterating the opposing army, sweeping war elephants, chariots, and men up into the vortex, destroying cities, poisoning food supplies, and forcing even the victorious soldiers to preserve themselves by washing their bodies, clothing, and equipment in rivers to avoid the fatal after-effects. These bombs whose explosions caused great "umbrellalike" clouds to spread out from the core were called "the Iron Thunderbolt[s]."

Coincidentally, when the ancient measurements and modern coordinates are compared, the findings indicate that the Iron Thunderbolt was a projectile of approximately the same shape and size as the atom bomb dropped on Hiroshima, marking the beginning of the end of World War II.

Not until 1945, when the first atom bomb was exploded in combat, were the descriptions in the *Mahabarata* considered anything but fervid dreams. And now that we have begun to consider the *Mahabarata* seriously, we must examine the possibility that these predictions were perhaps not visions of the future but of the past and that the writings referred to incidents of warfare that actually happened, perhaps over ten thousand years ago, between civilizations that no longer exist.

Perhaps the most inexplicable and mysterious incidents taking place in today's world purportedly occur in the night skies over the Earth. In the United States alone, it is estimated that more than 20 million persons claim to have seen unidentified flying objects (UFOs or OVNIs in Latin countries) and half of the total population believe in their reality.

Although objects in the skies have been seen since ancient times and have been randomly interpreted as divine lessons, signs, tests, and omens, UFO sighting has only gripped the general attention of the world's nations since 1947, when pilot Kenneth Arnold encountered and pursued a group of unknown objects spinning over the Cascade Mountains of Washington, which, he observed, resembled "flying saucers." It is notable that these unexpected visitors, have, from the first wave, been seen over the southwestern United States, especially in Arizona, at times that concurred with government experiments concerning the elemental forces of the universe, as if the occupants of the craft, whether from Earth or space, were especially interested in them.

Today UFOs receive worldwide notice and press coverage. They are reported by people all over the world and regularly over the Bermuda Triangle, which, because of its magnetic anomalies and sudden climatic aberrations, has been considered by some a cosmic gateway for visitors from space.

UFOs have been reported to be of different shapes, although they are usually said to be round. They have been observed and photographed from planes, merchant ships, and naval craft. They buzz planes and seem to interfere with tracking radar. They also seem to be capable of inconceivable speeds and are able to vanish at will.

Suppose they *are* real; why are they flying through the skies of Earth? Do they come for new materials, water, exploration, conquest, or, more altruistically, have they come to warn us about our blowing up our planet? (If this last is true, such a benign approach has rarely been evident in our own historical records of human invaders.)

Mankind is approaching maturity and is preparing to face mysteries not only concerned with the exploration of the earth but also with that of the solar system, the stars (and planets?) of the galaxy, and the universes beyond and the possible entities that we may meet there, as well as those which, in our airspace, appear to be investigating *us*.

The great mysteries of our time, those which affect us most deeply, do not deal, as in an earlier age, with the unknown parts of the Earth but with the cosmos, our planetary system, the galaxy, and the universe beyond. The mysteries of today also concern the human mind, its communicative powers, and even its physical powers, of which we are just beginning to be aware. We are becoming more serious in our study of such things as prescience, coincidence, dreams, reincarnation, inherited memories from ancestors, psychic manifestations, and UFOs. The witchcraft of former times is now the object of scientific inquiry.

We have long embarked on the study of life and how to prolong it, but now we are developing functional forms of invented life, namely robotics, and soon we may be able to create life itself, which the magicians of former centuries tried unsuccessfully to do. We are now able to control or destroy large sections of the Earth. But even the ancient magicians did not contemplate the destruction by man of the Earth itself.

To protect what we have and to further our capabilities, we still possess a potent shield—the largely untapped potential and the positive power of the human mind in its search for the solution to the mysteries that surround us.

Murdered and Reincarnated

Dr. Ian Stevenson is the world's foremost expert on reincarnation, a specialist in tracking down cases of children who seem to remember past lives. Particularly striking are those cases in which the child is born with birthmarks seemingly inherited from his or her past existence. One of his most dramatic cases is that of Ravi Shankar, who was born in Kanauj in Uttar Pradesh, India, in 1951.

From his earliest years, Ravi claimed that he was really the son of a man named Jageshwar, a barber who lived in a nearby district. He also claimed that he had been murdered. His present-life father did not believe a word and started beating him to make him stop talking such nonsense. The beatings did little to suppress Ravi's memories, and he became more obsessed with his past-life revivifications the older he grew. He even developed the strange delusion that his former murderers were still out to get him. While the entire story was fantastic, Ravi had, in fact, been born with a bizarre birthmark. It was a two-inch long serrated mark under his chin that resembled some sort of knife wound.

Ravi's memories and obsession were eventually traced to a murder that took place in the local region six months before his birth. On July 19, 1951, the young son of Jageshwar Prasad—a local barber—was murdered by two men, who decapitated him. The men, actually relatives, wanted to inherit the father's estate. Even though the murderers were taken into custody, they had to be released because of a legal technicality.

When Jageshwar Prasad learned of Ravi's claims, he decided to visit the Shankar family to check out the reports personally. The barber conversed with Ravi for an extended period of time and Ravi gradually recognized him as his former father. Ravi even offered him detailed information about his murder, information known only to Jageshwar and the police. And to this day, Ravi still shows that strange birthmark under his chin, a remnant of his past-life murder in India.

The Self-Propelled Coffin

Many critics contend that coincidence is nothing more than an artifact of human consciousness. Separate incidents simply float to the surface of our awareness, goes the argument, where they are noticed and turned into coincidences. In other words, we remember the so-called coincidence but forget a myriad of other occurrences that have no obvious connection.

What is one to make, then, of the curious coffin of Charles Coughlan? Coughlan was born in the Canadian province of Prince Edward Island, on the northeastern seaboard. But the end of the nineteenth century found him in Galveston, jewel of the Texas Gulf Coast, performing in a traveling actors' troupe for his daily bread. The year was 1899; Coughlan collapsed and died, perhaps from one of the tropical fevers rampant in the era before autopsies.

Coughlan was laid to what was supposed to be perpetual rest in a lead-lined coffin and buried in the community cemetery. Galveston itself, then Texas's most populous and prosperous city, was built on what amounted to a big sandbar, a precarious position that left it vulnerable to hurricane and high sea alike.

On September 8, 1900, hundred-mile-an-hour winds pushed a twenty-foot wall of water into the town, submerging all but the highest structures. The town was totally destroyed. Somewhere between six and eight thousand Galvestonians perished, drowned in their shoes, their bodies washed out to the open sea by the returning swell.

The dead were disturbed, too. The cemeteries were churned open by battering waves, coffins left their graves and floated away with the tide. For eight years, Coughlan's lead-encased corpse bobbed in the warm waters of the Gulf Stream. Eventually, it made its way around the tip of the Florida Keys and into the Atlantic, where the prevailing currents carried it north along the Carolinas and the New England coast.

In October 1908, a small fishing vessel off Prince Edward Island spotted the battered box awash in the tide. Attaching a grappling hook, the crew hauled it aboard. A copper nameplate revealed the weatherworn coffin's contents.

The coffin was washed ashore less than a mile from the small church were Coughlan had originally been christened. His remains were removed and buried again, right where his journey had started so many years and miles before.

Musical Mystery

Rosemary Brown, a London widow, owned a piano but was not very accomplished at playing it. She knew only one musician—a former church organist who was trying to teach her to play. The music world and the rest of London was hard-pressed to explain then, how, in 1964, she began writing pieces of music that seemed to come from the masters themselves.

Indeed, Brown was a self-proclaimed clairvoyant, whose mother and grandmother were also alleged to be psychic. She said that Franz Liszt, who had "visited" her once before in a vision when she was a child, appeared to her and began bringing music from the likes of Beethoven, Bach, Chopin and others. Each dictated his own music. Sometimes, she said, they controlled her hands, moving them to the proper keys; sometimes they only dictated the notes. But among the works she produced were the completion of Beethoven's Tenth and Eleventh Symphonies, which had been incomplete at the time of his death; a forty-page sonata by Schubert; and numerous works by Liszt and the others.

Musicians and psychologists alike examined the material and investigated every line of music and every line of Brown's testimony. Although some music critics dismissed the work as copied, and not copied well, others were amazed at the quality of the work. All agreed that each piece she produced was definitely written in the style of the composer to which it was attributed. No one has found evidence that she was lying, and most investigators pronounced her to be sincere. Quality music or not, it was music well beyond Brown's capability.

Liszt, however, had failed Brown in one respect. In his final visit to her, the clairvoyant claimed, Liszt had promised to make her a great musician one day. Yet she remained an unaccomplished pianist. Perhaps that is why, Mrs. Brown's story goes, the composers, who dictated to her in English, would often raise their hands and yell "Mein Gott!"

I Came Back for My Dog

Joe Benson of Wendover, Utah, was a spiritual leader of the Goshute Indians. His constant companion was a magnificent German shepherd he called Sky.

As Benson grew old and his vision failed, Sky guarded his steps and kept him from harm. Benson's health continued to decline and one day in late 1962 he told his wife Mable that he was about to die. She notified the relatives and soon they and their children had come to his bedside. But because they no longer followed the Indian traditions, they insisted that he be taken to the hospital in nearby Owyhee, Nevada. They ignored his protests and Sky's deep-throated growls and carried him away.

Benson stayed at the hospital for only a short time. When the doctors saw there was nothing to be done, they sent him back home, where soon afterwards, in January 1963, he died.

After the funeral ceremonies several of the mourners asked if they could have Sky. Mrs. Benson, who saw that the dog seemed to be grieving even more than she was, sensed that this would be wrong, so she kept him.

Ten days later she happened to look out the window to see someone coming up the road to the house. She built a fire in the cookstove and put on some fresh coffee. When she looked up, she saw someone she recognized in the doorway: her late husband.

True to her people's traditions, she gently told him he was

dead and had no business in this world. Joe Benson nodded and said only, "I am going. I came back for my dog."

He whistled and Sky, his tail wagging furiously, came running into the kitchen.

"I want his leash," Benson said. His wife took it down from a hook on the wall and handed it to him, taking care not to touch him. He snapped the leash on Sky's collar and the old man and his dog went out the door, down the steps, and on to the path that wound around the hill.

After hesitating for a few moments, Mrs. Benson ran outside to the other side of the hill. Joe and Sky were nowhere to be seen.

As it happened, Joe and Mable's next-door neighbor, their daughter Arvilla Benson Urban, witnessed this strange visitation and swore to it in an affidavit. She said, "I saw my father enter the house and not more than a few minutes later I saw him leave with his dog on a leash. I saw my mother go after him and I, after I could think, went after her.

"When I reached the top of the hill, my father and his dog were gone."

For the next several days the young men of the family searched for the dog without success. It appeared that Sky had vanished, with his beloved master, into another world.

A Vengeful Ghost

The strange story began on February 21, 1977, when the body of Teresita Basa was found by police. The forty-eight-year-old woman was lying on the floor of her high-rise Chicago apartment, stabbed to death and partially burned.

Like so many other hopeful immigrants, Basa had come to

the United States from the Philippines seeking employment and a better quality of life. She had been working as a respiratory therapist at Edgewater Hospital, and the police didn't have a clue toward solving the crime. Their initial impression was that perhaps she had been killed by a boyfriend. The real solution to the case, however, would eventually come from Basa's ghost.

Dr. José Chua and his wife also worked at the hospital, though they hadn't been particularly close to Teresita. But one evening while home together in Skokie, a small city just outside Chicago, Mrs. Chua unexpectedly entered a strange sort of trance. She got up and walked into the bedroom, where she lay down. Then a strange voice, speaking in Tagalog (a Philippine language) issued from her mouth: "I am Teresita Basa." After the strange voice accused a hospital orderly of the murder, Mrs. Chua emerged from the spell. But she suffered similar spells during the next several days, declaring in the murdered woman's voice, that the orderly, a black youth named Allen Showery, had taken her jewelry and given her pearl cocktail ring to his common-law wife.

Dr. Chua, terrified by the claims, was left with no alternative but to contact the local police. His call was turned over to Joseph Stachula and Lee Epplen, two veteran detectives.

The detectives were naturally skeptical of Dr. Chua's story, but with no other leads in the case, decided to follow it up. When they met with the Chuas, they questioned them minutely about the deceased Teresita Basa's claims. They especially asked the couple if Teresita claimed that she was raped as well as murdered. No rape had actually taken place and the detectives asked this question to see if the couple would follow the spurious lead. But the Chuas didn't take the bait. The investigators were also impressed by how much the Chuas seemed to know about the murder.

"To this day," Detective Stachula wrote some time later, "I'm not quite sure that I believe how the information was obtained. Nonetheless, everything [was] completely true."

Working with these clues, the Evanston police searched Showery's apartment and found Teresita's jewels. They even found her pearl cocktail ring in the possession of his girlfriend.

When confronted with the evidence, Showery confessed to the murder and was later convicted of the crime. The case was officially closed in August, apparently solved by the ghost of Teresita.

The Slow but Sure Bullet

Henry Ziegland of Honey Grove, Texas, walked out on his girlfriend one day in 1893. Her brother did his "heroïc" duty and shot Ziegland. Ziegland, however, was barely injured by the bullet, which only left a small scar on his face before embedding itself in the trunk of the tree in front of which Ziegland was standing. The brother, thinking himself avenged, ended his own life with the same weapon.

Twenty years later, in 1913, Ziegland decided to remove the tree from his property. Unable to perform the task manually, he decided to use dynamite. In the explosion, the bullet, which had originally been intended for Ziegland, became dislodged with such a catapulting jolt that it was shot violently into Ziegland's head, killing him at last.

The Strange Moons of Mars

It was not until 1877 that the astronomer Asaph Hall, while observing the night sky through instruments, first saw two moons circling Mars, moons that no other astronomers had previously reported seeing.

But Jonathan Swift, the author of the pre-science fiction fantasy *Gulliver's Travels*, wrote about them long before Hall, even nonchalantly giving their proportions and orbits. But this was in a fictional narrative, written in 1726, some 151 years before Asaph Hall "officially" discovered them.

Swift wrote of "two lesser stars or satellites, which revolve about Mars. The innermost is distant from the center of the primary planet exactly three of its diameters, and the outermost five; the former revolves in the space of ten hours, and the latter in twenty-one and a half."

How did Swift know? Had he read about it somewhere in some ancient commentary unknown to science or literature? Or if he imagined it, how did he get it right? He never said.

The moons are now an accepted truth of astronomy. Asaph Hall, in a graceful tribute to antiquity, called them Phoebus (Terror) and Deimos (Rout), which were the ancient names of the *horses* of Mars, the god of war, for whom the red planet was named several thousand years ago.

But an even greater mystery, suggested by the form and eccentric behavior of the moons, is yet to be solved. It has been theorized by some observers that they may be controlled or artificial space stations. This question may be cleared up within the next few years, if space exploration continues its rate of development.

James Chaffin's Second Will

James L. Chaffin was a North Carolina farmer who died in 1921. His family was no doubt surprised and depressed when they learned the terms of his will. The elderly man left his entire property to his third son Marshall, disinheriting his wife and three other sons completely. The will had been written and properly witnessed in 1905.

Four years later, however, son James P. Chaffin began dreaming that his deceased father wanted to talk to him. He would see the farmer by his bedside, dressed in his old black overcoat; and one day the figure finally said, "You will find my will in my overcoat pocket," and disappeared.

Chaffin was puzzled by the experience, but felt that he should check out the ghost's strange claim. It turned out that the overcoat was in the possession of another brother, so he made the trip to his brother's residence where he found the coat and ripped open its seams. There, hidden in the lining of a pocket, was a piece of paper upon which was written, "Read the twenty-seventh chapter of Genesis." Chaffin realized he was onto something, and so he went to his mother's house accompanied by several witnesses—to whom he eagerly told his story. The Bible wasn't easily found but eventually turned up. The book was so dilapidated that it fell to the floor in three pieces when handled. Thomas Blackwelder was one of the witnesses, and he picked up the portion of the Bible containing the Book of Genesis. He immediately discovered that two pages had been folded together to make a pocket. When he opened it, the surprised witnesses found a handwritten will dated 1919. It appeared that the deceased farmer had reconsidered, for this new document stated in part, "I want, after giving my body a decent burial, my little property equally divided between my four children, if they are living at my death, and the personal and real estate divided equal and if not living, give share to their children. And if she is living, you must take care of your mammy. Now this is my last will and testament."

By this time, Marshall Chaffin had died and his property was controlled by his widow, so James P. Chaffin took the will to court. Several witnesses testified that the 1919 will was truly in the handwriting of the deceased farmer. Marshall's widow didn't try to fight the case and the small estate was properly redistributed.

Occupants of a Different Kind

UFO occupants commonly fall into two broad, but distinct categories—extraterrestrial beings virtually indistinguishable from humans in appearance and size, and "humanoid" entities that are typically gray-skinned, thin-limbed and short, with large fetal heads and dark, wrap-around eyes.

But there may be a third category as well. Consider the bizarre beings seen near a Kelly, Kentucky, farmhouse the night of August 21, 1955, by eight adults and three children. This scary episode began when the house's owner, Billy Ray Taylor, rushed inside saying he had seen a flying saucer with a rainbow-colored exhaust land in a nearby forty-foot deep gully. The others laughed at first. Then the dog began barking.

Taylor and Lucky Sutton went to the back door, where they watched in awe as a hideously strange, glowing figure approached across the fields. Only three-and-a-half feet tall, the silvery entity supported a bulbous head with huge, flared ears and long arms ending in sharp talons reaching nearly to the ground. Sutton and Taylor both grabbed guns and fired, knocking the creature backwards, head over heels. Instead of falling to the ground, however, it scurried away.

Back in the living room a few minutes later, the men said they saw a similar creature and fired again. Apparently, they were now under siege, for when Taylor walked out onto the front porch to survey the damage, another one of the entities clawed at him from the roof.

Shortly before midnight, both families piled into two cars and hurtled into nearby Hopkinsville. The police returned to the farmhouse, but could not substantiate the story. One of the searchers stepped on a cat's tail in the dark, however, and nearly ignited a fatal panic. Finally, around 2 A.M., the police left.

The creatures came back once more, the group claims. But when the sun finally came up, they were gone for good.

We Interrupt This Program for a Special Premonition

Disasters are sometimes preceded by visions, dreams, or nightmares that foretell the event. Most of these premonitions come during sleep, but Mrs. Lesley Brennan's incredible vision came over the telly, as it is called in England.

On the morning of Saturday, June 1, 1974, the movie she was watching was interrupted by a special bulletin announcing that an explosion had ripped through the Flixborough Nypro plant, a nearby chemical plant that produced materials used in nylon, and that several people had died. About noon that day, two friends paid her a visit, and she asked them if they had heard about the accident. They hadn't.

And neither had anybody else, because the explosion actually took place at 4:53 P.M. The death toll was twenty-eight, and many were injured. When they heard later newscasts about the explosion, the three women at first thought the newscasters were stating the details incorrectly. But a check of the paper the next day showed the actual time of the explosion.

Brennan could offer no explanation. Perhaps she had fallen asleep and actually dreamed the telecast. Whatever happened, she had relayed the story of the event to two friends almost five hours before it actually occurred.

A Human Lightning Rod

Roy Cleveland Sullivan, a retired forest ranger from Waynesboro, Virginia, was known as the Human Lightning Rod because he had been struck by lightning *seven* times in the course of his thirty-six-year career.

The first strike, in 1942, caused the loss of a big toenail. Twenty-seven years later a second bolt of lightning burned his eyebrows off. The following year, in 1970, a third bolt seared his left shoulder.

After Sullivan's hair was set afire by a fourth strike in 1972, he began hauling a bucket of water around with him in his car. He was driving on August 7, 1973, as a bolt came out of a small, low-lying cloud, hit him on the head through his hat, set his hair on fire again, knocked him ten feet out of his car, went through both legs and knocked his shoe off. Sullivan poured the bucket of water over his head to cool off.

Sullivan was struck for the sixth time on June 5, 1976, hurting his ankle. The seventh blow from above hit Sullivan on June 25, 1977, while he was fishing. He required hospitalization for stomach and chest burns on that occasion.

Though he was never able to explain his peculiar attraction for lightning, Sullivan once said that he could actually see the bolts as they headed for him.

At 3 A.M. on the morning of September 28, 1983, Sullivan, aged seventy-one, took his own life with a bullet. Two of his Ranger hats, burned through the crown by lightning blasts, now reside in Guinness World Exhibit Halls in New York City and Myrtle Beach, South Carolina.

A Chilling Escape

The winter of 1984-85 set numerous cold-wave records across the continental United States from Michigan to Texas. It also saw one of the most remarkable survivals in the annals of modern medicine.

By the morning of January 19, 1985, the temperature in Milwaukee, Wisconsin, had dropped to a bone-numbing sixty degrees below zero. While his parents slept, two-year-old Michael Troche, dressed in light pajamas, wandered outside into the snow.

Found by his frantic father several hours later, Michael had quite literally frozen stiff. He had stopped breathing; ice crystals had formed both on and beneath his skin; and his limbs were rigid as sticks.

Rushed to Milwaukee's Children's Hospital, Michael was treated by a team of twenty nurses and eighteen doctors, including Dr. Kevin Kelly, a specialist in hypothermia. When Michael arrived at the hospital, Kelly pronounced him "dead, extremely dead." Physicians could actually hear his poor, frozen body cracking as they lifted it on to the operating table. And Michael's inner core temperature had fallen to sixteen degrees Centigrade; a precipice from which no one had ever returned alive.

The team set to work immediately, hooking Michael up to a heart-lung machine to warm his blood, injecting drugs to prevent his brain from swelling, thawing his body, and making incisions along his limbs as tissue filled with water from frozen cells and threatened to burst.

For three days the boy lay in a semiconscious state, hovering between life and death. Then, miraculously, Michael recovered almost as quickly as he had been frozen. He suffered some minor muscle damage to one hand and had to undergo skin grafts to patch the long incisions made in his arms and legs, but other than that was remarkably unaffected by his ordeal.

And at last report, the amazing Michael Troche failed to display any evidence of the feared brain damage that would have turned him into a vegetable. Ironically, doctors said he probably survived *because* he was so young and small; he had literally been flash-frozen by the wind-chill factor. His tiny brain and reduced metabolism required little oxygen to operate. A little older and larger, and Michael would have been another winter statistic.

Target: Tunguska!

Shortly after sunrise on June 30, 1908, something from space struck central Soviet Siberia. The eruption, detected on seismographs as far away as the United States and central Europe, was one of the largest explosions the world has ever known. For weeks afterwards, dust and debris thrown up by the gigantic conflagration colored skies and sunsets around the globe. Magnets were affected throughout the world at the moment of impact and horses stumbled and fell in cities thousands of miles distant.

The immediate area, that of the stony Tunguska River basin, was largely devastated. Acres of permafrost instantly turned to steam. Trees were flattened for twenty-five miles, and at ground zero their trunks were sheared of limbs and bark. The forest itself burst into flames. Herds of animals and a few scattered human settlements were incinerated where they stood. The Tungus tribesmen who returned home "found only charred corpses." That night in Europe no night fell. In London a paper could be read at midnight; in Holland pictures could be taken of ships sailing the Zuider Zee.

Because of Tunguska's remoteness, the first scientific investigator did not arrive at the scene of the tragedy until Dr. Leonid A. Kulik, a meteorite specialist from Petrograd, led an expedition there in 1927. Sixty years later the origin of the gigantic Tunguska explosion is still hotly debated.

Was it a wayward comet? A tiny mass of anti-matter that hit and possibly passed *through* the Earth? Or the nuclear generator of a crippled spaceship, swerving to miss the Earth's population centers? Each theory has its proponents and its problems. Some witnesses interviewed by Kulik and later investigators reported a fiery ball trailing a tail, an image conceivably consistent with either a meteorite or comet. But if the Tunguska object was a meteorite, what happened to the crater, and more importantly, the meteorite itself? None was found. And if it was a comet, why was it not seen sooner on approach? Moreover, since comets are mostly gaseous, "dirty snowballs," where did the immense energy, estimated at thirty megatons, come *from*?

Particle physicists have long prophesied the presence of what they call anti-matter, mirror images of ordinary matter, but negatively charged. Anti-matter as we know it, however, is extremely short-lived. A small body of anti-matter coming into contact with normal matter would indeed result in a sudden, tremendous release of energy. Unfortunately for the hypothesis, no one expects to find lumps of anti-matter floating through this part of the universe.

The Tunguska event *could* have been caused by an extraterrestrial spaceship, but again the evidence is largely inconclusive. Some Soviet researchers have found anomalous radioactivity readings at the devastated site, others have not detected any. A craft would also have to have been completely vaporized in the explosion, because no unusual metal fragments were ever found.

The Bleeding Walls

Atlanta homicide detectives are accustomed to blood. It comes with the territory, along with shot, stabbed and battered bodies. But they weren't prepared for blood *without* a body, especially blood that poured from walls and pooled on the floors of an elderly Georgia couple, William Winston, seventy-nine, and wife Minnie, seventy-seven.

Minnie Winston first noticed the blood spouting from the

bathroom floor "like a sprinkler," when she went to take a bath in their three-bedroom brick house of twenty-two years in September of 1987. The couple called the police shortly after midnight on the ninth, when they found more blood oozing from walls and floors in five separate rooms.

"I'm not bleeding," said William Winston. "My wife's not bleeding. And no one else is here." Winston had gone to bed about 9:30 that evening, after locking the doors and activating a security alarm system. Neither of the Winstons heard any intruders, nor did the alarm go off.

Steve Cartwright, an Atlanta homicide detective, admitted the police found "copious amounts of blood" splattered throughout the house, but no corpse, animal or human, that would have accounted for it. The Georgia State Crime Laboratory confirmed the blood as human the following day.

Cal Jackson, Atlanta police spokesman, said the department was treating the incident "as an unusual circumstance because we don't have a body or a cause for the blood."

Spontaneous Human Combustion

Some people say the kitchen is the deadliest room in the house. But on January 8, 1985, seventeen-year-old Jacqueline Fitzsimons, a cookery student at Halton Technical College in Widnes, Cheshire, England, had left the kitchen and was talking to classmates in the corridor when she abruptly burst into flames.

Jacqueline first complained of a burning sensation in her back while talking to a girlfriend, Karen Glenholmes. "Suddenly,

Jacqueline said she did not feel well,'' Karen said. ''There was a smell of smouldering and we saw her shirt burning. She screamed to us for help and said she was burning all over. In a moment even her hair was on fire.''

Staff members and other students in the hallway ripped away Jacqueline's apron, then beat her burning clothing in an effort to stifle the flames. She was then rushed to hospital, where the devastating damage of her injuries became evident: 18 percent of her skin was burned away. After fifteen days in intensive care, she died.

Cheshire fire prevention officer Bert Gilles admitted he was as baffled as anyone. ''I have interviewed seven eyewitnesses,'' he said. ''So far, there is no clear explanation of the fire, though spontaneous combustion is a possibility that should be examined.''

A jury in the subsequent coroner's inquest later ruled that Jacqueline Fitzsimons had died of ''misadventure,'' which was certainly true enough.

Cosmic Nemesis

Sixty-five million years ago the dinosaurs disappeared from the earth in the comparative twinkling of a geological eye. Some 165 million years before that, the dinosaurs had been the ruling species of the land, sea, and air.

Paleontologists have long pondered their disappearance, proposing abrupt changes in the earth's climate as the most likely suspect. But what caused those catastrophic changes in the first place? A gradual alteration of the atmosphere or environment should have allowed the dinosaurs ample time to adapt.

The first clue of a cosmic culprit came from the collaboration of a scientific father-and-son team at the University of California Berkeley campus. Geologist Walter Alvarez had been studying deposits near Gubbio, Italy, in 1977, when he discovered a layer of sediment rich in the rare element iridium, not usually found in the Earth's crust. His father, Luis Alvarez, a Nobel laureate in physics, suggested an explanation: A huge, extraterrestrial object, perhaps a comet or asteroid, could have struck the Earth and thrown up a massive amount of debris, raining down a layer of iridium. Fossils in the clay in which the younger Alvarez found iridium dated the deposit to 65 million years ago, the exact time of the great dinosaur extinction.

Other mass extinctions, moreover, seem to occur periodically every 26 million years, give or take a few thousand millennia. Could some recurring cosmic cycle account for such widespread extinctions, including the one that wiped out Tyrannosaurus Rex and his kin?

Some scientists think so. In 1984, Berkeley astrophysicist Richard Muller and astronomer Marc Davis, along with another astronomer, Piet Hut, of Princeton's Institute for Advance Study, proposed the existence of a solar companion known as the Death Star, or Nemesis, circling our sun every 26 or 30 million years. As it nears the solar system, Nemesis' gravitational field might dislodge asteroids in their orbit or drag comets in its wake, sending them crashing into the Earth's surface.

If real, our sun and Nemesis would be bound together in a binary system. In fact, most stars in our galaxy *are* binary, but none are known to have such long periods of revolution. Their orbits are usually measured in weeks or months. Moreover, any such companion star should be readily visible. Muller believes Nemesis may be a small red star, which would render it much harder to detect. Longer periods of revolution among binary systems might be common, too, says Muller. We just haven't recognized them for what they are *because* of their extreme orbits.

A team of astronomers led by Muller has already eliminated all but three thousand candidate stars visible from the Northern Hemisphere. If Nemesis is not found among those, says Muller, they will turn their attention toward Southern Hemisphere stars.

We needn't worry about the Death Star sneaking up on us in

the meantime. Present calculations put Nemesis at the far side of its orbit, meaning it won't return for another 10 to 13 million years.

Firestarter

Nothing is more terrifying than a fire on the rampage, especially if—in the true tradition of Stephen King's *Firestarter*—the arsonist lurks subconsciously within the mind. That's the problem the Willey family faced on their Macomb, Illinois, farm in 1948. Mr. Willey operated the farm with his brother-in-law and two children. Rounding out the household was his little niece Wanet. Nothing seemed out-of-the-ordinary there until curious brown spots began appearing on the wallpaper in the house. These spots would become incredibly hot, often reaching 450 degrees Fahrenheit before breaking into flames. The fires were so frequent that the Willeys' neighbors would stay in the house with buckets filled with water, waiting to douse each fire as it erupted. Several of these blazes broke out each day.

Nobody could figure out the cause of the blazes, not even the local fire department. "The whole thing is so screwy and fantastic that I'm almost ashamed to talk about it," admitted local fire chief Fred Wilson to reporters.

As the days rolled by, the fires became more frequent and bizarre. Soon they began to blaze from the porch, curtains, and other places in the house. And explanations began flying about. Representatives from a nearby Air Force base thought that high-frequency radio waves were causing the problem, while fire officials suggested that combustible gas was building up in the farmhouse walls. Despite these clever explanations, no practical answer to the Willeys' problem emerged.

Finally, after witnessing the fires for days, the tired and frustrated fire department badgered a confession from little Wanet. She had started the fires, the department told news reporters, by flicking lighted matches when no one was looking.

Nobody believed that explanation. The best evaluation came from Vincent Gaddis, who studied the case in 1962. Writing in his book *Mysterious Lights and Fires*, he stated that little Wanet must have had "incredible persistence, an unlimited supply of matches, and exceptionally nearsighted relatives and neighbors." In other words, like the heroine of *Firestarter*, he suggested she might have caused the fires through paranormal means, in a way far beyond the comprehension of the local officials.

Life at Stake

Humans have at one time or another survived almost every catastrophe imaginable, from falling out of an airplane without a parachute to impalement by an assortment of sharp instruments. Among the latter category consider the case of English motorcyclist Richard Topps, twenty-one, of Derbyshire, who survived an unwanted encounter with a fence post.

In August of 1985, Topps's motorcycle was involved in a collision with a car, seriously injuring his passenger. Richard himself hurled over the handlebars and into a fence, where he was impaled diagonally from chest to hip on a wooden post four feet long.

Because of the confusion Richard was left hanging for more than an hour, completely conscious but unable to help himself, until he was found by his brother. To free the stake piercing his torso required a two-hour operation, during which surgeons found that all his internal vital organs had escaped damage. Topps quickly recuperated from the surgery and went his way.

Eighteen-year-old Kimberly Lotti of Quincy, Massachusetts, suffered a similar impalement in December 1983 while driving her pickup home from work, and also lived to talk about it. Her truck swerved and cut into a chain-link aluminum fence. One of the two-inch diameter poles broke loose and shattered her windshield, passing all the way through her left upper chest.

"It was eerie," Kimberly said later. "I didn't feel any pain at all. I thought the pipe was just pressing against my arm. I guess I was in shock."

Rescue workers cut the pipe off about five inches from the front and back of her body and hauled her to the hospital, where the rest of the aluminum stake was safely removed.

Lady in Blue

The canon of Catholic miracles bulges with documented historical reports that are of peculiar interest to parapsychologists. For sheer quantity, however, few spiritual careers can match that of the humble Lady in Blue, Suor María Coronel de Agreda. By her own account Suor María bilocated, or appeared in two places at the same time, on some five hundred occasions between the years of 1620 and 1631.

Born in Spain in 1602 to a religious middle-class family, Suor María experienced intense visions while still a child. As a teenager she lapsed easily into ecstatic trances. As a young woman she joined the Franciscan convent of the Immaculate Conception at Agreda.

There she opted for a self-imposed regimen that included long periods of fasting, sleeplessness, and self-flagellation. Among the miracles attributed to her during this time was the uncanny ability to respond to the unspoken thoughts of others and to levitate her frail body above the convent floor.

But it was for her astounding facility of bilocation that Suor María is known. Her ghostly projections, it is said, hurled her across the Atlantic Ocean and into the desert environment of seventeenth-century west Texas, where she ministered to the physical and spiritual needs of a red-skinned, nearly naked people.

Of all the native Indian tribes that inhabited the American Southwest before the coming of the conquistadors, the least is known about the poor Jumanos, who lived along the Rio Grande River near what is modern-day Presidio, Texas. Early in the Spanish migration from Mexico they were encountered by Father Alonzo de Benavides, a Franciscan priest. To his great surprise, he found the mostly hunting-and-gathering Jumanos already converted to Christianity. What's more, they claimed that they had been directed to the meeting by a mysterious "woman in blue," the same gentle soul who had given them rosaries, nursed their wounds, and originally introduced them to the message of Jesus Christ.

Almost as perturbed as he was startled, Father Benavides fired off letters to both Pope Urban VIII and King Philip IV of Spain, demanding to know who had preceded him in his ministry. He did not receive an answer until 1630, on his own return to Spain, when he heard of Suor María's miracles, visited her convent in person, and learned that the habit of her order was blue.

Inside a Tornado

Nature presents numerous violent spectacles, but few compare with the destructiveness and intensity of the tornado, in which centrifugal winds can reach two hundred miles per hour.

Despite a plethora of still and video pictures of tornadoes, however, upclose eyewitness accounts are scarce. But an extremely rare observation of the *interior* of a tornado comes from a storm that blew through McKinney, Texas, north of Dallas, on May 3, 1943. "The bottom of the rim was about twenty feet off the ground," said a startled Roy Hall, whose house the tornado had just destroyed. "The interior of the funnel was hollow; the rim itself appeared to be not over ten feet in thickness and, owing possibly to the light within the funnel, appeared perfectly opaque. Its inside was so slick and even that it resembled the interior of a glazed pipe." The outer rim rotated in front of Hall's eyes with dazzling rapidity.

"I lay back on my left elbow, to afford the baby better protection, and looked up," he continued. "It is possible that in that upward glance my stricken eyes beheld something few have ever seen before and lived to tell about. I was looking far up the interior of a great tornado funnel.

"It extended upward for over a thousand feet, and was swaying gently, bending slowly toward the southeast. Down at the bottom the funnel was about one hundred and fifty yards across. Higher up it was larger, and seemed to be partly filled with a bright cloud, which shimmered like a fluorescent light. This brilliant cloud was in the middle of the funnel, not touching the sides."

Only one other account of the inside of a tornado is known, and that comes from a Greensburg, Kansas, farmer, Will Keller, who watched in awe as one of the terrible twisters skipped over the storm shelter in which he stood on June 22, 1928. The surrounding air, said Keller, was as still as death. The interior of his tornado was lit up, with lightning crackling from side to side. From the ragged rim at the bottom of the funnel, smaller tornadoes formed and whirled away, like an aerial Moby Dick giving birth to a litter of baby whales. The interior also contained a solitary cloud like the one Hall witnessed.

Neither man had anything to gain from fabrication. If true, however, their stories should result in a revision of what we know about tornadoes, particularly since present theory fails to account for such a complicated internal structure, especially one containing clouds and lightning.

A UFO at Socorro

The afternoon of April 24, 1964, found police officer Lonnie Zamora of Socorro, New Mexico, behind the wheel of his white Pontiac patrol car. A black Chevrolet whizzed past the small town courthouse and Zamora took off in chase. Instead of issuing a simple speeding ticket, the five-year veteran policeman took a detour through the Twilight Zone.

He was heading south on Old Rodeo Street in hot pursuit of the offender, when he "heard a roar and saw a flame in the sky to the southwest some distance away." Now outside the city limits, Zamora turned off paved streets onto a rough gravel road leading into the hills and toward the roaring flame.

Zamora slid and swerved up the steep hill. Then he "suddenly noted a shiny type object to the south about one hundred fifty to two hundred yards away." At the bottom of an arroyo, Zamora saw what he first thought was an overturned car "standing on radiator or on trunk." Beside it were "two people in white coveralls. One of these persons seemed to turn and look straight at my car."

Hoping to help, Zamora drove ahead, radioing headquarters about a possible accident. But when he heard the loud roar again, he dove for cover behind his car, knocking his glasses off in the process. Zamora said he could now see that the oval-shaped object was not an automobile at all, but an aluminum-white craft balanced on four landing legs. Its surface was smooth, with no visible doors or windows. Centered on one side was a red insignia, a bisected triangle two-and-a-half feet high and two feet wide. The thing rose out of the arroyo on a tail of fire, Zamora said, as the roar turned to a high-pitched whine.

When he went back to investigate the sighting sometime later, Zamora found some charred greasewood bushes and, more importantly, four podmarks indicating, he believed, the spot where the thing had landed.

Zamora's sighting was later investigated by several military and government officials, including Dr. J. Allen Hynek, then an astronomy consultant for the Air Force's Project Blue Book (a compendium of UFO sightings). Hynek tried to char the bushes with matches and create podlike impressions with a shovel, but found he couldn't satisfactorily reproduce the physical evidence himself. He also interviewed Zamora's old schoolteacher and a number of townsfolk, concluding that Zamora was a "solid, unimaginative cop."

The landing at Socorro, Hynek maintained until the day he died, was one of the most compelling pieces of evidence ever to fit into the puzzle of UFOs. Even more skeptical colleagues at Blue Book were swayed; some Air Force personnel spent years trying to prove Zamora's experience was the result of a secret government weapon gone dangerously awry.

Tucson's Rock-Throwing Phantom

A nightmare began for Mr. and Mrs. Berkbigler and their five children early in September, 1983. They had just moved into their large, but only half-finished desert home when large rocks started smashing into the structure every night. The rocks seemed to come out of nowhere and even the police couldn't find who was responsible. In short, the Berkbiglers were suffering from a rock-throwing poltergeist, a particularly bothersome sort of spook that likes to pelt houses with stones. The family members invariably ran outside to catch the culprit responsible, but there was never anyone in sight. The attacks would usually start between 5:30 and 7:00 P.M. when the family arrived home from their jobs or school. The stones would come in brief flurries and then stop, only to resume. Sometimes the family heard a mysterious knocking on the doors and windows as well.

The Berkbiglers originally felt that a vagrant was responsible for the mischief, but Mrs. Berkbigler was less sure of the cause. "Maybe it's a spirit," she finally told reporters from the *Arizona Daily Star*. "Maybe we've built over some sacred burial grounds or something."

Soon the local press was calling the Berkbigler's problem the "phantom stone-thrower." During the following weeks, the local sheriff's department visited the house and called in helicopter surveillance to solve the mystery. They ended up being struck by the rocks themselves, often in broad daylight, and became reluctant to visit the property.

The most frightening episode of the case occurred on Sunday,

December 4. The rocks had been active but sporadic all that day, so two reporters from the *Star* visited the house to interview the family. By 6:10 that evening, rocks were being hurled against the side door of the house with such viciousness that the reporters couldn't leave. The siege lasted for two hours until the family finally called in the police, who escorted the reporters away.

What was so bizarre was that, to hit the side door, the rocks had to travel through the house's open garage. Since a van was parked there that evening, the rocks had to be thrown with uncanny accuracy through a slim, two-foot opening between the garage's ceiling and the roof of the van. Yet the phantom stone-thrower accomplished this superhuman feat without any difficulty.

The case came to its climax on December 6 and 7, when scores of people began showing up at the house to help the family trap the culprit. Despite the constant patrols of the property, the rocks were thrown as usual, picking off people in the pitch black desert with astonishing skill. The self-styled posse succeeded in chasing an intruder from the property, but he turned out to be from the sheriff's office.

But then the rock-throwing simply stopped. The daily sieges ended after the second night of the search, and the case of Tucson's mysterious stone-thrower was left unsolved. It remains so to this day.

From Dream to Reality

One of the worst disasters in aviation history struck Chicago's O'Hare Airport on May 25, 1979. That was the terrible day an American Airlines DC-10 crashed on take-off, killing all of its crew and passengers. The accident stunned the entire country, but came as little surprise to a middle-aged manager in Cincinnati, Ohio. Beginning on May 16, Dave Booth, who worked with a car rental agency, had dreamt of a terrible airline crash every night.

"The dream would start," he later stated in writing, "with me looking out onto a field from the corner of a one-story building. The building was made of yellow tile bricks and had a gravel roof. The windows facing the field appeared to have paper cutouts pasted in. The impression I received of the building was that it was a school. However, I also associated a factory of some kind with the building. Behind the building was a gravel parking lot with a driveway coming around in front of the building then going back around to the main road behind me. As I'm looking out over the field I see a tree line running from northwest to southeast. All the trees and the grass are green. It is afternoon because the sun is in the west and it is setting, as opposed to rising. Looking over the tree line in a northeasterly direction I see this big airplane in the air. The first impression I get is that for being so close to the airplane it should be making a whole lot more noise than it is making. I keep sensing that something is wrong with the engine. The plane then starts to bank off to the right in an easterly direction, the left wing is going up in the air, very slowly, not in slow motion, the plane rolls over on its back and goes straight down into the ground. As I see the plane hit, it is as though I'm looking at the plane from straight ahead, not a side or rear view of the plane. When the plane hits the ground, there is a huge explosion. I can't think of any words to describe the explosion except that it was awesome. . . . As the sound of the explosion is dying out, I would wake up. The airplane I saw was an American Airlines three-engine jet."

This disaster struck nine days after Booth's dreams began, when an American Airlines DC-10 crashed after taking off at 3:03 P.M. in Chicago. The plane lost an engine just after takeoff, then lost altitude and crashed into an abandoned airport adjacent to O'Hare. Bystanders reported the plane's uncanny silence, as though its remaining engines had failed. The plane also rotated perpendicularly to the ground and hit with its left wing first.

Next it struck a hangar and exploded, billowing flames 400 feet into the sky.

Luckily, evidence for Mr. Booth's prediction doesn't rest solely on his personal word. When the dreams began recurring, he became so upset that he contacted both American Airlines and the Cincinnati Aviation Administration. They didn't know what to make of his call, so Booth next called the FAA, where representatives took detailed notes of his call and dreams. Their detailed notes were turned over to the Institute for Parapsychology in Durham, North Carolina, where researchers investigated the case.

Booth's disturbing dreams ended on the day of the crash.

Some Dramatic Deaths

The Greek playwright Aeschylus is known as the Father of Tragedy. History so honored him because of his plays, but the same honorific might equally have been bestowed because of the dramatic manner of his demise. According to legend, he was killed when an eagle mistook his bald pate for a rock and let drop a tortoise shell, cracking both open.

Modern victims of fate have suffered similarly ironic demises. Consider the case of the Prague, Czechoslovakia, woman who leapt out a third-floor window after learning of her husband's unfaithfulness. The husband, entering the building just as she jumped, broke her fall. She survived. He died on the spot.

Then there's the thirty-six-year-old San Diego woman who, in 1977, plotted to kill her twenty-three-year-old Marine drill instructor husband for his $20,000 insurance policy. She dropped the venom sac from a tarantula in a blackberry pie she baked, but he only ate a few bites. Next she tried electrocuting him in their shower, but that failed, too. So did attempts to kill him with lye, run him down in a car, inject an air bubble into his veins, and slip amphetamines in his beer while driving in hopes he would hallucinate and crash.

Exasperated, she enlisted a twenty-six-year-old female companion in crime. Together, they beat the husband over the head with metal weights as he slept. It was only at that point that he finally succumbed.

Finally on Memorial Day, 1987, a forty-year-old Louisiana lawyer stood up in his boat as a thunderstorm approached. "Here I am," he taunted the skies, raising his hands over his head. A bolt of lightning struck, killing him instantly. The lawyer's first name was Graves.

Falling Frogs

In May of 1981, residents in the southern Greece city of Naphlion woke up to a rain of green frogs. Thousands of the little amphibious creatures, weighing only a few ounces each, plopped out of the sky and flopped in the streets.

Scientists at the Greek Meteorological Institute, Athens, trotted out the usual explanation. A whirlwind out of North Africa had sucked the frogs from a marsh and wafted them some six hundred miles across the Mediterranean to drop them at Naphlion's doorstep.

Remarkably, few of the frogs died from the violent journey. In fact, they adapted quite well to their new surroundings. Some of the local citizens, however, report trouble sleeping at night: Their amphibious immigrants make too much noise.

Languages Reincarnated

What would happen if you hypnotized somebody and they started talking in ancient Norsk? That's just what happened to Dr. Joel Whitton, a prominent Canadian psychiatrist and skeptic exploring the issue of reincarnation.

Ever since the famous Bridey Murphy case back in the 1950s, New Age psychologists have tried regressing their subjects back to their previous lives. Few of them ever seem to come up with anything of interest, but that didn't prevent Whitton from trying, too. The psychiatrist's star subject was a professional psychologist who, during their hypnotic work together, began remembering and hearing foreign languages he apparently spoke during two past lives. What gradually emerged were memories of a Viking existence about A.D. 1000, and an earlier incarnation in Mesopotamia.

Reporting the case to the Toronto Society for Psychical Research, Whitton said his subject successfully recalled some twenty-two words of Norsk, the precursor of modern Icelandic and the language used by the ancient Vikings. Many of these words, including those that concerned the sea, have been identified and translated by two experts conversant in Norsk.

Whitton's subject, whose identity has not been revealed, never successfully spoke in seventh-century Mesopotamian, but he did write out some scattered scripts that resemble Sassanid Pahlavi, a dead language common to Persia between the third and seventh centuries A.D.

Whitton is not certain that this unique case proves the existence of reincarnation. It's possible, he concedes, but not likely, that his subject picked up the words and scripts from some normal source.

Sugar, the Homing Cat

Science is far from certain that it understands just how animals "home." Navigation by the position of the sun or by the earth's magnetic field represent two possibilities. But what about lost animals who find their way to their owners through unfamiliar territory? The case of Sugar, the homing cat, represents just such a mystery.

Sugar, a cream-colored Persian cat, was the pride and joy of Mr. and Mrs. Stacy Woods of Anderson, California. The couple decided to leave the area in 1951, but since Sugar was frightened by cars, they reluctantly decided to leave her behind with neighbors. Driving to their new residence on a farm in Oklahoma would be difficult enough without a troublesome cat to contend with. The Woods set out for the town of Gage and probably thought little more of Sugar while setting up their new house. But one day fourteen months later, Mrs. Woods was standing near the barn when a cat leapt through the window, landing right on her shoulder. Mrs. Woods was naturally startled and brushed the cat aside. But in taking a more careful look, she saw that it uncannily resembled Sugar. Both she and her husband soon adopted the feline and often commented on the resemblance.

Despite the coincidence, neither Mr. nor Mrs. Woods really believed the cat *was* Sugar until several days later. Mr. Woods was petting the feline when he noticed the cat's deformed hipbone. This was the exact same defect from which Sugar suffered. When they finally contacted their former neighbors in

California, the Woods learned that Sugar had disappeared a few weeks after their departure. The neighbors had not told the couple about the disappearance, fearing they would be upset by the news.

The Bélmez Faces

One of the craziest hauntings on record was originally reported from Spain in 1971, when strange faces began appearing in a small house in Bélmez.

The case first came to wide public attention in August, when Maria Pereira, a housewife in the small village, discovered that a female face had "formed" on the hearthstone of her kitchen fireplace. She tried to scrub the face from the stone but it seemed to emerge directly from the concrete. She even had the face covered by a second layer of cement, but it showed through that. Then faces began appearing on the kitchen floor, sometimes disappearing later in the day or changing expressions.

The house soon became a local tourist stop and Mrs. Pereira began charging an admission fee to see the faces. Hundreds of people began flocking to the house, until local political and religious authorities ordered the sight-seeing to stop.

Luckily, by this time Dr. Hans Bender of the University of Freiburg in Germany had learned of the case. Germany's leading parapsychologist, Bender decided to investigate the cause célèbre in collaboration with Spain's own Dr. German de Argumosa. In order to test the faces, the two investigators fastened a plastic plate over the kitchen floor. It was left there for several weeks and removed only when water condensed under it. The faces continued to form even under these controlled conditions. They consistently appeared through 1974, and although Mrs.

Pereira had a new kitchen built onto the house, it didn't take long before the faces began appearing there, too.

Professor Argumosa personally witnessed the materialization of a face on April 9, 1974, and photographed it, which was fortunate, since it later disappeared. The use of photographic documentation rules out any suggestion that the faces were hallucinations or chance configurations in the concrete.

In order to test further for fraud, Argumosa and his colleagues checked to see whether the faces were fashioned from artificial coloring. The results of this chemical study were published in November 1976 in the *Schweizerisches Bulletin für Parapsychologie* and it showed nothing suspicious.

The cause of the curious haunting has never been firmly established. Some of the local townsfolk dug up Mrs. Pereira's kitchen and found some old bones buried there. Rumor has it that the house was built over an ancient cemetery, a resting site for Christian martyrs killed by eleventh-century Moors.

The Ghost Wore Blue

Today, Dr. Julian Burton works in Los Angeles as a psychotherapist helping people with their problems. His dissertation for his graduate work, however, dealt more with the supernatural than the pathological, since it was devoted to the subject of spontaneous contact with the dead. Burton surveyed hundreds of people during his research, only to learn that communing with deceased friends and relatives is not unusual at all. This came as little surprise to the psychologist, since the idea for the project emerged from his own personal experience.

Burton's mother died in 1973 at the age of sixty-seven after suffering a massive stroke. He took the death hard but recovered by the following September, though the bond between them was to continue long after her death.

"One evening that September," recounts Burton, "my wife and I were entertaining relatives. I was in the kitchen cutting a pineapple when I heard what I thought were my wife's footsteps behind me to the right. I turned to ask the whereabouts of a bowl but realized that she had crossed to the left side outside my field of vision. I turned in that direction to repeat my question and saw my mother standing there. She was fully visible, looking years younger than at the time of her death. She was wearing a diaphanous pale-blue gown trimmed in marabou, which I had never seen before."

As Burton looked on, the figure simply dissolved, and the next morning he phoned his sister to report his experience.

"She was upset," continued the psychologist, "and began to sob, asking why our mother had not come to *her*. I felt bad about this and asked her if she believed what I had told her."

It turned out that, two weeks before her stroke, the two women had gone shopping and their mother had seen that same pale-blue gown. She had wanted to buy it, but didn't want to spend the two hundred dollar price for it.

The experience profoundly influenced Burton, who at the age of forty-two decided to go back to school to finish his doctorate. "I felt," he said, "that many people probably had similar experiences to tell."

A Miraculous Cure

Leo Perras can walk today even though he was a hopeless cripple for years. The story of his miraculous healing begins with a modern miracle worker, Father Ralph Di Orio, whose ministry is still going strong.

Father Di Orio was born in Providence, Rhode Island, in 1930 and was ordained a Roman Catholic priest in 1957. A linguist as well as an educator, Di Orio was quite conventional in his theological views and practices until 1972. That's when his predominantly Spanish-speaking congregation decided to become charismatic, a form of worship that emphasizes personal religious expression and spontaneous experience. Father Di Orio was resistant to the change and modified his services only with the approval of his bishop. Finally getting into the swing of things himself, the middle-aged priest began to practice laying-on-of-hands during the services and soon discovered that he possessed the power to heal. He was conducting his healing services at St. John's Church in Worcester, Massachusetts, when he first met Leo Perras.

Perras, from the nearby community of Easthampton, had been crippled in an industrial accident years before when he was only eighteen. Surgery failed, leaving him paralyzed from the waist down and confined to a wheelchair. Muscular atrophy eventually set into his legs, which damaged them even further and left Perras in considerable pain. He was taking pain medication daily when he sought out the New England priest.

When he first met Father Di Orio, Perras had been confined to his wheelchair for twenty-one years. The priest prayed over his visitor during the service, and the results were nearly instantaneous. The paralyzed man simply got up from his wheelchair and walked out of the church. The muscles of his legs apparently strengthened spontaneously and his long-endured pain vanished.

The story sounds too good to be true, but it is particularly well documented. The man's own physician, Mitchell Tenerowicz, chief-of-staff at Cooley Dickinson Hospital in Northampton examined the patient shortly after the healing and found that his legs were still atrophied, making it physically impossible for Perras to walk. But walk he did. Perras's legs strengthened over the next several weeks and on September 29, 1980, NBC-TV's

That's Incredible interviewed him and broadcast his story nationwide.

The Thirteenth Print

Nobody knew his real name. He called himself Cheiro the Great, and by the time he came to New York City from London in 1893 he had already established himself as the best-known, best-paid fortune-teller in the world.

Several years earlier he had made the headlines in English newspapers by deducing the identity of a murderer after studying a bloody handprint on a grimy wall. Now, the cynical New York reporters demanded proof of Cheiro's skills. They invited him to look at thirteen palm prints, then to describe the various people who had made these prints.

Within ten minutes, he had correctly described the donors of twelve of the prints, including that of the celebrated performer Lillian Russell, whom he correctly identified as a child of fate with great talent and ambition, but with great unhappiness as well.

But what about the thirteenth palm print? Why did he hesitate before getting to it?

Finally, he explained. "I refuse to identify this print to anyone but the owner," he said, "because it is the mark of a murderer. He'll give himself away through his own self-confidence and he will die in prison."

The thirteenth print was that of Dr. Henry Meyer, who was then in Tombs prison charged with murder. Meyer was convicted, and died a few months later in an institution for the criminally insane.

A Psychic Nightmare

Sometimes a psychic experience will take the edge off an otherwise shattering tragedy. When nineteen-year-old Wendy Finkel was killed in a car accident near Point Mugu on the southern California coast, her mother didn't need to hear about it from the police. She already knew. The date was Thursday, November 19, 1987.

It was the day before Wendy's birthday. The college coed and three of her friends had driven in from Santa Barbara to take someone to the Los Angeles airport. Two of the students planned to attend a rock concert. They took Wendy out for dinner and dancing, and then visited her sister, who lived near UCLA. The Finkels were looking forward to Wendy's birthday that Friday and especially to having their children home for Thanksgiving. The tragedy struck sometime early in the morning, when the car carrying the students apparently drove off the Pacific Coast Highway, and plunged down the embankment into the sea. A fisherman happened to see the 1986 Honda Civic floating in the water upside down the next morning, and the bodies of Wendy's three friends were soon recovered.

At the same time as the accident, Mrs. Finkel had awakened suddenly in her Woodland Hills home gasping for air. "I felt like I was drowning," she later told reporters. "I couldn't get any air in my lungs. I looked at the clock and it said two something. I'm assuming that's when the car got to Point Mugu and went off the cliff."

Wendy's body has not yet been recovered, though her mother has little doubt about her fate.

The Ghosts of the S.S. *Watertown*

Tragedy struck the oil tanker S.S. *Watertown* when it sailed from New York City to the Panama Canal early in December 1924. Two seamen, James Courtney and Michael Meehan, were cleaning a cargo tank when they were accidentally killed by gas fumes. Their bodies were buried at sea in proper maritime tradition on December 4.

The ghosts of the S.S. *Watertown* appeared the next day, but not in the form of sheet-clad phantoms stalking the ship's decks: The faces of the two unfortunate men were seen following the ship in the water. The disconcerting phantoms seen day after day by the ship's captain, Keith Tracy, and by the entire crew, seemed determined to follow the ship right through the canal.

Captain Tracy reported these eerie events to his head office when the ship docked in New Orleans, and officials from the company suggested that he try photographing them. He eventually delivered a roll of film with six exposures to the Cities Service Company, which had it commercially developed. While five of the shots revealed nothing unusual, the sixth exposure clearly showed the two faces lugubriously following the ship.

Interestingly enough, the Cities Service Company didn't try to play down the fascinating story or hide it from the public. They reported it openly in their own company magazine, *Service*, in 1934, and even displayed a blowup of the photograph in the main lobby of the Cities Service Company in New York.

Viewing the Future

Every student of the paranormal knows that ESP is not constrained by distance. Considerable research has shown that it can travel between two rooms as easily as halfway around the world. Even more amazing is the power of ESP to transcend the fabric of time itself. Some research conducted at Mundelein College in Chicago in 1978 certainly demonstrated this eerie fact.

The researcher in charge of the program was John Bisaha, who has long been interested in *remote viewing*, during which a subject tries to "see" what is taking place miles away. The experimental procedure is really quite simple. The subject merely sits with the experimenter while a target person (called the outbound experimenter) drives to some location either in the vicinity or even miles from where the subject is being tested. The subject is then asked to make contact with, or visualize, the outbound experimenter, and describe where he is. Bisaha used this procedure but added a significant revision. He asked his subject to describe the place the outbound experimenter would visit *the next day*.

For the most important part of his tightly controlled tests, Bisaha suggested that his star subject describe his upcoming sightseeing adventures in eastern Europe. For five consecutive days, Brenda Dunne—back in Chicago—tried to see where Bisaha would be visiting twenty-four hours later. At no time were the two participants in contact during the experiment.

The results were truly remarkable. When the sightseeing expedition took Bisaha to a circular restaurant built on some pillars rising from the Danube River, Brenda Dunne had already seen him "near water . . . a very large expanse of water." She also envisioned "vertical lines like poles . . . a circular shape like a merry-go-round." Similar successes were reported for the other days as well.

When the researcher returned to the United States, he took the records of the five sessions and turned them over to an independent judge, who was also provided with photographs of the target cities. His job was to match each of the reports given by Dunne to the correct photograph—and he didn't have any difficulty doing it.

Seagoing Pleisiosaur

In April of 1977, the nets of the Japanese fishing vessel *Zuiyo Maru* reeled in a strange haul off the coast of New Zealand—a forty-four-foot long, unknown marine animal that looked for all the world like a primordial monster of the deep. The crew hoisted the carcass out of the water and took color pictures of the bizarre catch before the captain, fearing a contaminated cargo, ordered it dropped overboard.

Professor Tokio Shikama, a student of ancient animals at Yokohama National University, studied the pictures and declared that the corpse was neither that of a known mammal nor of a fish. In fact, he compared its body to that of an ocean-dwelling *pleisiosaurus*, thought to be extinct for more than 100 million years.

Several other vessels in the area searched for the creature's remains after it was dumped by the Japanese, but without success. The tragedy is that even a single specimen of a pleisiosaur would have been worth far more than the captain's catch of normal fish.

Hog-Tied and Died

UFO occupants have reportedly demonstrated more than a passing interest in cattle and equines over the years. If Norway, South Carolina, farmer Richard Fanning is to be believed, their activities may extend to pork-on-the-hoof, too.

On the evening of December 6, 1978, the twenty-one-year-old Fanning, his wife and two other companions, spotted a ten-foot-diameter, white circle of light hovering over their hog pen. Beneath this object were two pairs of red and green lights, each about the size of automobile headlights.

"That doesn't look right," Fanning told his companions. "Let's leave." As he drove away, the silent lights followed, the white circle skimming the road at car-height and keeping fifty yards away, while the red and green lights pulled alongside.

Fanning headed for his house, where he kept a gun. But, he said, "All of a sudden the big white light made a U-turn behind my car and went back above the hog pen." The smaller, accompanying lights turned around as well. Fanning and the others watched the display until "after three or four minutes, all the lights went out." Fanning said, "I was scared, and I'm not scared of many things." He was so scared, in fact, that he and his wife stayed with relatives for the next two nights.

Three days later they went back to feed their stock and Fanning found one animal lying dead on its side. Another hog was "standing up dead," said Fanning. "I kicked him and he fell over."

An examination of the hog on its side revealed a missing jaw bone and a carcass "sort of like a sponge, with all the weight gone, kind of like jelly." Fanning said the animal alive had tipped the scales at 250 pounds, but that its remains weighed only about 50 pounds. "It was," he added, "the weirdest thing I've ever seen in my life."

Holes in the Head

Some strange rituals evolved out of the Flower Power of the sixties, but few were as bizarre as the practice of drilling a hole in one's head in order to achieve an expanded state of awareness.

Trepanation, the artificial opening of the skull, was common among some primitive societies for reasons not completely understood. Rationale for the risky, but survivable operation was probably both medical and religious in nature. Today's trepanners generally hold the same opinion.

The modern movement began in 1962, when a Dutch doctor, Bart Huges, claimed that the degree and state of one's consciousness depended foremost on the brain's blood volume. Things were different when we walked around on all fours, according to Huges, before we evolved the upright stance that separates us from most of nature. Problem was, the brain became encased in a confining, rigid structure; worse, gravity reduced the flow of oxygen and nutrients to the brain.

Huges's solution to the dilemma was to take an electrical drill and remove a small circle of bone from his cranium. The result, he said, was an increased blood flow and the ability of the now-freed brain to palpitate in rhythm with the heart. His consciousness returned to the childlike state he sought, in which the unfettered mind remained in touch with its primal dreams, imagination, and intense sensations. Adults lost this ability, Huges thought, as their skulls slowly solidified.

Trepanation as a solution to the human condition, however, did not set well with the local Dutch authorities, who promptly sentenced Huges to an insane asylum for observation. His ideas fared a little better, though, among the emerging hippies, for whom any kind of new "awareness" seemed worth the risk.

Huges's hole through the cranium directly into the brain promised a permanent mental stimulation. The trouble, of course, was finding someone to perform the operation, ancient witch doctors and shaman priests being in short supply. The answer was every handyman's dream: do-it-yourself.

Huges's foremost disciple was Joseph Mellen, a London accountant who had graduated from Oxford and met the Dutchman in Ibiza in 1965. Huges turned him on to the idea of trepanation. (Huges's own philosophy by this time had been encapsulated in a single word: "Brainbloodvolume.")

Mellen's own self-inflicted trepanation, following three aborted tries, was so "successful" that he later wrote a book about it, *Bore Hole*, the first sentence of which nicely sums up its contents: "This is the story of how I came to drill a hole in my skull to get permanently high."

Mellen reported a newfound sense of well-being from the trepanation that he claims remains with him today. His girlfriend, Amanda Fielding, subsequently undertook the cure, too, though instead of writing a book about her ordeal, she filmed it, calling her small movie *Heartbeat in the Brain*. Together, the two modern-day trepanners presently operate a London art gallery.

Power of Prayer

Many people think that science is the enemy of religion, but the tools of experimental research have sometimes documented the power of faith. Just such a project was recently undertaken by Dr. Randy Byrd, a cardiologist and a devout Christian. Byrd was so intrigued by the possible power of prayer that he decided to conduct an experiment to test it.

Since he was working at San Francisco General Hospital at the time, he certainly had enough patients to choose from. He began by programming a computer to choose 192 cardiac patients while an additional 201 similar patients were chosen to serve as his control group. Byrd wanted to see if those patients who were prayed for would recover from cardiac surgery better than the controls. He didn't perform the praying himself, but asked selected people and prayer groups across the country to participate in the study. The participants came from several different denominations and were provided with the names of the patients, but never met or otherwise contacted them. Nor did any of the patients ever know that the study was in progress.

The experiment took a year to complete and fully supported the belief that prayer really works. Byrd reported the amazing results of his study to the 1985 meeting of the American Heart Association, which convened that year in Miami. To a statistically significant degree, he told the group, prayed-for subjects required less postoperative antibiotic treatment and developed less pulmonary edema (the formation of water in the folds of the lungs). He also found that fewer prayed-for patients died during the study, although this trend wasn't statistically significant.

The reaction to this study by other physicians was surprising, to say the least. Many of them loved it. Probably the most surprising reaction came from Dr. William Nolan, the author of *The Making of a Surgeon* and an outspoken skeptic and critic of unorthodox medicine—and especially religious healing. Even he was impressed by the Byrd study.

"If it works, it works," he said of the power of prayer, when asked to comment on Dr. Byrd's study by the *Medical Tribune*.

The Real Dracula

The most famous horror novel of all time, Bram Stoker's *Dracula*, was based on the bloodthirsty career of a real person, Wallachian Prince Vlad IV, or Vlad the Impaler, who ruled fifteenth-century Rumania with an iron fist and sharpened stake.

Also known as Dracula, or "son of the devil," Vlad was one of the most ruthless rulers the world has known. A survey conducted in 1981, in fact, ranked him with only Idi Amin, Hitler, and Caligula in terms of total disregard for human life and suffering. He earned the soubriquet of Impaler because of his penchant for the wooden stake as a favorite tool of torture. Thousands of Turkish soldiers and civilians, thrust on poles staked in the ground, died in agony at his hands.

Vlad would dine among his writhing victims, supping or bathing in their life-fluid. So tightly did his terrible reputation grip the countryside that when he died in 1477, rumors surfaced that he rose from the dead in search of even more blood. Such stories may have contributed to the popular notion that the only way in which to stop a vampire's deadly depredations was to plunge a wooden stake through its still-living corpse. In an often overlooked tidbit of trivia, however, Stoker's original Count Dracula was only killed after his head was severed and a Bowie knife plunged in his chest—by a Texan. An almost incredible coincidence came to light in modern times.

A blood descendant of the real Dracula was located in Communist Rumania—working in a blood bank.

A Historical Female Vampire

History hints at other suspected vampires hidden among European royalty, too. The beautiful Elizabeth Bathory, born in 1560, and married to the Carpathian Count, Ferencz Nadasdy, at the age of fifteen, is a prime example. A wily wizard known only as Thorke reputedly tutored the young Elizabeth in the black arts. When the count was called off to war, his bride eloped with a stranger who had pointed white teeth and pale countenance, dressed in black. Elizabeth returned alone, sunk in savagery and given to torturing her servants. Back from battle, the count's protestations were of no avail.

Faced with her fading beauty, Elizabeth's mind became unhinged. She ordered a young housemaid murdered, her blood drained in a vat. The bath rejuvenated Elizabeth, temporarily. Now the need for youthful victims and their restorative bloodbath drove her beyond all bounds of humanity. With her own stock of servants exhausted, Elizabeth lured other prospects to the castle with the prospect of employment. Finally, she resorted to kidnappings, but one would-be victim escaped and alerted authorities.

Her confreres confessed to their crimes and were summarily

executed. Elizabeth herself was judged insane and walled up in her rooms for life, dying in 1614.

Hypnotic ESP

Back in the days of Franz Anton Mesmer, it was widely believed that hypnotized people automatically became psychic. The mesmerists claimed they could prompt their subject to see into the future, envision distant places, and diagnose the sufferings of people standing before them. These claims died out, however, as hypnosis became better understood.

But that doesn't mean these claims have disappeared.

While a doctoral student in psychology at Cambridge University, Carl Sargent decided to see whether there was any truth behind these fantastic eighteenth-century claims. To implement his experiment, the young experimental psychologist recruited forty subjects, mostly college students. One half of them were hypnotized and tested for ESP with standard ESP cards. The other subjects were tested with the same cards while totally awake.

The results of the experiment indicated that good old Dr. Mesmer may have been right. The hypnotized subjects scored well above chance, which would normally be five hits per run of twenty-five cards. They averaged a whopping 11.9 hits. The control subjects scored right at chance.

Sargent says his experiment shows something important about the nature of ESP. It is obviously enhanced by a relaxed, perhaps altered, state of mind.

The Buttercup Mammoth

Mammoths appear to have vanished from the face of the earth some ten thousand years ago, victims of climatic change wrought by the last great Ice Age and growing bands of aboriginal hunters who slaughtered them for their meat, tusks, and hide. Since the turn of the century literally hundreds of their frozen carcasses have been found in the frigid tundras of Alaska, Canada, and Soviet Siberia.

At least one of these finds, on the banks of the Beresovka River, Siberia, threatens to overturn the conventional wisdom of how mammoths became extinct. Half-kneeling and half-standing, the Beresovka mammoth was in an almost complete state of preservation. So solidly was its flesh frozen that investigating scientists actually feasted on its flanks. Even more amazing, however, was the fact that buttercups were discovered in the creature's mouth.

The great mammoth had itself been feeding on temperate temperature plants at the time of its death. What froze it to the bone in mid-bite, as suddenly as if it had been dipped in liquid nitrogen? The prevailing notion of a gradual climatic change to which mammoths could not adapt won't wash in this case.

Slow freezing would have formed ice crystals and subsequently resulted in putrefaction of the thawing flesh. But the Beresovka mammoth was fresh enough to eat without ill effect. The temperatures necessary to achieve such a flash-freeze have been estimated at minus 150 degrees Fahrenheit, readings never even recorded in the natural icebox of the nearby Arctic.

What could have accounted for such a catastrophic drop in the temperature of the surrounding air? In the absence of a nuclear winter brought on by atomic bombs, we must look for an alternative scenario. Forest fires and volcanic eruptions also throw huge amounts of heat and light-blocking debris into the atmosphere, as recent studies have shown.

One theory suggests that a mighty earthquake, the largest Earth had ever known, rent the world ten thousand years ago. Occurring along the junction of two tectonic plates, the quake resulted in the massive release of lava and accompanying volcanic gases. These gases rose high in the atmosphere and circulated toward the poles. Super-chilled, they plummeted back toward the earth, losing even more ambient heat in their rapid descent. Finally, they pierced the warmer air below, flash-freezing the Beresovka mammoth and others of its kind as they dined on a meal of flowers.

Psychic Archaeology

Jeffrey Goodman began his career as an executive with a small oil company in Tucson. With a degree in business, he wasn't particularly prone to wild flights of fancy. That's why it's so surprising to find him, these days, championing the new field of psychic archaeology, in which gifted psychics help find promising dig sites.

Goodman's psychic odyssey began in 1971, when he learned that conventional anthropologists believed mankind first appeared in the Americas sixteen thousand years ago. Goodman felt the date to be too recent. In fact, he felt sure he could find evidence of an earlier civilization right in Arizona if only he knew where to look. So in order to explore his hunch further,

Goodman consulted with Aron Abrahamsen, a well-known psychic from Oregon. Working from his home there, the psychic offered several clairvoyant descriptions that helped Goodman locate a dry riverbed in the San Francisco Peaks outside of Flagstaff. It was an unlikely place to look for a lost civilization, since no archaeological finds had ever been unearthed there. But not only did Goodman simply ignore that inconvenient fact, he even asked his psychic to predict the geological formations they would find while digging.

By digging just where the psychic directed, Goodman unearthed man-made artifacts dating back at least twenty thousand years. What was even more surprising was that 75 percent of Abrahamsen's geological predictions were completely correct, even though two local geologists had originally scoffed at them. The Oregon psychic predicted, for instance, that the excavators would hit one-hundred-thousand-year-old strata at the twenty-two-foot level. And that's just what they did.

Precognition and the Races

Skeptics like to scoff at psychics, saying that if ESP really works, why haven't they made a killing at the races? In fact, there is good evidence that some of them really have.

The British Broadcasting Company aired a series of talks on psychical research in 1934. Among the participants was Dame Edith Lyttleton, a former delegate to the League of Nations, who was herself a gifted psychic. Lyttleton devoted her presentation to the subject of precognition, ending the broadcast by urging her listeners to report their own experiences to her. She then systemically followed up the more promising cases, especially those for which outside documentation could be found. Surprisingly, an extraordinary number of cases were submitted by people whose precognitive experiences focused on horse races. Many of the witnesses had even used the information to place bets.

For example, one of Lyttleton's correspondents was a Mrs. Phyliss Richards, whose experience had occurred the year before.

"I crossed from Belfast to Liverpool on the night of Thursday, March 23, 1933, in order to see the Grand National which was being run the next day," Richards said. "On the boat I discovered that I had forgotten my mackintosh and felt a little worried. I went to sleep and dreamt that I was at the race, that it was pouring with rain and that a horse whose name began with 'k' and ended with 'jack' had won the race, although he was not the first horse past the winning post."

Richards ultimately placed a small bet on Kellesboro Jack, who ended up passing the winning post only after a riderless horse. And she won.

After hearing this account, Lyttleton and a colleague tracked down one of the people to whom Richards had told the dream before the race took place. He fully corroborated the incident and verified the winnings, too. Lyttleton published several similar cases in 1937, concluding that perhaps some people really can profit (in every sense of the word) by paying attention to their dreams.

A Phone Call From the Dead

Karl Uphoff, onetime rock musician, today believes in life after death. The reason: a phone call from his deceased grandmother, received in 1969.

Karl was eighteen years old when his maternal grandmother died. There had been a special bond between them, and when the old woman grew deaf in her later years, she often wanted Karl's help. Since Karl wasn't always home, she had a habit of calling his friends to find him. And because she couldn't even hear if anyone picked up the receiver, she would simply dial a number, wait a few moments and then say, "Is Karl there? Tell him to come home now." She would repeat the message a few times and then terminate the call, proceeding on to the next number on her list. These calls had ceased, however, two years before her death in 1969, when Karl's sister began taking care of her.

Two days after the woman's death, Karl decided to pay an impromptu visit to the home of Mr. and Mrs. Sam D'Alessio in Montclair, New Jersey, whose son, Peter, was a friend of his. Peter and Karl were downstairs in the basement talking when the upstairs phone rang. The two boys could hear Mrs. D'Alessio talking impatiently with the caller and becoming rather miffed. Karl was stunned when she called down to him.

"There's an old woman on the phone," she yelled. "She says she's your grandmother and she says she needs you. She just keeps saying it over and over."

Karl dashed up the stairs to grab the receiver, but by the time he reached the phone, no one was on the line. But that night, back home, Karl received a series of phone calls. Nobody was ever on the line when he picked up the receiver.

Was the call a hoax of some sort? This possibility seems extremely doubtful. When questioned by an investigator, Karl claimed that none of his current friends knew of the calls his grandmother used to make, and the D'Alessios were recent acquaintances. He also added that he had gone to visit them spontaneously, and that nobody could have known his whereabouts when the call was received.

Psychic Vision

When a housewife in Watts, a predominately black inner-city part of Los Angeles, had a vision that a body was buried in her yard, the coroner's office became interested.

The story began on July 17, 1986, when the woman, who was studying to be a minister, told police about the body. She had been having psychic visions for some time, and she had finally decided to act. When she and a friend began digging, they soon found part of a human skull and some other bone fragments. These finds were so provocative that the L.A. Police Department and some Explorer Scouts continued the dig and found even more.

Where did the bones come from? Police authorities aren't yet sure. From the scattered remains, it isn't possible to determine the sex of the person buried, or the cause of death, or how long the bones have been there. Dr. Judy Suchy, a forensic anthropologist with the coroner's office, is in charge of running experiments on the fragments in hopes of answering some of these questions.

Pitchforked Witch

The police were perplexed by the brutality of the murder. Charles Watson, a harmless old man, had been pinned to the ground by the two-prong pitchfork thrust through his throat. From his chest protruded a hedge-slashing hook, another familiar tool of Warwickshire farmers.

Locals bruited darkly of a ritual witch murder, but there weren't supposed to be any witches in February of 1945, not even in war-ravaged England. Since the Bobbies had few clues to go on, they called in the famous Superintendent Fabian of Scotland Yard. Although Fabian spent months on the case, he was never able to bring a suspect to justice.

Who killed old man Watson, then, remains a mystery. But, Scotland Yard finally figured that he had been perceived as a witch. Certainly Watson's eccentric behavior aroused the suspicions of his neighbors. He kept mostly to himself, sharing a thatched cottage with his niece. Spurning the camaraderie of pubmates, he bought his cider by the gallon jug and drank alone.

Gossip, however, centered around Watson's other peculiar habits. He was given to solitary wanderings in the wilds of Warwickshire, where he was frequently seen and heard communing with the birds of the air. Watson said he had his own understanding with them.

He also raised toads in a small garden. Rumor had it that he hitched them to miniature plows and followed them across the fields at night.

Rumors and innuendos were one thing, but what about reality? Could Watson really have been a witch, practicing his craft openly and holding his neighbors in fearful thrall? Regardless of one's beliefs, on a cold winter's day Watson was brutally murdered beneath a willow tree. The only motive Scotland Yard could uncover was that of witchcraft in the first degree.

The Headless Ghost

An early settler in the small Illinois town of McLeansboro, a man named Lakey, was found dead. His body was discovered by a passerby, his head chopped off, apparently by the ax that was still stuck in the stump next to his body. No one could understand the crime since Lakey appeared to have no enemies at all.

One day after his funeral, two men were riding horseback near the Lakey cabin site, along what is now known as Lakey's Creek. They had probably gone fishing on the Wabash River and were passing the cabin just as night fell, when they were joined by another, a headless horseman on a large black steed. Unable to speak, the men rode on fearfully, down the bank and into the creek. Suddenly the mysterious rider turned off, moved downstream and seemed to disappear into a pool of water below the crossing.

At first afraid to tell their story, the men soon found that others had seen the same apparition. The ghostly rider's trail was always the same. He joined riders coming from the east, turned near the center of the creek, and then disappeared.

Today, a concrete bridge carries automobiles over the same spot where riders once forded Lakey's Creek, and motorists have yet to see the restless ghost. The mystery of Lakey's death has never been solved.

Lost and Found

As a girl growing up in Yorkshire, England, Kate dreamed that she would marry "an army officer who wore gray flannels and tweed jackets, had a mustache, smoked a pipe and drove a sports car."

In her young adult life she moved to Toronto, where she met a man fitting that description. He was John Tidswell, an officer in the Canadian army and an amateur race-car driver. He divorced his first wife and married Kate on November 24, 1956. In due course the couple had three children—two boys and a girl. Their marriage seemed to be a happy one.

One day during the last week of July 1970, though, John took his sloop for a cruise on Lake Simcoe, thirty-five miles from the couple's home. He did not return. Searchers eventually found the disabled craft. There was no sign of John Tidswell, and on October 8, 1971, a court declared him legally dead.

And so matters remained until a few years later, when Kate Tidswell suddenly began having vivid dreams about her late husband. They were so disturbing that in 1979 she went to visit a psychic, seeking an explanation. The pyschic told her that John was still alive, living elsewhere and using the name "Halfyard."

Kate began a search that took her across thirteen states. She did not find her husband, but her dreams and the psychic's words left her convinced he was out there somewhere.

Meanwhile, a Denver man named Robert Halfyard was having legal troubles. He had won a trip to Europe but when he applied for a passport, authorities checked into his background and found out who he really was: John Tidswell. He had faked his death and abandoned his Canadian family to start a new life in the United States.

His "widow" promptly lost her pension from her husband's military career. Just as promptly she sued him for $100,000 in alimony and child support.

She told reporters she was trying hard to "see the humor" in the situation.

Proving Near-Death Experience

Opinion is certainly divided when it comes to the near-death experience. Some experts believe that it's a genuine preview of the afterworld, while others dismiss it as an hallucination. Can the reality of the near-death experience ever be proved? A recent attempt has been made by Kimberly Clark, a social worker at Harborview Medical Center in Seattle, Washington.

Clark's first encounter with the NDE came while she was working with a patient named Maria. Maria was a migrant worker visiting relatives in the city when she suffered a heart attack. She survived the crisis but suffered a second close call with death while recuperating in the hospital. Since so much medical technology was close by, she was easily and expertly revived.

The social worker saw the patient later that day. She was taken aback when the woman suddenly said, "The strangest thing happened while the doctors and nurses were working on me. I found myself looking down from the ceiling at them working on my body." Not impressed by the story, Clark assumed Maria was confused by her ordeal. But the social worker grew more interested when Maria said that while functioning out-of-body she "flew" up to the third-floor ledge on the northern side of the building, where she spotted a tennis shoe.

"She needed someone else to know that the tennis shoe was really there to validate her out-of-body vision," said Clark, who went upstairs to hunt for the tennis shoe with mixed emotions.

"Finally," she reported, "I found a room where I pressed my face to the glass and looked down and saw the tennis shoe. My vantage point was very different from what Maria's had to have been for her to notice that the little toe had worn a place in the shoe and that the lace was stuck under the heel and other details about the side of the shoe not visible to me. The only way she would have had such a perspective was if she had been floating right outside and at very close range to the tennis shoe. I retrieved the shoe and brought it back to Maria. It was very concrete evidence for me."

The Money Hole

Off the coast of Nova Scotia lies tiny, irregular-shaped Oak Island. Far out of proportion to its size, however, is the awesome enigma of what lies hidden beneath the deceptively innocent surface. Rumors hint of a fabulous pirate treasure of almost unimaginable wealth. Exploratory findings speak of a potential for tragedy and an engineering feat by whoever hid the treasure unrivaled in its almost supernatural ingenuity.

Whatever the eventual outcome, for almost two hundred years Oak Island has frustrated every single attempt to pry loose its secret. The first to try was sixteen-year-old Daniel McGinnis and two companions who rowed across Mahone Bay from the Canadian mainland in 1795. In a clearing on the wooded eastern end of the island they discovered an old ship's tackle block hanging from a single tree above a filled-in depression. Intrigued, they dug down, uncovering the opening of a thirteen-foot-wide circular shaft. At a depth of ten feet, the boys encountered the first of the thick oak platforms. Twenty feet down, they found a second platform, and at thirty feet, a third.

Digging through the flinty clay exhausted the young treasure hunters, both physically and spiritually. But there would be others to take their place. Work next resumed in 1804, financed by Simeon Lynds, a well-to-do Nova Scotian. Lynds's diggers found five more oak platforms, each at depths of ten-foot increments, three of which had been sealed over with ship's putty and a layer of coconut fibers. At ninety feet, they found what became known as the "cipher stone," inscribed with obscure symbols that one source interpreted to mean "ten feet below, $10 million are buried." The amount would be exponentially greater in today's dollars.

Eight feet under the cipher stone a miner's crowbar struck something solid, thought to be a treasure chest. Lynds's men broke off for the day. The following morning the pit had filled with water to a depth of sixty feet.

The Money Pit broke Lynds, as it broke the back of any number of similar expeditions since. Over the years just enough tantalizing evidence has been pulled out of the pit to keep treasure hunters coming back, including bits of gold chain and indications of chambers containing wooden chests.

The mystery of what the Money Pit holds deepened when two channels connected to the pit were discovered at the 111- and 150-foot levels. Filled with coconut fibers, both led to the island's beaches, where they seem to serve as sponges, soaking up the sea, and forever flooding the shaft with water. The coconut fibers hint of a South Pacific origin for the hidden treasure.

Treasure hunters continue to sink money into the frustrating hole, risking their lives in the process. Daniel Blankenship, a former Miami contractor, is director of Oak Island excavations from Triton Alliance Ltd., a forty-eight-member consortium of wealthy Canadian and U.S. backers. Blankenship was once deep in the pit when steel casings holding back the sides fifty feet above his head began collapsing. Workers winched him out of the hole only seconds before the shaft gave way.

Having already sunk $3 million in the site, Blankenship and Triton vow to fight on. Now in the works is what Triton president David Tobias calls "in all probability the deepest and most expensive archaeological dig ever made in North America." The new plan calls for sinking an immense steel and concrete shaft, sixty to seventy feet wide and two hundred feet deep, that will reveal, once and for all, what lies at the bottom of the Money Pit. Estimated cost? Ten million dollars.

Haunting the Rich and Famous

Ghosts don't haunt just broken-down old houses. Even the superchic of Hollywood sometimes get stuck with them. That sad situation was a constant nuisance to German-born actress Elke Sommer and her husband, writer Joe Hyams, back in the 1960s.

The couple came to realize that their house was haunted shortly after buying it in 1964. The first witness was a German newspaperwoman who was lying by the pool when she saw a stranger in the yard. Apparently in his fifties, he was neatly dressed in a white shirt, tie, and black suit. The guest reported the stranger to her hosts, who were baffled by the incident since they knew of no such person matching the description. But two weeks later the stranger appeared a second time when Elke Sommer's mother woke up to see the same figure. The elderly woman was getting ready to scream when the figure simply vanished.

The two visitations only represented the beginning of the couple's problems. From that time forward, strange noises were often heard in the house late at night. There was an odd rustling, and sometimes it even sounded as if the dining room chairs were being shuffled about.

At first, Hyams didn't think the problem was caused by the supernatural, so he cut back the trees and bushes to stop the rustling. But his efforts did little to eliminate the problem. Every night before retiring, he would carefully lock the doors and windows, only to find one particular window downstairs unlocked in the morning. Often, Hyams would hear the front door open and shut throughout the night, only to find it bolted in the morning. The frustrated writer finally planted three miniature radio transmitters around the property, but failed to catch any prowler responsible for the disturbances.

Finally, in the spring of 1965, the couple left the house in the care of a friend during a trip to Europe. No matter how carefully this caretaker locked the front door, it would be standing wide open the next day. And that August, the ghost made a repeat visit when the couple's poolman saw a stranger lurking in the dining room. The intruder was six feet tall, heavily built and wore a white shirt and tie. The poolman thought the stranger was a prowler until the man disappeared before his eyes.

With no end to the problem in sight, Joe Hyams finally contacted the Southern California Society for Psychical Research, which turned the case over to Dr. Thelma Moss. Then a psychologist at the UCLA Neuropsychiatric Institute, Moss took several psychics to the house, including such well-known local sensitives as the late Lotte van Strahl and Branda Crenshaw. Some of the psychics immediately sensed the ghost's presence, and their combined descriptions tallied with the reports of the eyewitnesses. Since all information concerning the case had been kept from them, Moss felt these correlations were extremely significant. The sensitives described the ghost as a gentleman in his fifties who had died of a heart attack. He was somehow attached to the house, they felt, and didn't want to leave.

While the investigation was still in progress, Hyams checked with the house's previous owners. It seems that they, too, had experienced similar trouble while they lived there. The house seemed to be permanently haunted, but the California writer wasn't intimidated by the discovery.

"Whoever or whatever the ghost is," he stated in a report published in the *Saturday Evening Post*, "we do not intend to be frightened out of our house."

But leave the house they ultimately did. After Moss completed her investigation, Sommer and Hyams brought in yet another psychic to explore the situation. Jacqueline Eastlund toured the residence in 1966 and then warned her hosts, "I see your dining room in flames next year. Be careful." The exhausted couple finally decided to sell the house in 1967, but a mysterious fire broke out in the dining room before they could leave. The cause of the blaze, like the haunting itself, has never been explained.

The Blue-Eyed Indians Who Spoke Welsh

Shortly after the American Revolution, when the lands west of the Mississippi were still claimed by Spain or England, an English surveying party visited a camp of Mandan Indians in what is now Missouri. When the officer in charge spoke to his orderly in Welsh (they were both Welshmen), they were astonished when a nearby Indian suddenly joined in the conversation. Apparently the two palefaces were speaking the Indian's language. They started to compare words and found that the Mandan language was about 50 percent Welsh. (*English*: bread, paddle, great, head, etc. *Mandan*: bara, ree, ma, pan, etc. *Welsh*: barra, ree/rhwyf, mawr, pen, etc.)

In addition, many of the Mandans did not resemble the other Indian tribes. They had blue eyes and their skin was of a lighter color than that of other Indians. The Mandan women, found to be "exceeding fair," were especially pleasing to the British explorers.

Then the English officer remembered that a Prince Madoc of Wales in A.D. 1170 sailed with his retinue to the west into the unknown ocean. Could he and his followers have sailed into the Gulf of Mexico and up the Mississippi and then stayed there?

Some time later most of the Mandans including the elderly "storytellers" and "rememberers" were wiped out by a plague brought by the whites. The few who survived were absorbed by other tribes. The chances for ever finding out why the Mandan Indians spoke Welsh are very slim, since all pure-blooded Mandans have now disappeared.

It All Depends on How You Look at It

A mysterious stone carved with letters in an unknown alphabet was excavated in Bat Creek, Tennessee, in the late 1800s. A report and reproduction of the inscription was sent to the Smithsonian Institute in Washington, attributing its origin to the Cherokee tribe. However, after fifty years of mystery as to what it meant, Joseph Maker of Georgia observed upon viewing it, "It's upside down. Turn it rightside up. It's Canaanite Hebrew." It turned out to mean "Year one of the Golden Age of the Jews," thereby solving one mystery and initiating another. A message from ancient Israel? In Bat Creek, Tennessee?

Guided by a Voice

Romer Troxell, a 42-year-old resident of Levittown, Pennsylvania, was devastated by his son's murder. Charlie Troxell's body had been found by a roadside in Portage, Indiana. All identification had been removed from it, and robbery had been the probable motive for the crime. But the murdered youth was now seeking revenge.

While driving through Portage to claim the body, Troxell kept hearing his son's voice inside his mind, and he kept his eyes open hoping to spot someone driving his son's stolen car. The voice, he said, started telling him where to look and Troxell finally found the vehicle.

"I made a U-turn and followed the car about a block behind," Troxell said. "I wanted to crash into the car but Charlie warned me against it."

So instead, Troxell merely trailed the vehicle until its driver stopped and stepped out. He then engaged the suspect in conversation while another relative driving with Troxell summoned the police. The officers later arrested the man, whom they quickly recognized as a suspect in the crime based on their own confidential information.

After the suspect was taken into custody and charged, Charlie's voice no longer echoed in his father's head.

"Charlie's in peace now," Troxell stated. "The police were onto the killer, though. I came to realize that when they later showed me what they had uncovered in their investigation. But when I heard my son guiding me, I acted. Maybe the Lord wanted it that way."

Swallowed by a Sperm Whale

The case of James Bartley, a seaman on board the whaler *Star of the East*, is a fairly convincing answer to doubters of the biblical text concerning Jonah.

According to British Admiralty records, in February 1891 Bartley left the ship as part of a longboat crew during a whale hunt. The sea was rough. The harpooner made a strike, the whale dove and suddenly came up under the longboat wrecking it and scattering the crew. All of the sailors were picked up except Bartley. The whale then died and its body floated. It was cut and sectioned with the long flensing knives of the crew. A shoe attached to a foot and leg appeared during the flensing. Then Bartley was extracted from the whale's stomach, alive but unconscious. He regained consciousness but could not speak for several weeks. He remembered little except the opening of enormous jaws and sliding down a long tube on his way to the whale's stomach, where he remained for fifteen hours, as attested to by the signed declaration of the ship's doctor and all hands.

Bartley's sight was affected by his experience and his skin was bleached. He spent his remaining years on land and died at the age of thirty-nine.

Previews of the Hereafter

All over the world, people have long noted and taken seriously the visions of those who approached death. During World War II, supplemental records were kept in at least one field hospital in the U.S.S.R. concerning seriously wounded soldiers who had literally been brought back to life from the edge of death. According to one study of numerous cases concerning those who had "returned" from being very close to the "other side," most individuals received a quick vision of a religious nature according to their individual religions. Among the principal groups, the Orthodox Catholics glimpsed visions of ancient saints and heard hymns, the Moslems found themselves at the edge of a verdant and promising paradise, whereas the dedicated Communists remembered nothing. Many persons also remembered seeing family members who were already dead.

The case of Thomas Edison is especially interesting since, as a scientist, he would be likely to report his last impression with a certain detachment. As he lay dying he seemed to be in a coma. Suddenly he raised himself up and said in a clear but wondering tone, "I *am* surprised. It's very beautiful over there." He made no further comment about what he had seen and died shortly thereafter.

Voltaire, the famous French philosopher and critic of the established church lay in a semicoma, dying. During his productive and contentious life, his enemies had frequently threatened that he would receive a just punishment after his death, presumably in hell. Just before he died the smouldering logs in the fireplace of his chamber burst into vigorous flames. He looked up and, with his accustomed wit, observed to his friends: *"Quoi! Les flammes déjà?"* ("What! The flames already?")

A Tale of Three Titans

The greatest maritime disaster of all time befell the greatest man-made behemoth of all time—the White Star Line's tragically ill-fated *Titanic*. The real-life tragedy was matched only by that of the *Titan*, a fictional luxury liner that also went down with a terrible loss of life in April 1898, fourteen years before the *Titanic* struck the iceberg that sent her to a watery grave, also on an evening in April.

The *Titan* sailed only in the pages of Morgan Robertson's novel, aptly named *Futility*. But the parallels between the two gigantic passenger ships stagger the imagination. Robertson's prophetic *Titan* departed Southampton, England, on her maiden voyage, as did the "unsinkable" *Titanic* herself. Both ships were the same length, 800 feet and 828½ feet long, and of comparable tonnage—70,000 and 66,000 tons respectively. Each had three propellers and carried 3000 passengers apiece.

Each ship was jammed to the gunwales with wealthy citizens. Both struck an iceberg at the same spot and sank. And both boats suffered terrible casualties because neither carried enough lifeboats. In the case of the *Titanic*, 1513 passengers died, most from exposure in the frigid Atlantic.

One of those who died aboard the *Titanic* was famous spiritualist and journalist W. T. Stead, who had written his own short story foretelling a similar sinking in 1892. But neither *Futility* nor Stead's story could save the doomed *Titanic*. Another premonition, however, *did* avoid a tragedy. In April 1935, seaman William Reeves was standing the bow watch aboard the tramp steamer *Titanian*, bound for Canada from England. The similarities and memories of the *Titanic* tragedy preyed on young Reeves's mind and sent a shiver up his spine. His boat's bow was cutting through the same still waters the *Titanic* had. And as midnight, the hour of the great ocean liner's end, approached, Reeves remembered that the date the great ocean liner sank—April 14, 1912—was his own birthday.

Overwhelmed by coincidence, Reeves called out, and the *Titanian* hove to, stopping just short of a looming iceberg. Soon after, other crystal mountains rose out of the night. The *Titanian* sat still, but safe, for nine days, until icebreakers from Newfoundland finally cut a swath through the deadly ice.

The Eels of Atlantis

The instinctive memory of animals causes them to gather in great numbers and to cross thousands and thousands of miles of earth and sea. The underwater migration of eels to a section of the mid-Atlantic Ocean is an outstanding and very curious example of this.

About every two years the eels from the lakes and rivers of Europe swim westward to the Atlantic where, in great living banks, they cross the ocean to the Sargasso Sea. There they meet with the great mass of eels from the American continent, which in turn have been swimming eastward to the same sea within the ocean. Aristotle, the ancient Greek philosopher and naturalist of the fourth century B.C., noted the eel migration from Europe but did not know about the west-to-east migration from the still unknown Americas. It is thought that the concentration of seaweed in the Sargasso Sea is the reason both eel populations make their pilgrimage to it, as the plentiful underwater seaweed would tend to protect their eggs. After spawning, the eels die and the young American eels, when sufficiently developed, return westward to the Americas, while the young European eels swim eastward to Europe. Both species are helped by the Atlantic current that flows clockwise.

Why is there so much seaweed in the Sargasso Sea? Is it perhaps possible that a mid-Atlantic continent, such as Atlantis, once existed there?

If it is true that Atlantis sank relatively quickly beneath the ocean, part of its vegetation may have adapted itself into seaweed still growing over what is now an underwater continent, the original spawning ground of the eels still alive in their ancestral and instinctive memory.

Possessed by a Murdered Man

Giuseppe Verardi was nineteen years old when his body was found under a bridge separating Siano and Catanzano, two small towns in Italy. His body was clothed only in undergarments, and the rest of his clothing was strewn nearby. The date was February 13, 1936, and the town authorities of Siano ruled that Giuseppe had killed himself. This pronouncement was greeted with skepticism by the boy's friends and family, who couldn't believe that a mere thirty-foot fall could explain the youth's injuries.

Giuseppe's death was history by January 5, 1939, when a strange drama unfolded in town. The prime player in the story was seventeen-year-old Maria Talarico, who had never known Giuseppe or his family. She was crossing the bridge with her grandmother when she suffered a strange spell, fell to her knees and became delirious. With the help of her grandmother and a kind passerby, she was taken back home. But when she recovered from the fit, she was no longer Maria. A strange masculine voice issued from her mouth, claiming to be Giuseppe Verardi himself.

The restless ghost of Giuseppe took complete control of Maria and even wrote a letter to his mother in his own, earthly, calligraphy. That same evening, the entity forced Maria to engage in a curious pantomime, in which "he" relived his last night in Siano. The spirit pretended to be drinking and playing cards, just as Giuseppe had done the night he died. The entity kept gulping down more and more wine, even though Maria never drank more than one glass with her meals. Then the entity began to reenact a fight with his fellow cardplayers, which presumably took place on the bridge.

Giuseppe's mother came to visit Maria the next day, and the possessing entity immediately recognized her and described the injuries found on his body. He also named his murderers, even though few of them still lived in Siano. Mrs. Verardi later returned home and prayed that her son's spirit would leave Maria. Later that day, Maria walked to the fateful bridge while still possessed by the murdered youth. She then took off her clothes and lay under the bridge in the exact position in which Giuseppe's body had been found. Within a few minutes Maria woke up with no memory of what had happened.

The psychic return of Giuseppe Verardi received a great deal of press coverage in 1939. Ernesto Bozzano, then probably Italy's leading psychical researcher, studied the case and issued a report of the occurrence in 1940.

Electrical Emission From the Brain

Hans Berger is best remembered today as the father of encephalography, the scientific study of brain waves. Few people realize, though, that Berger's interest in the brain's electrical emissions stemmed from his desire to explain ESP.

The scientist's interest in the paranormal stemmed from an experience he had when he was nineteen years old. A soldier taking part in some military exercises in Würzberg, Germany, Berger was riding his horse when it stumbled. He was nearly crushed by the wheels of a cart, but the horses were stopped just in time.

That same evening, Berger received a telegram from his father asking him if he were all right. It was the only time the youth had ever received such an inquiry. He later learned the reason for the communication. At the same time as the mishap, his eldest sister had a sudden presentiment that something was wrong with her brother, and she urged her parents to send the telegram.

"The incident was a clear example of the spontaneous transmission of thought," wrote Berger. "At the time of grave danger, I acted as some sort of transmitter and my sister became a receiver." Berger delved into the study of the brain in hopes of finding a physical explanation for telepathy. He failed, but his research helped scientists to better understand the brain's electrical rhythms.

The Clock That Stopped at Death

Every schoolchild learns to sing "My Grandfather's Clock," that wonderful German folk song about the clock that "stopped short, never to run again when the old man died." What few people realize is that this song is based on a genuine phenomenon. Clocks often stop when their owners die.

Several such cases were collected by the Duke University Parapsychology Laboratory, where Dr. Louisa Rhine worked for many years classifying reports of psychic phenomena sent in from the general public. Several of these cases concerned mysterious clock stoppings. For example, one gentleman from Canada explained to Dr. Rhine how he had helped his sister-in-law during his brother's last illness. When the patient died at 6:25 in the morning, he called the family and the doctor before helping to prepare a quick breakfast for everybody. The corpse had to be at the undertaker's by 9:30, so they had to watch the time carefully. When someone asked for the time during the meal, the witness took out a gold pocket watch. It had been a gift from his brother, and it had stopped at the exact time of his death.

"I called the attention of those gathered around the table to the phenomenon," wrote the witness, "and in order to show that it was no common occurrence, asked my [other] brother to wind the watch to make sure it had not run down. It was three-quarters wound."

The Too-Dangerous Machine Gun

It is rare in history when one finds that a new or suggested weapon has been considered by the controlling authority to be too cruel or destructive to use. Nevertheless, this is what happened when the inventor of a multiple firing weapon—or a sort of machine gun—was offered to Louis XVI of France in 1755 by an engineer named Du Peron. Louis and his ministers refused it as being too deadly because it would kill too many people at one time. Considering the opinion of Dr. Edward Teller, the so-called "father of the H-bomb," one realizes that Louis XVI would be considerably out of date in the world of modern warfare. Dr. Teller has estimated that an exploding H-bomb in a large metropolitan area would cause the death of about 10 million people, while a "bad nuclear war could kill a couple of billion."

A Real Ghostwriter

Sports figures and other public personalities frequently seek assistance for their autobiographies in the form of ''ghost'' writers, professional authors hired to whip their prose into shape. But real ghostwriters have plied their ethereal trade, too, as evidenced by the career of Mrs. J. H. Curran and her spiritual scribe, ''Patience Worth.''

Curran, of St. Louis, was originally distrustful of mediums and spiritualism, but on July 8, 1913, she attended a seance in which a Ouija board was employed. Placing her hands on the board, Curran spelled out the name Patience Worth. Patience revealed herself as a seventeenth-century English woman from Dorset, whose parents had emigrated to America, where she was killed in an Indian attack.

Intrigued, Curran continued her conversations with Patience. Over the next several years, and in the course of countless sittings, a remarkable sequence of poems, stories, and treatises poured from Patience, through Curran, and into print. A series of historical novels included *The Sorry Tale*, set in the first century, and the nineteenth-century *Hope Trueblood*. Her most celebrated spirit novel, *Telka*, was set in medieval England and penned in the language of the day, an archaic style Curran never studied.

Patience could ''dictate'' two or more novels simultaneously, shifting from one to another by chapter while never losing her train of thought. And Curran proved the perfect collaborator, dutifully recording Patience Worth's remarkable stories of days long gone by.

Angels in the Sky?

People who say they see angels are usually considered crazy. But it's hard to pin such a label on Dr. S. Ralph Harlow, a highly respected religion professor at Smith College in Massachusetts. His encounter of the angelic kind took place while he and his wife were walking in a wooded glen in Ballarvade, Massachusetts.

Harlow first heard some muted voices, the story goes, then declared, "We have company in the woods this morning." No source for the sounds could be found, so the couple proceeded with their walk. The voices seemed to grow closer, and finally emanated from just above. The perplexed couple looked up to behold an incredible sight: "About ten feet above us, and slightly to our left, was a floating group of spirits, of angels, of glorious, beautiful creatures that glowed with spiritual beauty," reported Harlow. "We stopped and stared as they passed above us.

"There were six of them, beautiful young women dressed in flowing white garments and engaged in earnest conversation. If they were aware of our existence they gave no indication of it. Their faces were perfectly clear to us, and one woman, slightly older than the rest, was especially beautiful. Her dark hair was pulled back in what today we would call a ponytail, and although I cannot say it was bound at the back of her head it appeared to be. She was talking intently to a younger spirit whose back was toward us and who looked up into the face of the woman who was talking."

Neither Dr. Harlow nor his wife could decipher what the beings were saying, though they both say they clearly saw and heard the beautiful phantoms. They watched in awe and exasperation as the "angels" passed by. Dr. Harlow, a careful observer, then asked his wife to tell him exactly what she had seen. Her description of the encounter matched his own.

Resurrection Roses

Dr. Nandor Fodor was both a psychoanalyst and psychical researcher, a man dearly loved by those who knew him. When he died on May 17, 1964, objects in his apartment mysteriously started to move, as if the deceased researcher was trying to demonstrate his continued existence to the world. But it was the behavior of the terrace flowers that most impressed his wife.

"On our terrace there are flowers," she exclaimed. "The climbing roses usually last four days, then lose their petals and new buds form. But after my husband's death the roses, about one hundred and fifty of them, bloomed at once and lasted for several weeks." The more Amaya Fodor observed the roses, the more her interest grew.

"For that period of time, no rose dropped a petal," she reported. "Then one day they all withered together. I cut them off and as I did so I asked for just one rose. I got it one week later—just one rose, which also lasted for several weeks."

Could these mysterious roses have bloomed by coincidence? That's a possibility, but for the fact that Fodor's case isn't unique. The well-known novelist Taylor Caldwell reports a similar experience in the October 1972 issue of *Ladies' Home Journal*. Ms. Caldwell and her husband, Marcus Rebak, had a shrub of resurrection lilies that never bloomed—not once in twenty-one years. Rebak used to quip to his wife, in fact, that "you can't prove the resurrection by these lilies." Yet when he died in April 1970, the lilies finally bloomed—on the day of his funeral.

Mark Twain's Premonition

Mark Twain, born Samuel Clemens, remains America's best-loved writer. Born in the little town of Florida, Missouri, and raised in nearby Hannibal, he was able to pen true Americana in such books as *Huckleberry Finn*. But few people know that beneath the humor and cynicism, Mark Twain was a serious student of the paranormal. His interest in the subject stemmed from personal experience, including the day in 1858 when he precognized his brother's death.

The writer was then working as a steersman on a packet traveling between New Orleans and St. Louis. One night while remaining ashore for a few days, he dreamt that his brother Henry was lying in a metal coffin dressed in one of Twain's own suits. The coffin was suspended between two chairs, and a bouquet of flowers—with a red rose in the center—rested on his chest. The dream was so vivid that when he awoke, Twain didn't realize that he had been sleeping and thought he was at home.

The dream had a tragic denouement two days later. While Twain remained in New Orleans, the packet on which he worked continued down the Mississippi. His brother also worked the boat and was continuing the journey when a boiler exploded. Henry was severely injured and taken to Memphis, where he died when the doctor accidentally injected him with too much morphine.

When Henry was prepared for burial, some kind ladies raised the money to procure a metal casket for him. His body was dressed in one of Twain's suits. While the writer was mourning his brother's death, a lady entered the room and placed a bouquet of white roses—with a red rose in the center—on the chest of the deceased. Later the casket was sent to St. Louis, where it was placed upstairs in his brother-in-law's home. When Mark Twain visited the room housing the body, he saw that the coffin had been placed on two chairs, just as he had seen in his dream.

A Shared Vision

Carl Jung, the famous Swiss psychiatrist, was equally well known for his interest in the occult. No subject within the realms of the paranormal bypassed his interest. He followed the burgeoning field of parapsychology, became a student of both astrology and alchemy, and carefully recorded his personal paranormal experiences. Many of these encounters are fully reported in his autobiographical *Memories, Dreams, Reflections*.

He had what was probably his strangest experience in 1913, while visiting the tomb of Galla Placidia in Ravenna with a friend. The psychiatrist was particularly impressed by a mosaic of Christ holding his hand out to Peter sinking beneath the waves. Jung and his woman friend examined the mosaic for twenty minutes and discussed the original rite of baptism in some depth. Jung never forgot that work of art. He had wanted to buy a photograph of it, but couldn't find one.

When Jung returned to his home in Zurich, he asked another friend, who was going to Ravenna, to obtain a picture of the mosaic. The upshot was both surprising and mystifying: The mosaic Jung and his friend had seen didn't exist. Jung reported this discovery to his former companion, who refused to believe that they had shared some sort of hallucination or vision. But the truth of the matter couldn't be countered: No such mosaic had ever been located on the baptistry wall.

"As we know," wrote Jung, "it is very difficult to determine whether, and to what extent, two persons simultaneously see the same thing. In this case, however, I was able to ascertain that at least the main feature of what we both saw had been the same."

Jung later characterized his experience in Ravenna as "the most curious of my life."

The Night Visitor

Dr. Michael Grosso was teaching a course in parapsychology at Jersey City State College in 1976 when he met Elizabeth Sebben, a bright anthropology major who had experienced many psychic encounters and was glad to find someone she could talk to. Grosso was especially interested in her out-of-body experiences. He suggested that she try to visit him should she find herself traveling out-of-body anytime soon. The visitation came in the autumn of 1976. Living by himself in a six-room apartment, he often passed his time practicing the flute. His musical exercises were usually placed on a music stand, which always stood near a particular bookcase. Grosso realized that something was peculiar one morning when, upon waking, he found the music stand in the middle of the room, even though he had never placed it there.

Grosso didn't think much of the incident until later that day, when Elizabeth called. She had tried to contact him the night before while out-of-body and wanted to tell him what she perceived. Without prompting from her friend, she told the following story: She had been studying the night before when she started feeling that she was leaving the body. She recalled that

The Pearl Tiepin

Next to good old-fashioned Monopoly, the Ouija board is probably one of the most popular games in the world. Even though many people don't take the board seriously, claims are that sometimes it leads to genuine contact with the beyond.

Hester Travers-Smith was a British psychic and an expert at working the board. One of her most famous cases involved a curious incident she shared with Geraldine Cummins, an Irish woman and a gifted psychic herself. They were working with the board in London during the terrible years of World War I when a cousin of Cummins, recently killed in France, took control of the board. The entity spelled out his name and then wrote, "Do you know who I am?"

The communicator next wrote the following message: "Tell mother to give my pearl tiepin to the girl I intended to marry. I think she should have it." The lady's full name, totally unfamiliar to the psychics, was then spelled out. The entity also offered the lady's London address, but when the psychics sent her a letter, it was returned to them. Since the address was either wrong or fictitious, the psychics lost interest in the case.

Six months later, however, Cummins learned that her cousin *had* been secretly engaged, a fact unknown even to his immediate family. His fiancée's name was the same as that spelled through the board, and when the War Office sent the youth's effects back to England, the family found the pearl tiepin mentioned in a will he had written while in France. It instructed his family to send the tiepin to his fiancée if he failed to return.

The entire case was later certified by Sir William Barrett, a noted physicist of his day, who examined the original records.

Lifesaving Telepathy

Some critics claim that even if ESP exists, it has no practical value. John H. Sullivan would disagree with that sentiment, since telepathy probably saved his life.

The incident took place on June 14, 1955, when Sullivan was welding a water pipe in the West Roxbury section of Boston. When his trench suddenly caved in, Sullivan was buried by dirt and only his hand could be seen sticking out. At roughly the same time, Sullivan's friend and fellow welder, Thomas Whittaker, was working at a different site. But something kept preying on his mind. He finally stopped work early and told another employee that something was wrong at the Roxbury site. Whittaker found himself driving to the location, taking several roads he usually specifically avoided. When he reached the trench, he saw one of his company's trucks unattended, its generator running.

"I walked over and looked into the fourteen-foot trench," he later testified. "At first I could see only dirt. Then I realized it was a cave-in, and then I saw a hand."

Whittaker began digging out the buried man, and some firemen arrived in short order to help. Sullivan was badly injured and probably would have died had the rescue been delayed.

The Angels of Mons

On August 26, 1914, the defeated British Expeditionary Force at Mons, France, found itself outnumbered by Germans three-to-one, and in full retreat. Disaster loomed on the horizon as a unit of Emperor Frederick Wilhelm's cavalry blocked their path.

But the coup de grace never fell. Suddenly, the German horses panicked, rearing on their hind hooves, nostrils flaring. The German cavalary fled the scene and the retreating British poured through to safety.

What stayed the German swords and panicked their horses? An article published in London's *Evening News* a month after their miraculous survival said the English soldiers had been spared by the sight of a squadron of angels hovering over their heads. The author of the article was one Arthur Machen, a writer of occult horror tales who rubbed shoulders with Yeats and Aleister Crowley as members of the Hermetic Order of the Golden Dawn, the twentieth-century's most infamous magical society.

According to Machen's article, "The Bowmen: The Angels of Mons," when the Germans deployed their forces for the final kill they beheld a vision in the heavens of a ghostly army arrayed on the British side. Even more remarkable, the angels were in the form of British bowmen of yore, their long bows drawn and aimed directly in the face of the enemy.

The story caused such a sensation in England that Machen finally admitted the angels were totally a figment of his own active imagination. But the account of celestial saviors aiding the Tommies in the trenches refused to die. When the survivors of Mons began returning home, many told tales that corroborated the angelic bowmen. A flood of articles and pamphlets subsequently supported the story. The Reverend C. M. Chavasse, an army chaplain, said he had it firsthand from both a brigadier general and two of his fellow officers who had been at the battle.

Despite Machen's denials, the Angels of Mons took on a life of their own. Unaware of his own actions, perhaps Machen had tapped into the collective consciousness of war-torn England. Undoubtedly the angels boosted spirits in the darkest days of the war, when England's finest were being slaughtered pell-mell in the fields of France. And in the end the ruse, if it was one, worked. The English and their allies did emerge victorious. The angels had been on the winning side after all.

Jungle Visions

Some travelers along the Amazon have reported that the natives there sometimes become psychic when they ingest certain plant distillates.

Dr. William McGovern was an assistant curator of South American ethnography at the Field Museum of Natural History when he made his observations in the 1920s. He was exploring the native settlements of the Amazon River, where he watched the Indians concoct a psychedelic brew from an hallucinogenic chemical called harmaline, found in the *Banisteriopsis caapi* vine.

"Certain of the Indians," he said, "fell into a particularly deep state of trance in which they possessed what appeared to be telepathic powers. Two or three of the men described what was going on in *malokas* [settlements] hundreds of miles away, many of which they had never visited, and the inhabitants of which they had never seen, but which seemed to tally exactly with what I knew of the places and people concerned. More extraordinary still, on this particular evening, the local medicine man told me that the chief of a certain tribe in far away Pira Panama had suddenly died. I entered this statement in my diary, and many weeks later, when we came to the tribe in question, I found that the witch doctor's statements had been true in every detail.''

Harmaline was later imported to Europe, where researchers at the Pasteur Institute in France experimented with it. They reported that their subjects became so psychic after taking it that they renamed the drug ''telepathine.''

The Thompson-Gifford Case

The scene was New Bedford, a coastal town in Massachusetts where two very different people liked to take long exploratory walks. The first was a rather unremarkable craftsman and Sunday painter of sorts named Frederic Thompson, and the other was the internationally acclaimed artist Robert Swain Gifford. Frederic Thompson liked to hunt for game along the coast and on rare occasions met Gifford, who liked to paint scenes suggested by the local landscape.

Frederic Thompson's strange psychic odyssey began in the summer of 1905 when he suddenly developed the urge to paint and sketch. He was continually haunted by landscape scenes that invaded his mind, and even believed that part of his personality was somehow linked to R. Swain Gifford. He didn't know that the celebrated painter had died and it was only sometime later that he discovered this fact while working in New York. Walking down a street on his lunch break, Thompson discovered an art gallery where the *late* R. Swain Gifford's paintings were on display. The shock was so great that he blacked out. His last memory before entering this short-lived fugue was of a voice saying, "You see what I have done. Go on with the work."

By the end of the year, Thompson's personality had begun to disintegrate, and he could no longer perform his job. He still felt compelled to paint and sketch, and the results often mimicked Gifford's style. He finally sought out Professor James H. Hyslop, then in charge of the American Society for Psychical Research in New York.

Hyslop, well trained in the psychology of his time, wasn't impressed with Thompson's tale. He felt that the man was probably heading for a breakdown and little else; but the professor did feel that a simple experiment might be in order. Since he was scheduled to visit a psychic shortly after this interview, Hyslop decided to take Thompson with him. Perhaps, he reasoned, the psychic could help diagnose the man's problems. This sitting proved productive since the psychic immediately sensed an artist at the séance and even described a landscape that had been haunting Thompson's mind.

The mystery deepened in July 1907, when Frederic Thompson gave Hyslop a series of his sketches revolving around two different scenes: a group of five isolated trees, and two gnarled oaks by a wild shoreline. Hoping to investigate the case on his own, Thompson then went to visit Gifford's widow in Nonquitt, a small Massachusetts town. There he found that his sketch of the five trees exactly matched an unfinished painting in Mrs. Gifford's possession. Her husband had been working on it at the time of his death. The following October, Thompson discovered the scene that had inspired his sketch of the oak trees and shoreline just off the New Bedford coast.

James H. Hyslop published his study of the case in the *Proceedings* of the American Society for Psychical Research in 1909. Frederic Thompson himself later became a successful artist, exhibiting his work for nearly two decades in the well-known galleries of New York.

The Imaginary Ghost

A thought-form is a physical object materialized through the power of the human mind. But do thought-forms exist? In the summer of 1972, several members of the Toronto Society for Psychical Research decided to search for so-called thought-forms by conjuring up a ghost. After several false starts, the group finally worked out a procedure that looked promising: re-creating the atmosphere of a typical Victorian séance. To facilitate the experiments, the group decided to establish contact with a totally fictitious entity. So one of the members created a biography for the spook. Named Philip, he was a Catholic nobleman in seventeenth-century England who had killed himself when his wife exposed his mistress as a supposed witch.

The group met weekly and, while sitting around the table, would exhort Philip to reveal himself. When they placed their hands on the table, Philip would often respond by tilting it. The table eventually began moving about, emitting mysterious raps from its surface.

"I wonder if by chance Philip is doing it," one of the sitters finally asked. When a clear rap responded, the group became tremendously excited and began to converse regularly with the ghost by code.

As might be expected, the raps—for which no normal explanation could be found—would reply in complete accordance with Philip's fictitious biography. If the entity were asked a question for which the group had never created a proper response, the table would emit only weird sawing sounds.

The sound and movement grew stronger the longer the group sat. Members reported that the table raised upon one leg and even levitated. They also said it displayed a raucous sense of humor. If anyone tried to sit on the table to stabilize it, a sudden force would throw him or her to the floor. The raps would also sometimes leave the confines of the table and sound from elsewhere in the room.

Because of the spectacular nature of these experiments, the Toronto group began to doubt the existence of bona fide *spirits*. Instead, it declared, spiritlike behavior could be traced to thought-forms created solely through the powers of the mind.

Spontaneous Regeneration

Pierre de Rudder was a Belgian peasant who lived in Jabbeke, near the city of Bruges. His strange story began in 1869, when he fell from a tree and shattered his leg. The damage was so extensive that the leg couldn't be reset, and when the bone fragments were removed, over an inch separated the upper and lower parts of the limb. Dangling freely, de Rudder's lower leg was held in place only by muscle tissue and skin. His physician wanted to amputate the limb, but despite the pain de Rudder steadfastly refused. He suffered from the pain for eight years before he decided to visit the city of Oostacker, the site of a shrine in honor of Lourdes.

Riding to Ghent by train caused de Rudder intolerable pain. He was even lifted onto the train by three helpers, and the discharge from his injury was so objectionable that he was nearly thrown off.

Needless to say, de Rudder was in a terrible state when he finally arrived in Oostacker, but he made his way to the shrine and began to pray. That's when a sudden ecstasy overcame him and, according to reports, he stood up and walked without the help of his crutches.

De Rudder died in 1898 and Dr. van Hoestenbergh had his body exhumed two years after so that he could more closely examine his former patient's legs and their primary bones. Photographs of the bones clearly showed, the doctor declared, that new bone was used to fuse the irreparably broken leg.

Damascus Steel

Among the numerous magical methods that seemed to work in earlier days was the damascene process of hardening steel swords by thrusting a superheated blade into the body of a prisoner or slave and then into cold water. In the Middle Ages Christian knights learned, to their dismay, that swords made of Damascus steel were more resilient and also harder than those of European manufacture.

Five hundred years after the Crusades, however, experiments in Europe indicated that the process was not magic after all. The Europeans found that thrusting a red-hot sword into a mass of animal skins soaking in water had a similar effect to the Damascus method. The organic nitrogen given off by the skins in the water produces a chemical reaction in the steel.

Map Dowsing

Dowsers usually work by holding twigs or rods in their hands, waiting for them to bend near water or precious ores. But dowsing can be used to discover more than just substances alone. J. Scott Elliot, a retired British military officer and expert dowser, uses his skill to help uncover archaeological sites. Sometimes he doesn't even visit the locations he wants to probe, but merely holds a pendulum over a map.

One of his typical successes was reported in 1969, when he used map dowsing to predict that a large structure would be unearthed under a cottage in the town of Swinebrook. Local excavators were skeptical, since Scott Elliot had designated a town in which no buried ruins had ever been found. It was six months before a trial dig was made there, and sure enough, the structure pinpointed by the dowser was readily discovered.

By making a five by ten foot trial cut, the local excavators found postholes, bones, and some pottery. When the site was more thoroughly exhumed in 1970, they found the floors of a structure and even its hearth. Two highly polished Bronze Age tools capped the sensational find.

A Double Nightmare

Like the young George Washington, Steven Linscott, a twenty-six-year-old Bible student from Illinois, felt compelled to tell the truth—but Linscott ended up in jail for it.

The events leading to his incarceration began on October 4, 1980, when Oak Park, Illinois, police were searching for leads in the murder of Karen Ann Phillips. The twenty-four-year-old nurse had been killed the previous morning and the police were visiting the Good Neighbor Mission—a halfway house for ex-convicts—in hopes of finding some relevant information. That's when they met Linscott.

A highly respected Bible student at a nearby college, Linscott happened to work at the mission. And when the police explained their purpose, he began thinking about his recent nightmare—in which he saw a blond young woman beaten to death. It was only after considerable thought that he finally told the police about his dream.

"I suddenly became intrigued by the possibility of my dream being an inspired experience," he later said. "If nothing else, going to the police seemed like an interesting diversion from memorizing two chapters of Romans."

Linscott's dream certainly did prompt the interest of detectives Robert Scianna and Robert Grego, who questioned their informant in detail. Linscott apparently knew so much about the murder that he was taken into custody as a suspect. He was formally arrested and charged with the murder in November.

Even though the prosecution's case was wholly circumstantial, the jury found him guilty, despite the fact that he had no motive and the fingerprints found at the crime scene weren't his.

Linscott was shattered by the verdict. "Everybody trusts the system," he later explained. "Everybody trusts the fact-finding process. Nobody realizes that it's a slick pole once you start sliding on it and you can't get off."

Steven Linscott served three years of his forty-year sentence before the Illinois Court of Appeals released him. The state's Supreme Court reinstated the conviction later, but the Bible student is currently free on bond pending another appeal.

Food for Spanish Horses

When the Spanish conquistadors first reached Peru, center of the great empire of the Incas, the Peruvian Indians thought that the Spanish war horses were ferocious and deadly monsters, quite unlike their own gentle llamas, especially when the horses stamped their hooves, snorted, and shook their heads.

The Peruvians nervously asked the Spanish calvarymen through an interpreter, "What do these fierce animals eat?" The Spanish knew what to reply. Pointing to the gold jewelry and gold ornaments of the Peruvians they said, "They eat those things of yellow metal. They are hungry now but do not wish to be seen eating. Leave the food in front of them and go away." At this point the Indians would gather a pile of gold objects that the Spaniards would pocket and then, calling back the Indians, would say, "These fierce animals are still hungry. Bring more food."

Psychic Mind Control

Wolf Messing, who died in 1974, was undoubtedly the Soviet Union's most celebrated psychic performer. He was best known for his stage performances during which he would carry out telepathic commands suggested by members of the audience. Those who became his close friends, however, had more spectacular stories to tell, including tales of his power to control another person's mind—even from miles away.

One such story has been told by Dr. Alexander Lungin, whose mother was Messing's unofficial secretary for several years. The incident took place while Lungin was in medical school in Moscow. His anatomy instructor, a Professor Gravilov, had taken a fierce dislike to him, and continually warned the youth that he planned to fail him, regardless of the work he did. The day of reckoning came when Lungin had to take his final examination. Each student had to take an oral test by approaching a table at which several examiners sat. One of them would then proceed with the questions. Just before the test, Gravilov gleefully told Lungin that he would be personally examining him. Terror-stricken by the news, Lungin conveyed his fears to his mother who phoned Messing and asked him to intercede. The psychic, who lived miles from the school, called back later and made it clear that he would.

When the time finally came, Lungin walked up to the examiners to take his orals and Gravilov didn't say a word. Instead, he merely looked on while Lungin was examined by another professor. The vindictive teacher even watched as the other professor signed Lungin's record book to show he had taken the test.

Needless to say, the student was delighted by these events, but what happened next was even more bizarre.

Lungin left the classroom and went outside to talk to some of the other students. Professor Gravilov came stalking out imperiously a few minutes later to ask if everyone had taken the examination. When the students replied that they had, Gravilov glared at the student he despised.

"Lungin hasn't taken it yet," he growled.

When the students explained that he had taken it and passed, Gravilov became enraged. "How did he pass?" he demanded sternly. "It can't be. Who gave him the exam?"

When the professor checked the records, he became livid and scurried off. Alexander Lungin had somehow outwitted him—probably with a little help from his famous friend Wolf.

Dadaji's Strange Visit

Can a person be physically present in two places at the same time? The idea sounds totally preposterous, but just such a case was reported by two respected parapsychologists in 1975. Dr. Karlis Osis and Dr. Erlendur Haraldsson, visiting India in 1970 to study that country's holy men, were especially interested in Dadaji, a businessman-turned-saint. He had a large mass of followers in southern India, and while looking into his purported miracles, the two researchers uncovered the following story:

Sometime in the early part of 1970, Dadaji visited Allahabad, some four hundred miles away from his home, and stayed with a local family. During that stay, he went out to meditate and later told his followers that he had bilocated to Calcutta. He even told his hostess that she could substantiate his story by contacting her sister-in-law, who lived there. The holy man also gave her the address of the residence where he projected himself.

According to the family who lived in the house, they did in fact verify Dadaji's unbelievable story. Roma Mukherjee, a disciple of the holy man, explained that she was reading a book in the study when Dadaji appeared before her. His figure was transparent at first, she explained, but then more fully materialized. The phantom's sudden appearance so frightened her that she screamed, summoning her brother and mother to her side. Dadaji, in the meantime, did little but motion to the girl to bring him some tea.

"When she returned to the study with the tea," report the two researchers, "Roma was followed by her mother and physician brother. She reached in through the partly opened door and gave Dadaji the tea and a biscuit. The mother, through a crack in the door, saw Dadaji. The brother, standing in a different position, only saw Roma's hand reach in through the opening and come back without the tea. There was no place she could have set the cup without entering the room. Then the father, a bank director, came home from morning shopping at the bazaar. He didn't believe what they told him and, brushing away their objections, peeked in through the crack in the door, where he saw a man's figure sitting on a chair."

When the family finally entered the room, Dadaji had disappeared, but a half-burned cigarette was left on the study table. It was Dadaji's favorite brand.

Talking to Animals

Vladimir Durov was an exceptional circus performer and extraordinary animal trainer. Capable of making his show animals perform whatever stunts he wanted, he claimed that part of his success came from the ability to establish psychic contact with his beasts. This claim eventually came to the attention of Professor W. Bechterev, head of the Institute for the Investigation of the Brain in St. Petersburg.

Intrigued, Bechterev tested Durov's claim with the help of a fox terrier. The usual procedure was for Bechterev to choose a series of commands, then tell them to Durov, who would take little Pikki's head into his hands, stare into the dog's eyes, and impress the instructions onto his brain.

For the first trial, Bechterev suggested that Durov make his pet jump on a specific chair, climb over to a table right next to it, then scratch the painting positioned over it. Durov complied by impressing the signals onto Pikki's brain, a procedure that took several minutes, and the little dog went to work.

"Pikki, after a few seconds, jumped from his chair, quickly ran to one at the wall, then equally quickly jumped on a little round table," reported Bechterev. "Rising on his hind legs, he reached the portrait with his right paw, scratching it a little with his claws." Taking instructions from Durov, Bechterev even found he could communicate instructions to Pikki himself.

The celebrated scientist could not, however, rule out the possibility that he and Durov were unintentionally cuing the dog with eye movements, so he later sent two of his colleagues to work with Durov and Pikki in Moscow. Durov explained his procedure for impressing commands on the dog, and the scientists performed their experiments while wearing blindfolds or metal screens over their faces. Pikki was able to respond to their psychic commands despite the controls.

But one especially provocative puzzle remains. Could Durov really communicate with his pet by psychically impressing instructions to the dog's brain, or was Pikki merely an especially psychic dog?

Search for Sasquatch

Grover Krantz claims his chosen field of research has torpedoed his academic career and brought him nothing but ridicule from colleagues. An anthropologist at Washington State University, Krantz specializes in the study of the world's most elusive primate, the so-called Bigfoot, or Sasquatch, often reported as inhabiting the dense forests of the Pacific Northwest.

Stories of huge, hairy, apelike animals in the Blue Mountains of Washington and Oregon date back to the nineteenth century. Orthodox anthropologists tend to dismiss such tales as fanciful folklore, but not Krantz, who believes the Sasquatch may be our nearest living relative. Humans, in fact, may be directly descended from the shy interloper, remains of which have never been found.

The controversial primate draws its name from the gigantic footprints it leaves behind, prints two feet long in some cases, separated by a six-foot stride. According to eyewitnesses, Sasquatch stands as much as eight feet tall and may weigh as much as eight hundred pounds. The body is completely covered in dark-brown hair, save for the flat face, and the palms and soles of its hands and feet. The face is characterized by a receding forehead and prominent brow ridge. Sasquatch's proportions are roughly those of a human, except for its dangling long arms. For food it seems to prefer roots, berries, and an occasional rodent.

Serious interest in Sasquatch was revived in the spring of 1987, with the discovery of four new sets of prints and the published analysis of another set of prints made by U.S. Forest Service rangers in 1982. The latter set of tracks measured seventeen inches long. Moreover, said Krantz, they showed evidence of dermal, or skin, ridges on the soles of the feet, along with sweat pores and wear patterns, anatomical details almost impossible to duplicate, even by the cleverest of hoaxters.

Pointing to the bone impressions in the plaster casts, Krantz also noted that the ankle seemed to be moved further forward on the foot than that of any other known primate, man and gorilla included. Such an evolutionary shift forward, Krantz added, would be necessary to support the creature's immense weight, another key detail fake prints would probably overlook.

Krantz himself isn't taking any more chances with the evidence or his reputation. He has vowed to shoot Sasquatch on sight, believing the scientific value to be gained should outweigh any squeamishness at the act. "The only way to convince anyone is with a real specimen," Krantz said. Short of shooting a Sasquatch, he hopes to use a helicopter and infrared detector to try to locate the decomposing remains of one.

New Zealand UFO

Movies and still photographs of UFOs are relatively rare. The ones that stand up to scrutiny are scarcer still. But some of the best and most thoroughly analyzed UFO pictures ever were taken by an Australian network TV crew on the night of December 30, 1978, near Kaikoura, New Zealand.

UFOs had been repeatedly reported during the previous weeks, primarily in the area of Cook Straight, which divides New Zealand's North and South Islands. Smelling a story, reporter Quentin Fogarty and cameraman David Crockett flew to Wellington. From there, they boarded the freight plane *Argosy*, piloted by Captain Bill Startup, and bound for Christchurch, on the south of New Zealand's two largest islands. Also accompanying the crew were copilot Bob Guard and sound engineer Ngaire Crockett, David's wife.

Fogarty and Crockett were filming introductory material from the plane just before landing when the cockpit came alive. Startup and Guard spotted several UFOs and contacted air-traffic control in Wellington. Wellington, in turn confirmed the sightings on radar. By the time Fogarty reached the flight deck, five pulsating lights were visible, varying from a pinpoint to what looked like a large balloon filled with light.

At this juncture Wellington informed the plane that "you have a target in formation with you." Startup banked the *Argosy* in a 360-degree turn but nothing immediate could be seen until he finally switched off the navigation lights. Then everyone could make out a single, bright light hovering in the night sky. Crockett switched seats with Guard, his TV camera running all the while. On the return flight from Christchurch, more UFOs were seen.

The videotape of the "Kaikoura Lights" is probably the single most heavily analyzed photo in UFO history. Even so, the results are largely inconclusive. Several potential light sources, such as the planets Venus and Jupiter, and brightly-lit squad boats on the ocean's surface can be eliminated as candidates. But what the tape does show may never be known, except that it clearly portrays an unidentified flying object.

Young Dante's Dream

The Divine Comedy of Dante Alighieri is rightly regarded as one of the world's great spiritual masterpieces. But for the dream of the dead poet's son, Jacopo, however, the complete manuscript might have been lost forever.

When Dante died in 1321, Jacopo and his brother, Pietro, despaired, not only for the loss of their father, but for the incomplete manuscript of the *Comedy* he left behind. The two turned the house upside down and rummaged through his papers, but the elder Dante's missing papers were not to be found.

In the depths of their mourning, Jacopo had a dream. His father entered his room, arrayed in blazing white garments. When Jacopo asked if he had finished his masterpiece, Dante nodded yes, and indicated where the missing sections could be found.

With a lawyer friend of his father bearing witness, Jacopo entered Dante's chambers. Behind a small blind attached to the wall they found a tiny window. In the cubicle on which it opened they beheld the poet's final pages, covered in mold. *The Divine Comedy* was again whole, thanks to a faithful son's dream.

A Ghost With a Message

Early in the morning of December 6, 1955, Lucian Landau, a London businessman, had an unusual drama. He was sleeping in the home of Constantine Antoniadès in Geneva when he felt someone entering his room. When he turned over in bed, he saw a faint pool of light in which he gradually perceived the figure of his host's late wife. Next to her figure stood an Alsatian dog with an unusual brown coat. The apparition soon began to disappear, but while desolving, Landau heard it say, "Tell him."

The London businessman didn't hesitate to impart the information to his host when they met later in the day. But he didn't explain exactly what had occurred. Instead, he merely asked whether his host's wife had ever had an Alsatian dog.

"Oh, yes," responded Mr. Antoniadès. "He is still alive."

This response puzzled Landau, since there was no evidence of a dog in the house. Antoniadès then explained that he boarded the dog at a kennel when his wife became ill, since he couldn't look after it. When Landau finally told his host about the ghostly visitation, Antoniadès called the kennel, only to learn that the dog had been destroyed a few days earlier.

The words "tell him" were finally beginning to make sense.

When an investigator from the Society for Psychical Research in Great Britain looked into the case, Antoniadès corroborated the remarkable episode. "I affirm," he testified, "that there was not any photograph of my wife with the dog or the dog alone anywhere in the house where Landau could have seen it before the incident occurred."

Psychic Stock Market Tips

Beverly Jaegers isn't your typical psychic. She doesn't conduct séances. And she would probably wince if you gave her some Tarot cards. But she does live in a lovely St. Louis home, bought with the money she's made by using her sixth sense. In fact, Jaegers views psi with all the rigor of a Wall Street executive. It isn't a fleeting and unreliable capability, she says, but something we can use productively every day of our lives.

In order to prove her point, Jaegers helped the *St. Louis Business Journal* perform an unusual experiment in 1982. The paper wanted to see just how reliable Jaeger's powers really were, so they pitted her against the stock market. The experiment began when the *Journal* asked each of nineteen prominent stockbrokers to choose five stocks they believed would increase in value. These stocks were subsequently monitored for six months. Even though Jaegers had no business experience or training, she was asked to pick five stocks based purely on her sixth sense.

The result?

The stock market entered into a downtrend during the period of the test, and by the time the experiment was completed, the Dow-Jones industrial average had fallen by eighty points. Because of this unfortunate trend, sixteen of the stockbrokers lost their shirts. They were undoubtedly surprised to learn that, during this same period, the stocks intuitively chosen by Jaegers increased in value by 17.2 percent. Only one of the stockbrokers matched her uncanny success.

Corn From the Sky

Since 1982 kernels of corn have been falling on houses along Pleasant Acres Drive in Evans, Colorado, just south of Greeley. Gary Bryan, who lives there, says, "I'd probably have a ton of it if I picked it all up." Once in a while a pinto bean appears amid the corn.

The problem is that there are no cornfields near the houses, and the nearest grain elevator is five miles away. Nobody can figure out where the corn could be coming from. All the witnesses can say is that from time to time it is seen descending from the sky.

When the press heard the story in September 1986, reporters from area newspapers and television channels came to the site and saw the bizarre phenomenon for themselves. As the corn was falling, they searched for a prankster with a slingshot but found none.

People who hadn't seen the fall with their own eyes didn't believe it—until they saw it themselves. As one convert, Eldred McClintock, told the *Rocky Mountain News*, "It really came down. I've seen it now and I believe it."

Kangaroo Monster

"It was as fast as lightning and looked like a giant kangaroo running and leaping across the field," the Reverend W. J. Hancock said. Frank Cobb, who also saw it, said it didn't look like anything he'd ever seen, although in some ways it resembled a kangaroo.

Kangaroos, which are not native to Tennessee, are unaggressive, herbivorous animals. But this beast was a killer. In January 1934 the creature was terrorizing the tiny community of Hamburg, Tennessee, and had already killed and partially devoured several German shepherd dogs.

When the creature visited the Henry Ashmore farm on January 12, it left five-clawed tracks the size of a big man's hand. Will Patten saw the thing and chased it away. The next day he found a partially-eaten dog in his yard.

The creature was also killing geese and chickens and as armed parties searched for it without success, panic set in. A. B. Russell, chief of police of nearby South Pittsburg, Tennessee, tried to defuse the hysteria, calling it "superstition started by a mad dog." But those who had seen it knew better. They said it was huge—weighing at least 150 pounds—and incredibly agile, able to leap fences and other hurdles with ease. It ranged between South Pittsburg and Signal Mountain, which meant that to get around it had to cross two mountain ranges and two rivers.

Finally a bobcat was shot and killed on Signal Mountain on January 29, thirteen days after the creature's last appearance. The authorities and the newspapers declared that the mystery had been solved, but witnesses resolutely rejected that explanation. What they had seen, they said, was large and kangaroo-like.

The monster was never seen again and it has never been satisfactorily identified or explained.

The Dover Demon

For more than twenty-five hours in April 1977 a strange creature from another world made its presence known in the wealthy Boston suburb of Dover.

The Dover demon first appeared at 10:30 on the evening of April 21, when three seventeen-year-olds were driving north on Farm Street. The driver, Bill Bartlett, thought he saw something creeping along a low wall of loose stones to his left. Then his headlights illuminated something he had never imagined even in his wildest dreams.

The creature slowly turned its head and stared into the light, revealing two large, lidless eyes shining "like two orange marbles" and an otherwise featureless face with no apparent nose. It had a head shaped like an upright watermelon and nearly the size of the rest of its body, which was thin and spindly. The hairless skin had the apparent consistency of "wet sandpaper." About four feet tall, it had been making its way uncertainly along the wall, wrapping its long fingers around the rocks as it moved.

The sight struck Bartlett speechless and a few seconds later, when he found his voice, his headlights had passed the creature. His two companions, their attentions elsewhere, had not seen it at all.

Not long afterward, fifteen-year-old John Baxter was walking home up Millers High Road after dropping his girlfriend off at midnight. A mile later he saw a short figure approaching and assumed it was a friend who lived on the street. Baxter called out to him but got no response.

The two continued to approach each other until the short figure stopped. Baxter stopped too and asked, "Who is that?" The sky was overcast and he could see only a shadowy form. When he took one step forward, the form shot off to the left, ran down a shallow gully, and dashed up the opposite bank.

Perplexed, Baxter followed the stranger until he got to the gully. He looked across and thirty feet away saw something with a monkey-shaped body, a "figure-eight-shaped" watermelon-like head, and glowing eyes. Its long fingers were entwined around a tree.

Baxter felt suddenly uneasy and left the scene.

The next person to see the Dover demon was Bill Bartlett's friend, Will Taintor, eighteen. Taintor knew about the creature from Bartlett. Still, he was shocked when he and his friend Abby Brabham, fifteen, saw the thing along Springdale Avenue. Their description matched Bartlett's except that where he described glowing orange eyes, they swore the eyes were green.

When investigators interviewed the witnesses, they were impressed with the consistency of their testimony. They were also impressed when the police chief, the high school principal, schoolteachers, and the youths' parents all said the young people were honest and reliable.

As one of the investigators, Walter Webb, observed at the conclusion of his probe into the case, "None of the four was on drugs or drinking at the time of his or her sighting so far as we were able to determine. . . . None of the principals in this affair made any attempt to go to the newspapers or police to publicize their claims. Instead the sightings gradually leaked out. As for the idea the witnesses were victims of somebody else's stunt, this seems most unlikely, chiefly due to the virtual impossibility of creating an animated, lifelike 'demon' of the sort described."

What was the Dover demon? Some have suggested it was an extraterrestrial. Others say it may be something known to the Cree Indians of eastern Canada as the Mannegishi. Little people with round heads, no noses, long spidery legs, and six-fingered hands, the Mannegishi legend goes, live between rocks in the rapids of streams and rivers.

Hotel in Another Dimension

It all began innocently enough in October 1979, when two couples in Dover, England, set off on a vacation together intending to travel through France and Spain. It ended in a journey that took them to another world.

Geoff and Pauline Simpson and their friends, Len and Cynthia Gisby, boarded a boat that took them across the English Channel to the coast of France. There they rented a car and proceeded to drive south. Around 9:30 that first evening, October 3, they began to tire and looked for a place to stay. They pulled off the autoroute when they saw a plushlooking motel.

Len went inside and in the lobby encountered a man dressed in an odd plum-colored uniform. The man said there was no room in the motel but there was a small motel south along the road. Len thanked him and he and his companions went on.

Along the way they were struck by the oldness of the cobbled, narrow road and the buildings they passed. They also saw posters advertising a circus. "It was a very old-fashioned circus," Pauline would remember. "That's why we took so much interest."

Finally the travelers saw a long, low building with a row of brightly lit windows. Some men were standing in front of it and when Cynthia spoke with them, they told her the place was an inn, not a hotel. They drove farther down the road until they saw two buildings, one a police station, the other an old-fashioned, two-story building bearing a sign marked "Hotel." Inside, everything was made of heavy wood. There were no tablecloths on the tables, nor was there any evidence of such modern conveniences as telephones or elevators.

The rooms were no less strange. The beds had heavy sheets and no pillows. There were no locks on the doors, only wooden catches. The bathroom the couples had to share had old-fashioned plumbing.

After they ate, they returned to their rooms and fell asleep. They were awakened when sunlight filtered through the windows, which consisted only of wooden shutters, no glass. They went back to the dining room and ate a simple breakfast with "black and horrible" coffee, Geoff recalled.

As they were sitting there, a woman wearing a silk evening gown and carrying a dog under her arm sat opposite them. "It was strange," Pauline said. "It looked like she had just come in from a ball but it was seven in the morning. I couldn't take my eyes off her."

At that point two gendarmes entered the room. "They were nothing like the gendarmes we saw anywhere else in France," according to Geoff. "Their uniforms seemed to be very old." The uniforms were deep blue and the officers were wearing capes over their shoulders. Their hats were large and peaked.

Despite the oddities, the couples enjoyed themselves and, when they returned to their rooms, the two husbands separately took pictures of their wives standing by the shuttered windows.

On their way out Len and Geoff talked with the gendarmes about the best way to take the autoroute to Avignon and the Spanish border. The officers didn't seem to understand the word "autoroute," and the travelers assumed they hadn't pronounced the French word properly. The directions they were given were quite poor; they took the friends to an old road some miles out of the way. They decided to use the map instead and take a more direct route along the highway.

After the car was packed, Len went to pay his bill and was astonished when the manager asked for only nineteen francs. Assuming there was some misunderstanding, Len explained that there were four of them and they had eaten a meal. The manager only nodded. Len showed the bill to the gendarmes, who smilingly indicated there was nothing amiss. He paid in cash and left before they could change their minds.

On their way back from two weeks in Spain, the two couples decided to stop at the hotel again. They had had a pleasant, interesting time there and the prices certainly couldn't be beat. The night was rainy and cold and visibility poor, but they found the turnoff and noticed the circus signs they had seen before.

"This is definitely the right road," Pauline declared.

It was, but there was no hotel alongside it. Thinking that somehow they had missed it, they went back to the motel where the man in the plum-colored suit had given them directions. That motel was there, but there was no man in the unusual suit and the clerk denied such an individual worked there.

The couples drove three times up and down the road looking for something that, they were now beginning to realize, was no longer there. It had vanished without a trace.

They drove north and spent the night in a hotel in Lyons. Room with modern facilities, breakfast and dinner cost them 247 francs.

Upon their return to Dover, Geoff and Len had their respective rolls of film processed. In each case the pictures of the hotel (one by Geoff, two by Len) were in the middle of the roll. But when they got the pictures back, the ones taken inside the hotel were missing. There were no spoiled negatives. Each film had its full quota of pictures. It was as if the pictures had never been taken—except for one small detail that a reporter for Yorkshire television would notice: "There was evidence that the camera had tried to wind on in the middle of the film. Sprocket holes on the negatives showed damage."

The couples kept quiet about their experience for three years, telling it only to friends and family. One friend found a book in which it was revealed that gendarmes wore the uniforms described prior to 1905. Eventually a reporter for the Dover newspaper heard it and published an account. Later a television dramatization of the experience was produced by a local station.

In 1985 Manchester psychiatrist Albert Keller hypnotized Geoff Simpson to see if he could recall any more of the peculiar event. Under hypnosis he added nothing new to what he consciously remembered.

Jenny Randles, a British writer who investigated this bizarre episode, wonders, "What really happened to the four travelers in rural France? Was this a time slip? If so, one wonders why the hotel manager was apparently not surprised by their futuristic vehicle and clothing and why he accepted their 1979 currency, which certainly would have appeared odd to anybody living that far back in the past."

The travelers—perhaps time-travelers—have no explanation. "We only know what happened," says Geoff.

African Alarm Clock

Many people can wake themselves up at any time of night, just by giving themselves the proper suggestion before falling asleep. During the 1960s, a researcher in Cape Town, South Africa, proved that he could wake up given the correct *psychic* suggestion.

Mr. W. van Vuurde was the subject of these experiments, which were conducted in collaboration with Professor A.E.H. Bleksley of the University of Witwatersrand. Mr. van Vuurde had discovered that he could wake up to match the time set on a broken clock, even if he didn't look when he manipulated the hands while setting it. When he explained his peculiar talent to Dr. Bleksley, the professor was eager to test the subject under more stringent conditions.

For a series of 284 nonconsecutive nights, W. van Vuurde kept a careful record of each time he woke during the night. Meanwhile, elsewhere in the city, Professor A.E.H. Bleksley randomly set a clock to a different time each night the experiment was conducted. A trial was considered a success when van Vuurde woke on any experimental night within sixty seconds of the appropriate time. Since he typically slept for eight hours, the chances for any given night's success was 160-to-1.

Out of the 284 experiments, the subject woke to the correct time on eleven occasions. That may not seem like much, but because of the low odds, the chances of this success rate resulting from chance is 250,000-to-1.

Psychic Detective

No subject raises the skeptic's hackles like police who rely on psychics—especially when the officials go public with the news.

On Sunday morning, August 4, 1982, Tommy Kennedy went on a picnic near Empire Lake in New York and disappeared. Soon everyone was called in to help locate the missing five-year-old, from the lake's casual visitors to the Tioga County Sheriff's Department. Nobody could find a trace of the boy, and Tommy's mother grew increasingly frantic. By six o'clock that evening, nearly 100 people were exploring the nearby woods. Finally, Richard Clark, a fireman who was taking part in the work, suggested they call Phillip Jordan, a prominent local psychic, who happened to be the firefighter's tenant. Nobody thought much of the idea, except for Deputy David Redsicker, who had seen the psychic at work.

That evening, Phil Jordan visited the Clarks at their home in Spenser, New York. Without telling him anything, the fireman handed the psychic a T-shirt the lost boy had worn. After fingering it for several minutes, Jordan asked for a pencil and some paper. Then he began sketching a lake, some overturned boats, and a house by a rock.

"That's where they'll find the boy," he explained. "I can see him lying under a tree with his head in his arms. He's sound asleep."

This information was immediately forwarded to the sheriff's office. The next day, Richard Clark and Phil Jordan went to Empire Lake to continue the search. Tommy's mother was naturally present and cooperative, and this time the psychic gathered his impressions from a pair of the boy's sneakers. His second series of impressions matched the first, so the search party was directed into the woods to find the tree and house he had seen.

Tommy Kennedy was found within the hour, in the exact place identified by the psychic on his map. The boy had wandered off the day before, and subsequently walked in the wrong direction until he became hopelessly lost in the woods. He had spent the night crying and sleeping under a tree.

Phil Jordan was given an honorary deputy sheriff's badge from the Tioga County Sheriff's Department for his help on the case. "The boy had lain and slept under that tree for most of the twenty hours and we missed him," said Sheriff Raymond Ayres. "Phil Jordan simply used some kind of paranormal talent that the rest of us don't have. I would not hesitate to call on him again if I thought he could help."

Death Clicks

The Samoans believe that when death hovers near, paranormal raps will break out in the victim's home. This strange phenomenon has been called the death click or death rattle, and its existence represents more than mere folklore.

Genevieve B. Miller, for instance, often heard these strange sounds, particularly as a small girl. She first heard the raps during the summer of 1924 in Woronoco, Massachusetts, when her sister, Stephanie, was bedridden with a mysterious illness. While the girl remained in bed, knocking sounds, which sounded like knuckles cracking, echoed through the house. They would come in sets of three, with one drawn-out click followed by two shorter raps. Once, Mrs. Miller's father became so irritated by the sounds that he ripped out every window screen in the house, blaming them for the ruckus. But his little rampage did nothing to stop the noise.

By October 4, it was clear that Stephanie was dying. When the doctor arrived, he heard the noises too.

"What on earth is that?" he said while turning to find the source of the sound. When he turned back to his small patient, she uttered her last words and died.

The raps decreased their activity after the death, but never completely stopped. They erupted now and then when the family moved to a new home. Then, in 1928, Stephanie's brother broke through the ice while walking over a frozen river and drowned.

From that day forward, the death clicks were never heard again.

The Man With the Photographic Mind

Ted Serios has been called "the man with the photographic mind"—not because of his memory, but because of his ability to impress pictures on Polaroid film by pure concentration.

Most of what we know about the case comes from Denver psychiatrist Jule Eisenbud, who worked with Serios in the sixties. A former Chicago bellhop, Serios lived in Eisenbud's home for the duration of the experiments. His usual procedure was to stare into the camera lens, often through a black paper cylinder, and tell the experimenters when to snap the shutter. A blurry scene would often be found printed on the resulting snapshot.

Of course, skeptics howled that it was a fraud from start to finish, claiming the strange cylinder Serios liked to work with contained a hidden lens. But such criticism can't explain all of Serios's successes by any means.

An especially provocative experiment was designed by Dr. Eisenbud in 1965. Several witnesses gathered at his home and each wrote a target theme on a slip of paper. Serios, not told of the suggestions, was simply asked to imprint one of the suggested targets onto Polaroid film. This meant that some part of Serios's mind had clairvoyantly to receive the slips, choose one of the targets, and then imprint it onto the photographic paper.

Serios began his part of the experiment by drinking a few beers and then got to work by focusing into the Polaroid camera. The image that subsequently resulted looked like a blurry close-up of a spider. It didn't seem to match any of the suggestions offered by the guests. The only one that came close was a slip with the words "staggerwing airplane" written on it. Two years later, however, Dr. Eisenbud was looking through a copy of *The American Heritage of Flight*, where, to his surprise, he found a series of photographs of staggerwing planes—and Serios's previous photograph was identical to one of them.

Fire and Faith

The Free Pentacostal Holiness Church is a fundamentalist sect with branches scattered throughout the South. Its members take the Bible literally and seriously believe the Bible when it states that true believers can defy serpents, poison, and fire. So as part of the religious services, the congregation will whip itself into a frenzy, at the height of which they will handle rattlesnakes, drink strychnine and touch fire, without any discomfort or ill effect.

A scientific study of the Free Pentacostal Holiness Church was undertaken by New Jersey psychiatrist Berthold Schwarz in 1959. He visited Tennessee several times to observe the church meetings, and watched while the parishioners held kerosene lamps to their hands and feet without getting burned. "On three occasions," reports Schwarz, "three different women held the blaze to their chests, so that the flames were in intimate contact with their cotton dresses, exposed necks, faces, and hair. This lasted for longer than a few seconds. At one point, a congregation member picked up a flaming coal the size of a hen's egg and held it in the palms of his hands for sixty-five seconds while he walked among the congregation." Schwarz, on the other hand, could not touch a piece of burning charcoal for more than a second without developing a painful blister.

Dr. Schwarz believes that these worshipers probably enter some sort of trance during the proceedings. But what power prevents their clothing from burning remains a scientific enigma.

The Handprint in Cell 17

In the 1860s and 1870s, the United States was wracked by violent labor unrest. Working conditions in the Pennsylvania coal mines were terrible—one long, hazardous day's work paid an average of fifty cents—and the mostly Irish-immigrant miners were frequently at odds with their bosses, most of whom were of English and Welsh descent.

To fight the mine owners, a secret society called the Mollie Maguires was formed. The Mollie Maguires directed the first strike against mining companies in America. But their resistance went further: They incited riots and killed about 150 persons.

The owners bought the services of the Pinkerton Detective Agency, which placed undercover agent James McParlen in the ranks of the Mollies. McParlen's subsequent testimony would send twelve members of the group to the gallows. In 1877 "Yellow Jack" Donohue was convicted of the murder of a foreman of the Lehigh Coal and Navigation Company. Three other men were sentenced to hang as well for the murder of another mine foreman. Two of these men went stoically to their deaths. But one—Alexander Campbell—swore he was innocent.

As he was being dragged from his first-floor cell, number 17, Campbell rubbed his left hand in dust from the floor and pressed his palm against the plaster wall. "This handprint will remain here for all time as proof of my innocence," he shouted. He repeated this vow over and over again as he was led struggling to the gallows, where after the trap was sprung he took fourteen minutes to die by strangulation.

Campbell was gone but his handprint remained, just as he had said it would.

In 1930, when Robert L. Bowman was elected sheriff of Carbon County, he vowed to remove the handprint, which was being taken as proof of a terrible injustice in the county's history. In December 1931 a work crew came to cell 17 and removed the section of plaster wall containing the handprint, replacing it with a new wall of fresh plaster.

The following morning the sheriff entered the cell, where he was horrified to see the faint outline of a hand in the still-moist plaster. By evening a black handprint was fully visible.

Although the cell is now kept locked and is opened only to an occasional visitor, the handprint remains there to this day.

As late as 1978 a private citizen who sneaked into the cell tried to paint over it, only to have the print reappear minutes later in the fresh paint.

The Lifesaving Dolphin

One day in early August 1982, eleven-year-old Nick Christides was surfing in the Indian Ocean off the Cocos Islands when he was swept out to sea. For the next four hours he drifted helplessly in shark-infested waters as boats and airplanes searched for him in vain.

Fortunately Nick had a friend: a dolphin that joined him early in his ordeal and protected him from the sharks that were stalking him. The dolphin stayed at his side, fending off the would-be attackers and making sure he did not lose his strength and sink to the bottom of the ocean.

Eventually Christides was spotted from the air and rescued. His father told reporters, "The dolphin just stuck with him, either swimming beside him or going around in circles. He must have realized Nick was in trouble and being pulled out by the northerly current."

Dreams of the Dead

Many technologically unsophisticated cultures believe that we can contact the dead through our dreams. In fact, some anthropologists suggest that belief in a life beyond death stems from the fact that we commonly dream about our deceased friends and relatives. Some new research, however, suggests that some of these peculiar dreams could be literally true.

Several cases pointing in this direction have been collected by Helen Solen of Portland, Oregon, who has been particularly interested in the dream experiences of a housewife she calls Gwen. Gwen's postmorten dreams began in 1959, soon after her mother died. "I don't specifically remember if I ever dreamed of anyone dead or not," she explained to Solen. "However, I was very distraught over my mother's death at the early age of forty-nine. Many times after that she came to me in my dreams, especially when I was perplexed or disturbed."

Gwen soon learned that she could ask her mother for help in a crisis, and the phantom would reply in her dreams. One night, for example, Gwen dreamed of a room filled with coffins. The eerie dream suggestion: that her father was about to die as well. Her mother appeared in her dreams that night to comfort her, and to explain that she would personally help the elderly man make the transition. Gwen's father entered the hospital suddenly, two days later, and physicians advised that bypass surgery be performed. Gwen gave her permission for the surgery, but the denouement came two days after that.

Gwen's mother appeared in an early-morning dream to say the crisis was over at last. Gwen woke right after the dream and saw that it was 7 o'clock. Later in the morning, the hospital called to say that her father had died—at precisely 7:10 A.M.

ESP vs. Bombs

German-born anthropologist Ruth-Inge Heinze, a renowned student of religion and shamanism, today teaches at the California Institute of Integral Studies in San Francisco. But had it not been for her sixth sense, she would have lost her life in World War II.

The incident occurred during an air raid, when Dr. Heinze often had to scurry to bomb shelters during the Allied raids over Germany. During one raid, however, the bombing was so intense that she couldn't make it to a shelter. She sought safety in the entrance to a public building instead.

"Shrapnel fragments from the antiaircraft cannon fell like rain everywhere," she later explained. "Hundreds of guns, big and small, kept shooting at the multitude of planes. The entrance niche barely offered any cover. Suddenly, however, I felt compelled to go out on the street and run to the next house, approximately one hundred yards away. It was a miracle that I was not hit by any of the shrapnel pieces, which were falling all around me. The moment I reached the next building, the first house where I had been standing was hit by a bomb and completely demolished. I had somehow sensed the course of the oncoming bomb."

Today, Heinze simply scoffs when skeptics try to tell her that ESP doesn't exist.

The Little People

Stories of so-called "little people" who share space with us on this planet are so pervasive that we must conclude one of two things: Either earlier societies had a peculiar penchant for amusing themselves with similar fairy tales, despite vast differences in geography and culture, or some little-understood stimulus gave rise to the stories.

In Central America, for instance, diminutive, dwarflike humanoids are known as the *ikals* and *wendis*. In the Tzeltal Indian language, the ikals are hairy, three-foot-tall beings said to live in caves like bats. In fact, according to contemporary accounts collected by Berkeley anthropologist Brian Stoss, "about twenty years ago or less, there were many sightings of this creature or creatures, and several people apparently tried to fight it with machetes. One man also saw a small sphere following him from about five feet. After many attempts he finally hit it with his machete and it disintegrated, leaving only an ashlike substance."

Stoss was also told that the *ikal* paralyzed and kidnapped Indian women, who were then taken back to their caves and impregnated as often as once a week, giving birth to black offspring who were taught to fly.

These tales raise several curious comparisons with modern-day experiences reported by UFO abductees, who report small, humanoid entities that paralyze, probe, and impregnate their victims. Could the little people of yore be the forerunners of today's UFO occupants? If so, perhaps we should be looking to *inner*, as opposed to outer, space for their origins.

Carried Off by a Giant Bird

At 8:10 P.M. on July 25, 1977, ten-year-old Marlon Lowe of Lawndale, Illinois, had an experience that science says is impossible: He was snatched off the ground and carried through the air by an immense bird.

The first Lawndale resident to notice something unusual in the air was a man named Cox, who saw two large condorlike birds descending out of the southwest. At the time Marlon Lowe was running with some friends, unaware that just behind him the two large birds, unlike any known to exist in Illinois, were flying level at about eight feet above the ground. Marlon was still running when one of them snatched him with its claws and carried him into the air.

His mother Ruth Lowe, who watched this happen, screamed in terror and ran off after the birds. After carrying him for about thirty-five feet, the creature dropped Marlon, who fell unharmed to the ground. It and its companion then flew off to the northeast. In all, six persons witnessed the incredible event.

Mrs. Lowe thought the birds looked like enormous condors, with six-inch beaks and necks one-and-a-half feet long with a white ring in the middle. Except for the ring the birds were black. Each wing was, by the most conservative estimate, four feet long.

Even with six witnesses the story was so incredible that, though it attracted nationwide publicity, hardly anyone believed it and the Lowe family was subjected to vicious persecution. The local game warden called Mrs. Lowe a liar. Pranksters began leaving dead birds, including on one occasion "a big, beautiful eagle," on the Lowes's doorstep. Local youngsters teased Marlon and called him "Bird Boy."

The stress of the original attack and its aftermath was such that Marlon's hair turned from red to gray. For more than a year afterwards he refused to go outside after dark.

Two years later, looking back, Mrs. Lowe told investigators Loren and Jerry Coleman, "I'll always remember how that huge thing was bending its white-ringed neck and seemed to be trying to peck at Marlon as it was flying away.

"I was standing at the door and all I saw was Marlon's feet dangling in the air. There just aren't any birds around here that could lift him up like that."

John Lennon's Death Foreseen

Psychic Alex Tanous was being interviewed by Lee Speigel for NBC radio's "Unexplained Phenomena" show. The two were sitting in the office of the American Society for Psychical Research, located on West 73rd Street in New York City, just across the street from the Dakota Apartments.

Speigel asked for a prediction that would be of special interest to the station's listening audience, eighteen to thirty-four-year-old rock enthusiasts.

"The prediction that I will make," Tanous said, "is that a very famous rock star will have an untimely death and this can happen from this moment on. I say untimely death because there is something strange about this death, but it will affect the consciousness of many people because of his fame." Without mentioning a name, he added that the star might be foreign-born but living in the United States.

The show was aired on September 8, 1980. Three months later, John Lennon, the English-born rock star living in New York City, was shot and killed outside the Dakota Apartments, visible through the windows of the office in which Alex Tanous had been sitting when he foresaw the tragic event to come.

James Dean's Porsche

Sometimes it is the thing itself, a fabulous jewel or ill-fated ship, that seems to harbor and perpetuate a curse. Other times, a public figure may become inexplicably intertwined with a particular object, provoking the hand of fate.

This could be the case with the Porsche in which teen legend James Dean crashed and died in 1955, tragically ending what many considered one of the most brilliant and promising Hollywood careers of all time.

Whatever its previous pedigree, from the moment Dean died behind the wheel, the Porsche took on a jinx of its own. After Dean's death, car enthusiast George Barris bought it first, but as it was being removed from the tow truck it slipped and broke a mechanic's leg. Barris sold the engine to a doctor and amateur racer, who installed it in his car. The car subsequently went out of control during competition and killed its owner. Another driver in the same race was injured when his racer crashed while using the drive-shaft from Dean's Porsche.

The body and chassis of the Porsche had been so badly damaged during Dean's original accident that it wound up on display in a traveling road-safety campaign. In Sacramento it fell off its mounting, breaking a teenage viewer's hip. Then it was moved to the next stop aboard a trailer truck that was hit by another car from behind. The driver of the colliding car was thrown out, run over, and killed by the cursed Porsche.

Another race driver almost died after using two tires from Dean's death car. The tires blew out at the same time. Meanwhile, the touring display continued to suffer its indignities. In Oregon, the truck's emergency brake failed, sending it slamming into a storefront. While mounted on supports in New Orleans, the Porsche itself literally disintegrated breaking into eleven parts.

The sports car—and Dean's accompanying curse—disappeared while being shipped back to Los Angeles by train.

A Cathar Priest

He should have been a poor parish priest. Instead, François-Berenger Saunière kept company with a beautiful Parisian opera star and secreted away four bank accounts, with which he financed the restoration of an obscure French chapel at Rennes-le-Chateau. The church was decorated with a statue of the devil, causing people to ask whether Saunière's newfound wealth came from God or Satan.

The answer may be found among the legends of a heretical thirteenth-century sect known as the Cathars, which once controlled the French province of Languedoc, on the Mediterranean. The Cathars (Greek for ''purified'') believed that the world had been created by the Demiurge, God's competitor, so to speak. The Demiurge, an evil that had to be overcome in order to achieve salvation, was said to be as capable of bestowing favors on his servants as the Christian God.

On March 2, 1244, the last Cathar stronghold at Montségur

was overcome by orthodox forces. But rumor had it that Cathar treasure had been smuggled out before the final fall. Whispered gossip said it was the same treasure Saunière discovered shortly after he took charge of the small church of Sainte-Madelaine, in Rennes-le-Chateau, in 1885.

Soon after his arrival at Rennes-le-Chateau, Saunière visited Paris, and life was never the same for the poor country priest. His fellow parishioners were startled when the humble Saunière was subsequently visited in Rennes-le-Chateau by Emma Calve, the world-renowned soprano. She continued to see the priest, in fact, until her marriage to the tenor Gasbarri in 1914.

Whatever his unknown expenditures, Saunière spent more than a million francs restoring and transforming the previously obscure church of Sainte Madelaine, including the demons in stone. Over the front portico he had inscribed these words: "This is a fearful place."

Kirlian Photography

Serendipity plays an inescapable role in scientific discovery. As one example, consider Russian engineer Semyon Kirlian, who was repairing an electrotherapy device in 1939 when his hand brushed too near a live electrode. The resulting flash and shock piqued Kirlian's curiosity: What would happen if he used the electrical charge itself as a sort of flash photography aid?

To Kirlian's surprise, his first picture—of his own hand—revealed an auralike discharge streaming from the appendage. Kirlian photography had been born, and its chance discoverer would devote the next forty years of his life to plumbing its depths.

He soon found that, among other applications, his machine

could apparently determine the health of a particular specimen. This came about when a colleague tried to trick Kirlian by submitting two supposedly identical leaves for analysis. When their photographs showed dramatically different "auras," Kirlian checked his equipment closely, but to no avail. The trickster finally admitted that the sample with the weaker aura had been taken from a diseased tree, whereas the other leaf came from a perfectly healthy one.

Many theories have been propounded to explain the Kirlian effect, from electromagnetic fields surrounding the body to electrical charges coursing through a layer of sweat to the ethereal "life force" itself.

Human Batteries

In ways still unknown, the electricity in a wall socket seems intimately linked with the human nervous system, although science seems reluctant to acknowledge the biological equivalent. But there have been people whose "batteries" were of an unusual and supercharged nature, like that of Angelique Cottin, a fourteen-year-old French girl whose amazing electromagnetic properties were the subject of a study by the Academy of Sciences.

Beginning on January 15, 1846, and for the next ten weeks, Angelique drove compasses wild. Objects, including heavy furniture, would retreat from her touch and vibrate in her presence. Whatever her strange power was, the Academy equated it with "electromagnetism." The force seemed to stem from her left side, the experts said, particularly at the elbow and wrist, and to increase in intensity in the evening. During a seizure, Angelique herself would often go into convulsions, her heart pulsing at 120 beats per minute.

Another supercharged human was American teenager Jennie Morgan of Sedalia, Missouri, who allegedly sent charged sparks between herself and anyone who approached, sometimes knocking them unconscious. Animals became unfriendly and fled from her presence.

A London, Ontario, teenager named Caroline Clare exhibited similar symptoms following an undiagnosed illness during which she described places she had never actually visited. The illness lingered for a year and a half. When it disappeared, Caroline was so magnetized that cutlery stuck to her skin and had to be pulled off by another party. She, too, was the subject of a study, this one conducted by the Ontario Medical Association.

The most powerful human battery, however, may well have been Frank McKinstry of Joplin, Missouri, who became so energized he supposedly stuck to the earth. If McKinstry stopped walking, for example, he was unable to take another step unless others lifted his feet off the ground, breaking the circuit.

Nazi UFOs

Some theorists have long sought an earthly explanation for the elusive UFO. The similarities between the advent of the modern flying saucer in the summer of 1947, and the subsequent abrupt advances in both Soviet and Western aerospace technology, they argue, are simply too striking for coincidence.

In fact, scattered sources indicate that Hitler's *Luftwaffe*, which deployed the world's first jet fighter, was hard at work developing a range of supersecret aerial weaponry during the closing days of World War II. According to a report issued on

December 13, 1944, by Marshall Yarrow, a Reuters correspondent, "the Germans have produced a 'secret' weapon in keeping with the Christmas season. The new device, which is apparently an air defense weapon, resembles the glass balls that adorn Christmas trees. They have been seen hanging in the air over German territory, sometimes singly, sometimes in clusters. They are colored silver and are apparently transparent."

Were the flying Christmas balls the "Foo Fighters" of World War II fame, or had Nazi engineers developed something even more sophisticated? Italian author Renato Velasco alleges that the Germans produced a low-profile, disc-shaped flying machine they dubbed the *Feuerball*, or "Fire Ball," used both as an antiradar device and psychological warfare weapon against the Allied forces.

An improved version, the *Kugelblitz*, or "Ball Lightning" fighter, replaced the earlier gas turbine engine of the *Feuerball* with one employing jet propulsion. According to Velasco, the *Kugelblitz* was the first aircraft capable of "jet lift," vertical takeoff and landing. Its designer was Rudolph Scriever, and it was reportedly manufactured at the BMW plant near Prague in 1944. The craft was first flown in February 1945, over the vast underground research complex of Kahla, Thuringia, Germany. It was also in this same area of the Harz Mountains that Hitler reportedly intended making his last stand, fortified by the awesome array of new "secret weapons" *Luftwaffe* commander Goering had been repeatedly promising.

Time ran out for the secret Nazi armory. But if the Soviets or some other power managed to capture flying disc technology, it may have led to experimentation and development of something that gave rise to the frequent reports of early UFOs, starting in 1947.

Apocalypse Soon

Above all else, ancient myths around the world address two major matters: beginnings and endings. Concern with how the world and human life as we know it began, and, more importantly, how it will end, or what catastrophes it will have to suffer through to survive, is universal.

Prophets, both religious and secular, have likewise found themselves preoccupied with the approach of a global apocalypse. The sixteenth-century French sage, Nostradamus, customarily cryptic as to specific dates, chose to be uncharacteristically precise when it came to the following prediction:

> The year one thousand nine hundred ninety-nine,
> the seventh month
> A great frightening king will come from the sky.

We don't have to wait too long to learn what Nostradamus had in mind. What's more, other sources suggest that a terrible judgment or trial of sorts is at hand. Islamic theology prophesied that the Muslim religion would last until sometime after man walked the moon. A Tibetan tradition holds that Buddhism would end with the dethronement of the thirteenth Dalai Lama, and that, too, has come to pass. An Old Testament prophecy says the Messiah's second coming will be marked within a generation of the Jew's reestablishment in their homeland.

And that most magnificent creation of Mesoamerican civilization, the Mayan calendar, comes to a crashing halt on December 24, 2011, signifying the end of the present fifth age. The fifth cycle, called *Tonatiuh*, is scheduled to end in massive cataclysms or earthquakes.

The significance of these various myths and traditions of impending doom is not that they vary in date, but that they all converge so remarkably at the close of the present second millennium, 2000 A.D., the astrological Age of Pisces. Whether the ancients will be proven right remains to be seen.

Nostradamus

Of all prophets past and present, few have captured the public imagination like Michel de Nostredame, or Nostradamus, a Jewish physician born in Saint Remy, France, in 1503. In 1555, he published his *Centuries*, a series of prophecies written in three groupings of one hundred stanzas each, and almost immediately became what we today would call an overnight media success.

The prophecy that made his reputation went like this: "The young lion shall overcome the old on the field of battle in single combat; in a cage of gold he will pierce his eyes, two wounds in one, then he dies a cruel death."

Shortly after publication, Henry II of England, during wedding festivities, jousted with the younger Montgomery, whose lance shattered and pierced Henry's golden helmet, striking him in the eye. Ten days later, the king, who used a lion as his emblem, died an agonizing death.

The reputation of Nostradamus was assured. One might argue that the interpretation was made to fit the fact, especially as it related to events in his own time. However, Nostradamus's predictions anticipated people, places, and events centuries in the future, including the French Revolution, the ill-fated flight of

Louis XVI and Marie Antoinette, ending at the guillotine, the rise of Napoleon, World War II (he made puns on the names of both Hitler and Roosevelt), air raids on England, and even the use of atomic weapons. What mystery is there today in this couplet, for example?

> A Libyan prince shall become powerful in the West.
> France shall be preoccupied with the Arabs.

No imagination is needed to supply the name of the Libyan prince, only a copy of the latest headline. And the reemergence of the Ayatollah Khomeini, as well as the downfall of the Shah of Iran, is eerily foreshadowed in this stanza:

> Rain, hunger, and unceasing war in Persia.
> Excessive faith will betray the king.
> Finishing there—begun in France.

One remembers that it was during his exile in France that the Ayatollah laid the foundations for the revolution against the Shah and his own return to Iran.

Modern Prophecies

Prophecy is a long esteemed tradition. Thus, there is no reason to believe that there are not equally adept prophets practicing their prescient craft among us today. In fact, there could be even more than during the Middle Ages, given the simple increase in the human population.

H. G. Wells missed the predicted outbreak of World War II by a year and the location, a Danzig railroad station, although he had the correct country, Poland. (The Germans, in fact, used a radio transmitter as the excuse for their attack.) Homer Lee, a military commentator, accurately foresaw that the Japanese would use a pincer movement launched from the Lingayen Gulf to invade the Philippines and cut off the Americans at Corregidor thirty-two years before it came to pass.

The problem, of course, is that prophecies can be right but still have no effect on subsequent events if they are not acted upon. A case in point is the prediction told to Lord Kitchener, who was warned by the professional psychic, Cheiro, not to travel by sea in the year 1916. Kitchener ignored the warning by embarking for Russia aboard the H.M.S. *Hampshire* in the year foretold. The ship struck a mine and went to the bottom, taking Lord Kitchener with it.

Convulsions and Cataclysms

Geologists will be the first to admit that the planet Earth appears primed for an apocalyptic catastrophe of a global nature. The crust itself is under immense stress and strain as continent-sized tectonic plates collide with one another in a dangerous, immemorial dance accompanied by drums and torches, the grinding earthquakes, and volcanic fires that rim the deceptively "Pacific" Ocean.

In 1883, the world recorded its most powerful explosion in this area when Krakatoa erupted, literally vaporizing itself, and sending tidal waves around the globe. So much ash and dust were thrown into the upper atmosphere that sunsets changed color and climatic conditions were drastically altered for years to come. Because of our vast low-lying population, an explosion today would no doubt extract a toll of lives measured in the hundreds of thousands. Even the coastal regions of faraway Japan and Hawaii would be threatened.

The coastline of California stands perched on the edge of disaster, with an earthquake on the order of the one that destroyed San Francisco in 1906 expected at any moment. Pressure is also building up beneath Great Britain and Scandinavia. If released, it could flood portions of Scotland and turn London into a North Sea port.

Psychics have long warned of a global convulsion of nature that threatens the future of humanity on this planet. Now they are being joined by the scientists themselves, whose own predictions are just as dire. Beyond earthquakes and volcanoes, they see a rising "greenhouse effect" that could raise the world's ocean levels to encompass most present-day ports. This decrease in the protective ozone layer overhead could dramatically increase the incidence of cancer in the population. Some even predict a sudden reversal of the Earth's magnetic poles.

In fact, nearly all of these potential geographical catastrophes are in the natural order of things, including advancing and retreating ice ages, and bombardment by celestial bodies the size of a small country. What has changed most on a planetary scale is that there are immensely more people around now to suffer the consequences. The question is no longer whether the scientists or psychics are right, but whose crystal ball will shatter first?

Lost Continents Under Two Oceans

Atlantis is not the only ancient land purported to have sunk beneath the sea. Scholars and fabulists alike speak of two other sunken continents, the legendary lands of Lemuria and Mu.

The name Lemuria comes from the ancient family of lemurs, and was coined by nineteenth-century English zoologist P. L. Sclater to account for the similarity of lemur fossils found in the southern tip of India and the Natal province of South Africa. Sclater postulated the existence of Lemuria, a drowned continent that formerly spanned the Indian Ocean connecting Southern Africa and Southern Asia.

The notion of a tropical bridge once connecting the existing land masses captured the fancy and support of no less an evolutionary authority than Thomas Huxley. In Germany, biologist Ernst Haeckel went so far as to speculate that ancient Lemuria might have been the long lost Garden of Eden, the cradle of the human race.

The missing land mass of Mu has also been long sought by students of the unexplained. It first surfaced in a series of books authored by James Churchward, a retired British colonel who once served with the Bengal Lancers in India. While assigned to famine relief, said Churchward, he became acquainted with a rishi, or Indian high priest, who had in his possession a library of stone tablets written in Naacal, the native tongue of Mu.

According to Churchward's theory, based on the Naacal tablets and the oral traditions of the Pacific islands and parts of

South and Central America, the first humans originated in Mu some 200 million years ago. Their science, including the ability to manipulate gravity, had advanced far beyond what we know today. But approximately twelve thousand years ago, tragedy struck in the form of a cataclysmic gas explosion. Undermined, the continent of Mu collapsed into the Pacific Ocean. All that remained of the five-thousand-mile-long by three-thousand-mile-wide land mass were a few scattered islands surviving above the waves. The huge and unexplained remains on a number of Pacific Islands and the great head statues on Easter Island could not have been constructed by the manpower available on islands limited in population by their present size. It is also to be noted that the native Hawaiians still call this lost continent Mu.

Of the people of ancient Mu, 64 million are supposed to have perished in the cosmic explosion. Those who survived eventually colonized the other continents. Churchward died in 1936, aged eighty-six, after having written five books on the subject of Mu. Other written references to Mu are supposed still to exist in certain monasteries in the high mountains of Central Asia.

The Palatine Lights

More things sail the sea than Horatio ever imagined. Consider the story of the unfortunate brig *Palatine*, immortalized in John Greenleaf Whittier's stirring poem of the same name. In 1752, the story goes, the *Palatine* sailed from Holland with a load of immigrants bound for Philadelphia. According to the poem by Whittier, the crew mutinied off New England's Block Island after the ship ran aground. There they burned her, the cries of one poor woman passenger who remained behind rising above the crashing waves.

According to legend, the baleful brig periodically reappears as a blazing ball of fire out at sea. Whittier described it thus:

> Behold! again, with shimmer and shine,
> Over the rocks and seething brine,
> The flaming wreck of the *Palatine.*

Unfortunately, no register shows the *Palatine* ever sailing from Holland, or any other port of call. But in this instance, at least, the facts are as compelling as poetic legend. Records do show that a *Princess Augusta* weighed anchor at Rotterdam in 1738, destination Philadelphia, with a contingent of 350 German passengers from the districts of Lower and Upper Palatinate. The voyage was ill-starred from the start.

A tainted water supply soon killed half the crew and a third of the passengers in their bunks, including Captain George Long, who died from a deadly draught. Then the *Augusta* hit cold weather and rough seas that blew her off track. The crew added to her troubles by extorting money and possessions from the remaining passengers. Almost mercifully, she ran aground on December 27, on Block Island's north end. The islanders saved many of the passengers, but could not salvage any luggage due to the activities of the crew, who cut the *Augusta* loose, leaving her to crash and sink. Mary Van der Line, having lost her senses by now, went down with the ship, guarding to the end her chests of silver plate. Of the 364 who had set sail from Rotterdam, only 227 survived.

But what of the fire, "the shimmer and shine," of which Whittier wrote? Shortly after the *Augusta* went down, another captain passing through Block Island Sound reported a blazing ship at sea. According to his log, "I was so distressed by the sight that we followed the burning ship to her watery grave, but failed to find any survivors or flotsam."

What observers have seen ever since, however, became known as the "Palatine Light," a ghostly glow that manuevers in and around the waters near Block Island, whose residents take it almost for granted. Local physician Aaron C. Willey, writing in 1811, noted, "Sometimes it is small, resembling the light through a distant window, at others expanding to the highness of a ship with all her canvas spread. The blaze actually emits luminous rays.

"The cause of this 'roving brightness' " Willey added, "is a curious subject for philosophical speculation." And also for those who believe life imitates art, in all its ramifications.

The Crystal Skull

Crystal quartz is enjoying an immense revival in popularity today because of its alleged spiritual properties. But the same material fascinated our ancestors. The Greeks called it *crystallos*, or "clear ice." In Egypt, as early as 4000 B.C., foreheads of the dead were adorned with "third eye" quartz crystals thought to enable a soul to see its way to eternity. Traditionally, the preferred medium for the crystal balls used by seers and psychics has always been the highest-grade rock quartz.

But the single most compelling quartz object known is the so-called Mitchell-Hodges Crystal Skull, variously thought to be Aztec, Mayan, or Atlantean in origin. Even its original discovery is much disputed. It was reportedly found by eighteen-year-old Anna, the adopted daughter of vagabond adventurer F. A. Mitchell-Hodges, in 1927, while excavating the ruins of Lubaantun, "City of Fallen Stones," in the jungles of British Honduras. After three years of digging at the ancient Mayan site, Anna uncovered the life-size, rock-crystal skull in the debris of a collapsed altar and adjoining wall. A matching jawbone was found twenty-five feet distant three months later.

The Mitchell-Hodges team excavated extensively in the area. In fact, it contributed heavily to our present store of artifacts and knowledge about pre-Columbian civilization in the New World. But Mitchell-Hodges himself was also known to be a devout believer in the legend of Atlantis. Indeed, it was the faith that a link between Atlantis and the Maya could be confirmed that drove him to dare the jungles of Central America in the first place.

Rock crystal, unfortunately, cannot be dated by conventional means. However, the Hewlett-Packard laboratories, which studied the eerie skull, estimated that its completion would have required a minimum of 300 years' work by a series of extremely gifted artisans. On the hardness scale, rock crystal ranks only slightly below diamonds. Why was it so valued by whoever wrought it that they spent three centuries patiently polishing a piece of non-native stone?

The mystery of the crystal skull deepened when the two pieces were attached, and it was learned that the clear cranium rocked on the jawbone base, giving the appearance of a human skull opening and closing its mouth. It could have been manipulated by temple priests as a divinatory oracle.

Other properties attached to the crystal skull are even more peculiar. The frontal lobe, for example, is said to cloud over sometimes, turning milky white. At other times it emits an almost ghastly aura, "strong with a faint trace of the color of hay, similar to a ring around the moon." Whether the product of an overwrought imagination, or stimulated from within the skull itself, those who keep company with it for long periods of time report unnerving experiences that affect all five senses, including ethereal sounds, smells, and even ghosts. The skull's visual impact is hypnotic, even on the skeptical.

Whatever its powers, though, a fatal curse on its owner does not seem to be part of the parcel. Mitchell-Hodges himself hardly let the skull out of his sight for more than thirty years, during which time he survived three knife attacks and eight bullet wounds. At his death on June 12, 1949, aged seventy-seven, he bequeathed the crystal skull and its mysterious heritage to his adopted daughter, who first found it buried beneath an ancient altar in the Honduran jungle. The skull, with an estimated value of $250,000, has remained in private hands.

Flames From the Sky

Legend has it that the Great Chicago Fire of 1871 began when Mrs. O'Leary's cow kicked over a lantern, igniting her straw. The flames then allegedly consumed her barn, jumping from one wooden structure to another until virtually the whole city lay under flame. Before the flames were through, more than seventeen thousand buildings were destroyed, a hundred thousand people were left homeless, and at least two hundred fifty had died.

Less well-known is that the whole of the American Midwest fell victim to disastrous fires the night of October 8, 1871, from Indiana to the Dakotas, and from Iowa to Minnesota. All told, they represent the most mysterious and deadly conflagration in national memory. Eclipsed in history by the Chicago cauldron, little Peshtigo, a small community of two thousand near Green Bay, Wisconsin, fared far worse in terms of lives lost. Half the town—1,000 people—died that terrible night, suffocated where they stood, or consumed by flames whose origins remain unknown. Not a single structure was left standing.

Where did the fires come from, and why so suddenly, without any warning? "In one awful instant a great flame shot up in the western heavens," wrote one Peshtigo survivor. "Countless fiery tongues struck down into the village, piercing every object that stood in town like a red-hot bolt. A deafening roar, mingled with blasts of electric flame, filled the air and paralyzed every soul in the place. There was no beginning to the work of ruin; the flaming whirlwind swirled in an instant through town." Other survivors referred to the phenomenon as a tornado of fire, reporting burning buildings lifted whole in the air before they exploded into glowing cinders.

What eyewitnesses described was more like a holocaust from heaven than an accidental fire started by the nervous cow. And in fact, according to a theory propounded by Minnesota Congressman Ignatius Donnelly, the devastating fires of 1871 *did* fall from above, in the form of a wayward cometary tail. During its 1846 passage, Biela's comet had inexplicably split in two; it was supposed to return in 1866, but failed to appear. Biela's fragmented head finally showed up in 1872 as a meteor shower.

Donnelly suggested the separated tail appeared the year before, in 1871, and was the prime cause of the widespread firestorm that swept the Midwest, damaging or destroying a total of twenty-four towns and leaving 2,000 or more dead in its wake. Drought conditions that fall no doubt contributed to the extent of the conflagration.

History today concentrates on the Chicago Fire alone and largely overlooks the Peshtigo Horror, as it was then called. It ignores altogether Biela's comet and its unaccounted-for tail.

Lincoln's Precognitive Dream

Some premonitions come true and some do not, no matter how real and terrible the events they portray. Take, for instance, the case of the sixteenth president of the United States, Abraham Lincoln, who foretold his own assassination in a dream.

Lincoln recounted his nocturnal warning to a close friend, Ward Hill Lamon, who left a written account for posterity. In his dream, said Lincoln, "there seemed to be a deathlike stillness about me. Then I heard subdued sobs, as if a number of people were weeping. I thought I left my bed and wandered downstairs.

"No living person was in sight, but the same mournful sounds of distress met me as I passed along. I kept on until I arrived at the East Room and there I met a sickening surprise.

"Before me was a catafalque, on which rested a corpse wrapped in funeral vestments. Around it were stationed soldiers who were acting as guards. 'Who is dead in the White House?' I demanded of one of the soldiers. 'The President,' was his answer. 'He was killed by an assassin.' "

Within a few days of this dream, the president was dead, felled by the derringer of John Wilkes Booth. Mortally stricken, Lincoln was carried from Ford's Theater to a private house across the street. After his death, his body lay in state in the White House's East Room, just as it had in Lincoln's dream.

Phantom Hitchhikers

On a winter's eve in 1965, Mae Doria of Tulsa, Oklahoma, set out alone on the forty-three-mile drive to her sister's house in Pryor. "While driving on Highway 20," Doria remembered, "a few miles east of the town of Claremore, I passed a schoolhouse and saw this boy who appeared to be around eleven or twelve years old hitchhiking by the side of the road."

Concerned about someone so young on such a cold night, Doria pulled over and offered him a ride. "He got in the car, sat down next to me on the front seat," she said, "and we chatted about things that people who don't know each other usually talk about." Doria asked him what he was doing in the area, and he said, "Playing basketball at the school." Her passenger appeared to be about five feet tall and well built, "like a boy would look if he played sports and used his muscles." He was a Caucasian, with light-brown hair and bluish-gray eyes. But unbeknown to Mae Doria, she had just picked up a phantom hitchhiker.

The young man eventually pointed at a culvert outside Pryor and said, "Let me out over there." Not seeing any houses or lights, Doria asked where he lived, to which he replied, "Over there." She was trying to determine where that might be when her passenger simply disappeared. Doria stopped the car immediately and jumped out. "I ran all around the automobile, almost hysterical," she said. "I looked everywhere, up and down the highway and to the right and left, but to no avail. He was gone." Later, Doria remembered the hitchhiker had not been wearing a jacket, despite the winter chill. A chance conversation with a utility employee two years after the event revealed that the phantom figure had first been picked up at the same spot in 1936.

An even eerier encounter involved an accidental death for which a phantom hitchhiker was at least partially responsible. In February 1951, Charles Bordeaux, of Miami, was an officer in the Air Force's Office of Special Investigations in England. An American airman had been shot and killed under mysterious circumstances, and Bordeaux was ordered to investigate.

He learned that a security guard had spotted a man running between two parked B-36 bombers. He shouted "Halt!" three times, and when the figure refused to stop, shot at him. "I could have sworn that I hit him, but when I got to that area of the airfield, no one was there. He had disappeared." Instead, the guard's errant bullet struck and killed another airman.

Continuing his investigation, Bordeaux spoke to an officer who had also been on the flight line that fatal night. He had been driving by prior to the incident when he saw a man in a Royal Air Force uniform hitchhiking. After he climbed in, the officer said, he asked if he could spare one of his Camel cigarettes. Then the figure asked for a lighter. The officer saw the flash of flint out the corner of his eye, but when he turned his head the passenger had vanished into thin air, leaving his lighter lying on the empty seat.

The Castle of Unrequited Love

The lonely little Latvian toiled mostly at night, working in the humid air of Florida to erect a monument to a love that would never be his. From 1920 to 1940, diminutive Edward Leedskilnin (he stood only five feet tall and weighed 100 pounds) labored at massive coral blocks weighing as much as thirty tons, using techniques only he knew. The results, which look more cast or poured than carved, continue to amaze architects and engineers, as well as the one hundred thousand tourists who flock here every year.

The object of Leedskilnin's love and labor was a teenage bride he forever referred to as "Sweet 16." Spurned the day before the wedding, he left Latvia and settled in Florida. Using the native building blocks at hand, Leedskilnin began constructing Coral Castle on ten acres of land, presumably hoping to lure his reluctant love to America.

She never came, but Leedskilnin kept doggedly at work, weaving an impenetrable aura of mystery and majesty around his solo project. No one knew how he lifted the gigantic coral blocks off the ground and onto his flatbed truck, or how he shaped and maneuvered them into place, in one case balancing a nine-ton slab so delicately that it swung open at the touch of a single finger. If visitors called, Leedskilnin broke off work; when they left, he resumed.

When Leedskilnin died in 1951, his secrets died with him,

though he intimated that they related to the same techniques used to build the Great Pyramid of Cheops. All he would ever say for certain is that he had conquered the natural laws of weight and balance.

Leedskilnin was less lucky at love. Several years ago Sweet 16 was contacted and asked if she would like to visit Coral Castle. "I wasn't interested in him at sixteen," she retorted, "and I'm not interested in him at eighty."

Approximately eight thousand visitors now tour his handiwork every month, marveling at wonders like an eighteen-ton model of Saturn, complete with rings, perched atop three-foot-thick walls. Mars, also represented by an eighteen-ton coral globe, squats frozen in orbit nearby.

A monument built for love is reminiscent of the Taj Mahal, at Agra, India, a tomb that is considered the world's most beautiful building. It was built by the Mogul Emperor Shah Jehan, for his favorite wife Mumtaz Mahal. But the Taj Mahal was built by hundreds of skilled workers, assisted by the specialized hoists and derricks used to build the marvelous Mogul palaces, aided by unlimited funds and an army of suppliers and long lines of oxen for hauling, whereas the Coral Castle was built at night—by one single man.

Toads Sealed in Stone

Stories of living or mummified animals found encased in stone abound. An inordinate number of these involve frogs and toads. During construction of the Hartlepool Waterworks near Leeds, England, in April of 1865, for instance, quarry workers supposedly found a living toad entombed in 200-million-year-old magnesian limestone. The toad, at a depth of twenty-five feet, had left the form of a perfect mold in the limestone. According to newspaper accounts, the toad was quite lively, but unable to croak because its mouth was sealed shut. Instead, barking noises issued from its nostrils. Aside from the "extraordinary length" of its rear claws, it appeared to be a normal specimen, though it died within a few days of being freed.

About the same time, the magazine *Scientific American* reported how silver miner Moses Gaines split open a two-foot-square boulder to find a toad perfectly concealed inside, again as if the rock had almost been poured around it. The animal was described as "three inches long and very plump and fat. Its eyes were about the size of a silver cent piece, being much larger than those of toads of the same size such as we see every day." Gaines's toad was alive, too, albeit sluggish. "They tried to make him hop or jump by touching him with a stick," the magazine reported, "but he paid no attention."

These stories and others opened a scientific Pandora's box that has yet to be satisfactorily shut. A Dr. Frank Buckland tried replicating the feat by sealing six test toads in limestone and sandstone blocks, and burying them a yard deep in his garden. The following year, when dug up, the sandstone toads had all died. The limestone toads fared better; two were alive and had actually put on weight. But when Buckland repeated the experiment to be sure, all the toads died.

Undaunted, a Frenchman known as Monsieur Séguin went Buckland one better. In 1862, he encased twenty toads in plaster of Paris and allowed the block to set. Then he buried it. When Séguin opened the block twelve years later, the story goes, four of the toads were still alive.

What the Petrified Hand Held

In the summer of 1889, farmer J. R. Mote of Phelps County, near Kearney, Nebraska, was excavating a cave when he came across a "large brown stone weighing over twenty pounds. When the clay was removed from it," according to an article in the August 7 issue of the *San Francisco Examiner*, "a large fossil, representing a clenched human hand, was revealed. The specimen had been broken from the arm just above the wrist, and the imprint of a coarse cloth or some woven material was plainly outlined on the back of the hand. At the time of the discovery nothing was said of it," the article continued, since "Mr. Mote does not belong to the curious class of people."

That soon changed, however. "A small boy in the family, whose faculty for smashing things was just beginning to develop, conceived the idea of opening the hand. When broken, to his astonishment, there rolled out eleven brilliant transparent stones."

Mr. Mote did have enough curiosity over this unusual turn of events to seek out a jeweler, who proclaimed them genuine first-water diamonds, without a speck to flaw or mar their beauty.

"The jewels," the article continued, "are nearly all uniform in shape and are about the shape of lima beans. They have the appearance of being water worn, but are still beautiful stones."

Lincoln and Kennedy

Shortly before he departed for Dallas in November 1963, President John Fitzgerald Kennedy's secretary, Evelyn Lincoln, warned him not to go. Kennedy dismissed her premonition of tragic consequences. On November 22, he was slain when Lee Harvey Oswald fired a bolt-action, Italian carbine from a window on the sixth floor of the Texas School Book Depository.

The number of curious parallels between the American Presidents John Kennedy and Abraham Lincoln, also assassinated after a premonition warning of his death, strain the bounds of coincidence. Lincoln, for example, had been elected president on November 6, 1860, Kennedy on November 8, 1960. Both had also been first elected to Congress a hundred years apart, Lincoln in 1846, Kennedy in 1946. The two men who succeeded them as president were also born a century apart, Andrew Johnson in 1808 and Lyndon Baines Johnson in 1908. Their assassins, John Wilkes Booth and Oswald, were born 101 years apart.

Booth shot Lincoln in the head from behind, in a theater, and fled to a barn: Oswald struck Kennedy in the head from the rear, from a warehouse, and fled to a theater. Both assassins in turn were killed before they could come to trial. Both Kennedy and Lincoln were shot on a Friday, in the presence of their wives. Lincoln had been shot in Ford's Theater, Kennedy in a Lincoln made by the Ford Motor Company.

And both presidents foresaw their own deaths. Lincoln told a guard on the day he was assassinated that there were "men who want to take my life. . . . And I have no doubt they will do it. . . . If it is to be done, it is impossible to prevent it."

A few hours before he was felled by Oswald's bullets, Kennedy said to his wife, Jacqueline, and Ken O'Donnell, his personal adviser: "If somebody wants to shoot me from a window with a rifle, nobody can stop it, so why worry about it?"

The Coffins That Would Not Stay Still

Dead persons may not talk, but that doesn't mean they don't get around. The most moving case on record belongs to a burial vault on the island of Barbados, a former British colony of the Lesser Antilles, just off the coast of Venezuela.

The scene of the macabre happenings was the family burial vault of the Walronds, wealthy plantation owners who laid their dead to rest, or what they thought was rest, in a tomb hewn out of rock in Christ Church cemetery. Family member Thomasina Goddard was first buried there in 1807, but within a year the vault's ownership had been taken over by another generation of slave-owners, the Chases. Two of their daughters were buried in the tomb in the years 1808 and 1812.

Thomas Chase, their father, also passed away in 1812. When the massive marble slab covering the underground vault was drawn back for his burial, the workers recoiled in horror. The leaded coffins of both girls stood on their ends, upside down. No sign of a break-in or human tampering could be found. Somehow the coffins had moved themselves, but how?

A male relative died in 1816, causing the tomb to be opened again. And again, the coffins inside were found in a state of total disarray; that of Thomas Chase, which had required eight men to carry, was leaning upright against one wall.

Eight weeks later yet another intended interment drew a curious crowd. Though the vault had been sealed after the last discovered disturbance, the Chase coffins had *again* been moved around. Lord Combermere, the governor of Barbados, was called in. In 1819, he had the coffins stacked and seals placed around the covering marble slab. But the government proved no match for ghosts. When noises were heard issuing from the haunted tomb the following year, Lord Combermere ordered the vault opened for inspection. The expected ensued. After the governor's intact seals were removed, inspectors entered the damp darkness and found the lead caskets had done their deathly dance yet again. Only Thomasina Goddard's original wood coffin remained untouched.

Finally, the bodies were removed and reburied in a more restful corner of the cemetery. Today, the Christ Church vault remains open and abandoned, the dead driven out by powerful forces unknown.

The Powers of Uri Geller

The most widely celebrated psychic in the world today is Israel's Uri Geller, a former army paratrooper who continues to amaze audiences while amassing a considerable personal fortune, estimated in the millions, from private displays of his incredible powers.

Born in Tel Aviv in 1946, Geller demonstrated his psychic abilities as early as age three by reading his mother's mind. More tangible events emerged at age six, when he learned he could move the hands of a watch without touching them. Years later, similar demonstrations would bring him fame and fortune.

Geller first came to widespread attention in the early seventies, when public performances in Munich, Germany, resulted in a wealth of bent silverware and keys, two of Geller's favorite mental targets. He also caused watch hands to stop and start running again. Two of his more spectacular feats occurred when he drove through Munich's cobblestoned streets blindfolded, and stopped a cable car dead in its tracks in the Chiemagu Mountains.

Geller soon came to the attention of psychical researcher and author Andrija Puharich, who sponsored a visit to America so the Israeli psychic could be examined in a scientific setting. The results of experiments Geller did at the Stanford Research Institute under the guidance of physicists Hal Puthoff and Russell Targ seemed to confirm his paranormal abilities without doubt. He not only passed the carefully controlled protocol the scientists had set up, registering high scores in remote viewing, clairvoyance, and psychokinesis, but apparently was also able to affect a wide range of sensitive electronic instruments.

Another stellar Geller performance took place on November 23, 1973, during an appearance on BBC-TV's "David Dimbleby Talk-In" program. Following the show, hundreds of startled viewers called in to say their silverware and other metal objects at home had begun bending as they watched Geller. When the former paratrooper returned to America, he was an overnight celebrity.

Geller critics like professional stage magician James ("The Amazing") Randi, of course, contend that these purported psychic powers are nothing more than standard, stock-in-trade conjurer's tricks. And admittedly, Randi has shown himself adept at recreating several so-called "Geller phenomena," like the bending of spoons and keys, by sleight of hand and other techniques.

But Geller may have the last laugh, all the way to the bank. After a period of a few years, during which he dropped largely out of public view, Geller recently returned to the world stage with a new book and greatly enlarged bank account, including a palatial estate with helicopter pad outside London. Geller's latest gimmick, reportedly, is locating petroleum reserves and precious metal deposits from the air, simply by flying over the site in a small plane, with his hand held out. His earnings from these and other psychic activities over the past decade have been estimated at $40 million.

The Levitations of Peter Sugleris

Twenty-two-year-old Peter Sugleris has much in common with the famous Israeli psychic Uri Geller, including the ability to bend metal objects such as keys and coins, affect electromagnetic instruments at a distance, and start and stop the hands of watches. Sugleris also says he can levitate like the venerable Joseph of Copertino and the nineteenth-century medium D. D. Home.

Even as a boy, Sugleris's Greek mother, who thinks his ability to levitate may be inherited, referred to him as "Hercules" because of his peculiar powers. Her own maternal uncle was known to have levitated on at least two occasions while he was sixteen and eighteen years of age.

Sugleris says he most frequently levitates in the presence of family members in the course of ordinary life. But, he adds, he can levitate at will, though not on demand, for others as well. The feat involves immense concentration, he says, and he frequently prepares several months ahead by adhering to a vegetarian diet.

On the most recent occasion, videotaped by his wife Esther in late February 1986, Sugleris rose off his kitchen floor a distance of approximately eighteen inches, and remained suspended in space for forty-seven seconds. During the levitation, his face took on such a grimace that he frightened his wife. "I thought he would burst," she said, "he was so inflated."

Afterward, Sugleris described the experience, saying he broke into a profuse sweat accompanied by dizziness and drowsiness. "It took me ten to fifteen seconds to recover my consciousness," he noted. "I was confused and dizzy, and I felt that I would black out. This was done out of anger. I wanted to prove that I could do it."

The frightening grimace during levitation is at least partially reminiscent of the circumstances of St. Joseph of Copertino, the most frequent flier of all, who, witnesses agreed, would begin and end his flights with a shrill, piercing cry.

The Dreams and Premonitions of Chris Sizemore

People who suffer from multiple personalities have enough problems. But like Chris Sizemore, the real-life protagonist of *The Three Faces of Eve*, many multiples report being haunted by psychic images and dreams.

Sizemore says she had her most vivid psychic experience as a child, when her sister fell sick with pneumonia. At least everybody thought it was pneumonia, except for Chris, who reported a curious dream. She saw herself running down a green hill in a pasture. When she turned to climb up the slope, again,

Jesus appeared before her and said, "My child, your sister has diphtheria, not pneumonia. Go and tell your mother."

When Chris told her parents the story, they remained skeptical but finally summoned their physician. He reexamined the girl briefly before diagnosing the problem as diphtheria. Chris's dream probably saved her sister's life.

Even when this experience took place, Chris was already suffering from the competing personalities within her. She was never cured by her psychiatrists, despite the uplifting ending to both the book and movie made about her. She went through years during which her personality constantly changed, living at one period of her troubled life in Roanoke, Virginia, where her psychic experiences repeatedly occurred.

These incidents usually took the form of premonitions and invariably focused on her family. On one occasion, for instance, she had a vision in which her husband was electrocuted. She begged him not to go to work that day, and his replacement was sent to repair some power lines and was electrocuted on the job. Later, she became fearful when her daughter was scheduled to receive the Salk polio vaccine. Her husband refused to take the premonition seriously and the girl was later injected with spoiled vaccine, and became seriously ill, almost dying from the injection.

A UFO Landed at the Stonehenge Apartments, Jersey City

UFO landings are generally assumed to be furtive affairs, conducted in relatively isolated areas, far from prying eyes. No UFO, for example, has ever turned up on the White House lawn, or touched down in Red Square.

Nevertheless, UFOs have frequently been sighted in populated cities. A number of people claim to have seen one landing in the Stonehenge Apartments, in Jersey City, the night of January 12, 1975. The spherical object was seen by at least nine observers, including the doorman, both in and outside the apartment building.

According to published reports, after the UFO settled to the ground in the park, a hatch opened, and small humanoid occupants, dressed like "kids in snowsuits," descended a ladder. They then dug around in the grass with what looked to be shovel-like instruments. After dumping their soil samples into the equivalent of extraterrestrial pails, the tiny humanoids reboarded the UFO. It then lifted off with a bright flash of light and vanished in the night sky. The "dark, almost black" sphere made a droning noise, like a "refrigerator motor."

A year later, in January and February 1976, the UFO seemingly revisited the scene of its earlier excavations. It was seen on three separate occasions by Stonehenge Apartment tenants and pedestrians simply passing by. An improbable coincidence exists in the name of the apartments. For in England, on the Salisbury Plain, the strange and unidentified ruins of Stonehenge have often been supposed to have been constructed by or received visits from extraterrestrials.

Cannibalistic Coincidence

Fact often follows fiction. Take the uncanny case of the two Richard Parkers. The first was a cabin boy in Edgar Allan Poe's uncompleted adventure novel, *Narrative of Arthur Gordon Pym*, published in 1837. In the course of the story, four sailors are shipwrecked at sea and escape in a small lifeboat. Facing starvation, the four finally decide to draw straws to see who will be sacrificed and cannibalized by the other three. Parker draws the short stick and is promptly stabbed and eaten by the surviving trio.

More than forty years later, Poe's unfinished tale was repeated in amazingly accurate and grim detail. Four survivors of a shipwreck, adrift in an open boat, *did* draw straws to see who would survive and who would be eaten. And the loser was Richard Parker, the ship's cabin boy. His mates stood trial for his murder in England in 1884.

The macabre event might not have come to light at all but for a contest sponsored by the *London Sunday Times* seeking remarkable coincidences. Twelve-year-old Nigel Parker won the competition. The unfortunate cabin boy eaten by his comrades had been Nigel's great-grandfather's cousin.

Saving Dream

Great calamities have been foretold by dreams. But nocturnal visions have saved lives, too, including that of Captain Thomas Shubrick, whose ship set sail from Charleston, South Carolina, for London in 1740. Shubrick had barely cleared port when a terrible storm hit. The wind blew so viciously that friends and relatives in Charleston could only pray for the crew's survival. There was no hope that the vessel itself would emerge unscathed.

But that night, the wife of one of Shubrick's closest friends, a Mrs. Wragg, had a dream in which she saw the captain alive and clinging to floating flotsam. The vision so moved her she insisted her husband lead a search party. A small boat was sent out, but returned empty-handed.

The dream repeated itself a second time and so did the unsuccessful search. When the dream appeared yet again, Mrs. Wragg begged her husband to search one last time. On the final voyage, Captain Shubrick and another exhausted sailor were rescued from a piece of the ship's wreckage. Persistence paid off, and so did Mrs. Wragg's dream.

Caught by a Ghost

Frederick Fisher was drunk on the night of June 26, 1826, when he stumbled from a pub in Campbelltown, New South Wales. He had already led a checkered career that had seen his fortunes swing from prisoner to prosperous farmer. Only a few months before, in fact, he had been locked up for bad debts, leaving his estate in the hands of an ex-convict named George Worrall.

Local suspicions were aroused when Fisher disappeared after his night at the pub and Worrall was seen wearing a pair of his pants. According to the story told by Worrall, Fisher had sailed for England aboard the *Lady Vincent.* The police, however, were unconvinced and posted a $100 reward for information leading to the discovery of Fisher's body. Questioned again, Worrall admitted that four of his friends had killed Fisher. Still skeptical, the police arrested Worrall instead. But without a corpse they stood little chance of conviction.

The standoff between Worrall and the authorities persisted until that winter. One night James Farley, a well-respected farmer in the community, chanced to walk by Fisher's house. A sinister figure was sitting on the railing, pointing at a spot in Fisher's paddock. Convinced he had seen a ghost, Farley fled.

Farley contacted Constable Newland and the officer, in the company of an aborigine tracker, visited Fisher's property. The two turned up traces of human blood on the railing. At the spot the ghost had indicated, they dug down and found Fisher's badly shattered body. Worrall was sent to the gallows, convicted by the ghost of the friend he had murdered.

The Prophecies of Mother Shipton

Visitors to Knaresborough on the River Nidd, Yorkshire, are still shown the old well and cave where Ursula Sontheil once held court. Deformed at birth in July 1488, Sontheil became better known as Mother Shipton, the prophetess who foretold the deaths of kings, as well as the coming of the automobile, the telephone, and submarine.

Despite her physical deformities, young Ursula had an agile mind, learning to read and write far more easily than her peers. At the age of twenty-four, she married Toby Shipton of Shipton, York. Her reputation as a local psychic soon spread to encompass all of England and Europe, as hundreds of the curious flocked to her side to receive her often cryptic couplets.

Some pronouncements, though, were not so obscure, as when Mother Shipton predicted, "Carriages without horses shall go, and accidents shall fill the world with woe." The telephone and satellite television she prophesied with this refrain: "Around the world thoughts shall fly, In the twinkling of an eye."

Her contemporaries would have been equally confused when she penned this couplet: "Men shall walk over rivers and under rivers, Iron in the water shall float." Today, of course, we take submarines and iron battleships for granted.

Mother Shipton foresaw many of the historical events that shaped the modern world, including the defeat of the Spanish Armada in 1588: "And the Western Monarch's wooden horses," she said, "Shall be destroyed by Drake's forces." In longer lines she anticipated Sir Walter Raleigh's opening of the New World to English commerce:

> Over a wild and stormy sea
> Shall a noble sail
> Who to find will not fail
> A new and fair countree
> From whence he shall bring
> A herb and a root.

The herb, of course, was tobacco, the root, the potato.

Mother Shipton died in 1561, at age seventy-three, having precisely predicted the day and hour of her own death years before.

Spirit Voices on Tape

When Friedrich Jürgenson died in 1987, the Swedish psychic and filmmaker left behind a most unusual library. It contained thousands of tape recordings on which mysterious voices were imprinted—voices Jürgenson claimed had been produced by the dead.

Jürgenson began his research into the psychic world in the 1950s when he became interested in establishing contact with the dead. Wondering whether the dead could imprint their voices on magnetic tape, Jürgenson started sitting by his tape machine, invoking spirit presences to speak to him through the recordings. Nothing happened for months, until he tried to tape some bird songs near his house. Some strange interference came over the playback, suggesting to the filmmaker some otherworldly sounds.

"A few weeks later I went to a small forest hut and attempted another experiment," he explained in an interview with London's *Psychic News*. "I had no idea, of course, what I was looking for. I put the microphone in the window. The recording I made passed without incident. On playback I first heard some twittering of birds in the distance, then silence. Suddenly, from nowhere, a voice, a woman's voice in German: 'Friedel, my little Friedel, can you hear me?' "

At the time, Jürgenson didn't know he had embarked on a long-lived search to contact the dead. Even a few parapsychologists became interested in the project. William G. Roll of the Psychical Research Foundation then based in Durham, North Carolina, visited the filmmaker in 1964 to conduct some experiments. For these sessions Jürgenson would load his tape recorder with a blank cartridge, and then everyone in the room would engage in some casual conversation. When the recording was played back extra voices could clearly be heard darting in between the rest of the talk. An unusually conservative parapsychologist, Roll was impressed enough to issue a special report on his Scandinavian trip. Jürgenson and his "spirit" voices, he declared, certainly seemed for real.

The Archduke's Fatal Car

Environmentalists frequently assail the modern automobile as the curse of the twentieth century. Some cars have been indisputably cursed, but hardly in ways foreseen by the Sierra Club.

The open limousine in which Archduke Franz Ferdinand, heir

to the Austrian and Hungarian thrones, was assassinated seems to have been such a car. His wife died with him in the assassination, which led to the outbreak of World War I.

Shortly after the opening of hostilities, the car was taken over by Austria's General Potiorek, who was subsequently disgraced at the battle of Valjevo and died insane. A captain on his staff next assumed ownership. Nine days later the officer struck and killed two peasants, swerving into a tree and breaking his neck.

The governor of Yugoslavia acquired the cursed convertible after the end of the war, but fared little better, suffering four wrecks in four months. In one of the accidents, he actually lost an arm. The car was then passed on to a doctor, who six months later overturned in a ditch and was crushed to death. A wealthy jeweler then purchased it—and committed suicide.

The disasters continued when another owner, a Swiss race-car driver, crashed in the Italian Alps and was hurtled over a wall to his death. A Serbian farmer who forgot to turn off the ignition while the car was being towed became the next victim as the vehicle lurched into motion and ran off the road. The last driver was garage owner Tibor Hirshfield, who was returning from a wedding with four companions. Hirschfield's friends were killed when he tried to pass another automobile at high speed.

The car was subsequently installed in a Vienna museum, where its blood lust seems to be satiated, at least temporarily.

Tulpas

We know that the mind can create its own phantasms, but what about its ability to project these images into the exterior world outside the brain's boundaries? Where does one end and the other begin? More importantly, what happens when the mental projection takes on a life of its own?

The strange experience of Madame Alexandra David-Neel supplies a cautious answer and warning. David-Neel, who lived to the ripe old age of 101, was one of many adventurous women of the English Empire who braved the mysterious East alone and often left written records of their travels.

David-Neel not only traveled widely in primitive nineteenth-century Tibet, she studiously followed the religion and teachings of the Buddhist lamas with whom she lived. Her most trying ritual involved the creation of what the Tibetans called a *tulpa*, or phantom being generated by the mind. The lamas warned her that these "children of our mind" could sometimes turn dangerous and uncontrollable, but David-Neel persisted.

She shut herself away and began coalescing her concentration, having targeted for her *tulpa* the image of a fat, short monk "of an innocent and jolly type." Surprisingly successful, she was soon treating her new "companion" like any human guest in her apartments.

When David-Neel went on her next horseback adventure, the ethereal monk went along. From her saddle she would turn and look over her shoulder at the *tulpa*, engaged in "various actions of the kind that are natural to travelers, and that I had not commanded."

As testament to her success, others in her train began seeing the monk and mistaking him for a living being. At that point, her *tulpa* took a turn for the worse. His features took on a malignant, mocking countenance. Once the decision was made to banish the monk, however, his eradication proved almost as difficult as his original creation. In *Magic and Mystery in Tibet*, David-Neel recounts the six months of hard struggle that followed before her wayward *tulpa* finally vanished.

"There's nothing strange in the fact that I may have created my own hallucination," David-Neel concluded. "The interesting point is that in these cases of materialization, others see the thought-forms that have been created."

From Manila to Mexico City

On October 25, 1593, the fabric of space and time warped, depositing a Spanish soldier from the Philippine capital of Manila into the main plaza of Mexico City, nine thousand miles away. The soldier, dressed in a different uniform than those around him, quickly drew a crowd, and was forced to surrender his arms.

Asked for an explanation, the startled soldier could only stammer, "I know very well this is not the governor's palace in Manila," he managed, "but here I am and this is a palace of some kind, so I am doing my duty as nearly as possible." Pressed for additional details, he said that the governor of the Philippines had been killed the night before, and hence the need for additional guards.

Needless to say, the confused sentry was quickly thrown into prison, where he remained until a Spanish brig from the Philippines confirmed his account of the governor's assassination.

The teleported soldier, moreover, fared better than the man with a similar story arrested by Portuguese authorities in 1655. According to John Aubrey's *Miscellanies*, the man had been in the Portuguese colony of Goa, in India, when he found himself suddenly whisked through the air, back to Portugal.

Charged with witchcraft, because everyone knew only witches could fly, officials of the local Inquisition gave him a fair trial and expeditiously then ordered him burned at the stake.

Psychic Warfare

The days of casual interest in psychic phenomena are long departed, and the reason is not hard to fathom. If clairvoyance, remote viewing of targets, and psychokinesis are repeatable, controllable human faculties, as they appear, neither superpower can afford to let the other open a potential gap in the ability to wage psychic war.

According to Charlie Rose, a member of the United States House Select Committee on Intelligence, psychic sensing "would be a hell of a cheap radar system. And if the Russians have it and we don't, we're in trouble."

Rose also expressed concern about the discrepancies in levels of psychic research funding between the two competing superpowers. *Known* U.S. spending is between $500,000 and $1 million, whereas the Soviet budget is estimated to be at least ten, and perhaps as much as a hundred times that.

Nor do the Soviet studies concentrate solely on passive perception. For instance, a Defense Intelligence Agency document on "Soviet and Czechoslovak Parapsychology Research" detailed Russian experiments in which a gifted psychic was able to stop a targeted animal heart from beating.

According to the DIA report, the frog heart was placed in a glass 2½ feet from the psychic. As she concentrated on controlling its beat, the electrocardiogram showed, the rate of contraction actually decreased. "Five minutes after the experiment began," according to the report, "she stopped its beat entirely."

Using the mind to wage war opens a Pandora's box of possibilities. Not only would an individual leader be subject to remote assassination, but thermonuclear weapons could be held hostage to psychic threat, or even exploded. According to Ron Robertson, a security officer at the Lawrence Livermore Laboratory, "all that it takes is the ability to move one-eighth of an ounce a quarter of an inch." A similar scenario is painted by Texas A&M University military historian Robert A. Beaumont in *Signal*, the journal of the U.S. Armed Forces and Electronics Association. "An effective ESP system," said Beaumont, "would, depending on the nature of the phenomena, offer potential to the executor of a surprise attack, from the psychic influencing of targets through precognition and remote sensing, to message transmission below the detection and countermeasure threshold of a potential victim."

The Scientist Who Knew the Ultimate Secret

Robert Sarbacher, an American physicist who died in July 1986, claimed to have been privy to a secret that is "the most highly classified subject in the United States government, rating higher even than the H-bomb," as he described it to a group of Canadian scientists who met with him in his office at the Department of Defense on September 15, 1950.

What was this extraordinary secret? It was that the U.S. government possesses the remains of crashed extraterrestrial spaceships and the bodies of alien beings. Dr. Sarbacher told the scientists that the matter was being studied by a super-secret group headed by Dr. Vannevar Bush, who was President Truman's chief science adviser.

Sarbacher was not the sort of man given to wild exaggerations. His entry in *Who's Who in America* consists of three inches of tiny print, attesting to a richly successful scientific, academic, and business career. During World War II and after, he volunteered his services as a "dollar-a-year man" to the government and specialized in issues relating to guided-missile control.

The Canadians, who regularly met with Sarbacher to discuss matters of mutual interest to the national securities of the two countries, had asked their American colleague if there was any truth to persistent rumors of this kind of direct physical evidence of the reality of UFOs. Sarbacher confirmed there was but would provide no further details because of the subject's extreme sensitivity.

One of the Canadians, radio engineer W. B. Smith, was so impressed that when he returned to Ottawa he urged his government to begin its own UFO project. Soon afterwards such a project, code-named "Magnet," was put into operation, with Smith in charge. But he was unable to learn any more about the American government's alleged UFO secrets.

In 1983 UFO investigator William Steinman located Sarbacher, who was then living in Florida, and asked him about what he had told the Canadian scientists. Sarbacher replied that, while he had not been involved directly in the UFO-recovery project, he did recall that "certain materials reported to have come from flying saucer crashes were extremely light and very tough. There were reports that instruments or people operating these machines were also of very light weight, sufficient to withstand the tremendous deceleration and acceleration associated with their machinery. In talking with some of the people at the office," he said, "I got the impression these 'aliens' were constructed like certain insects we have observed on earth."

In a later interview with another investigator, Sarbacher said the craft were believed to be from another solar system. He said that he was invited to a conference at Wright-Patterson Air Force Base in Dayton, Ohio, where scientists and military officers were to report what they had learned from their analyses of the material and the bodies. Unfortunately, because of pressing other commitments, Sarbacher was unable to attend, though he later talked with those who did go.

Those who spoke with Sarbacher were struck by his obvious sincerity and his consistent refusal to embellish or elaborate on his story. His testimony may well represent a rare glimpse behind the curtain of secrecy covering the U.S. government's knowledge of what UFOs are.

Nova Scotia's Sea Serpents

For at least a century and a half the seagoing folk of Nova Scotia, on Canada's far eastern coast, have been encountering some very strange—and very large—creatures.

One of the first known sightings occurred in 1845, when fishermen John Bockner and James Wilson saw a 100-foot-long "serpent" in St. Margaret's Bay. They reported their sighting to the Reverend John Ambrose, who not long afterwards had his own run-in with the monster.

In 1855 residents of Green Harbour were terrified to see, in one citizen's words, "a hideous length of undulating terror" pursue local fishing boats, apparently intent on bodily harm. As the fishermen raced desperately for shore, their families watched helplessly. One observer described the creature in an issue of the nineteenth-century American magazine *Ballou's*: "Near what might be the head rose a hump or crest crowned with a waving mass of long, pendulous hair like a mane, while behind, for forty or fifty feet, slowly moved, or rolled, the spirals of his immense snakelike body. The movement was in vertical curves, the contortions of the back alternately rising and falling from the head to the tail, leaving behind a wake, like that of a screw-steamer, upon the glassy surface of the ocean."

As the creature got closer to shore, observers could hear a sound like escaping steam emanating from the beast. They could now see glistening teeth, protruding ridges over evil-looking eyes, dark-blue scales on the head and back, and dirty yellow on the bottom. The head they saw was six feet long.

The creature finally gave up the chase and the exhausted fishermen arrived safely on land. But it was seen again by three men in a boat the next day. They rowed away as fast as they could and were not pursued.

Then, in 1883, six military men fishing in Mahone Bay were startled to see what looked like an immense version of a "common snake" with a head six-feet long sticking out of the water. The rapidly moving creature had a neck as thick as a tree and was dark brown or black with irregular white streaks. Although they couldn't see all of its body, the witnesses agreed it must have been something like eighty feet long.

In 1894 a man named Barry observed a similar beast as he was relaxing on a wharf in the coastal town of Arisaig. About 120 feet away and approximately 60 feet long, the creature was moving with an "undulating" motion. A tail "like half of a mackerel's tail" was visible as well.

Reports of these giant "lunkers," as the Nova Scotians call them, have continued well into our own time.

On July 5, 1976, Eisner Penney of Nova Scotia's Cape Sable Island saw an enormous something and told some friends about it. They scoffed at him but a few days later one of them, Keith Ross, along with his son Rodney, had an encounter of their own. "It had eyes as big around as saucers and bright red-looking," he said. "I mean, you could see the red in its eyes like they were bloodshot. It had its mouth wide open and there were two big tusks—I call them tusks—that hung down from its upper jaw. It passed astern of us, so close. And we could see its body, about forty or fifty feet long with grayish, snakelike looking skin, full of lumps or bumps and barnacles. And it appeared to

us to have a fish's tail, a
whale's."

Ross's boat roared away a
He detected another boat on s
toward it. Ironically, Eisner Pe
told him what he'd just seen, they
not far away. The creature was see
fisherman Edgar Nickerson.

No one has any idea what these creatu ... ar beasts have been reported around the w ... os they were called "sea serpents" and were the ... of a spirited controversy among zoologists. Whatever the Nova Scotia lunkers may be, it seems safe to say they are not serpents, even oversized ones: Snakes cannot undulate vertically. Nor, of course, do they have fishlike tails.

Foo Fighters

Popular history dates the beginning of the modern UFO phenomenon to the summer of 1947, when Idaho businessman Kenneth Arnold saw nine silvery, crescent-shaped objects flying in formation like "a saucer skipping over water" near Mount Rainier, in Washington State. Several years earlier, however, at the height of World War II, similar flying saucers were reported by both Allied and Axis car crews in the European and Pacific campaigns.

On the Allied side, at least, such nocturnal lights and daylight discs were known as *Foo Fighters*, after a popular Smokey Stover cartoon character who was forever mumbling, "Where there's foo, there's fire." Foo itself, of course, was a play on the French word, *feu*, for fire.

Foo Fighter encounter occurred on ctober 14, 1943—when B-17 Flying For- American Eighth Air Force suffered disastrous during a daylight bombing raid on Schweinfurt's heav- defended ball bearing factories. Historian Martin Caidin called it "one of the most baffling incidents of World War II, and an enigma that to this day defies explanation."

As the 384th Bombardment Group completed its run over the target, numerous pilots and top-turret gunners in the staggered formation reported a cluster of small silver discs straight ahead. Plane Number 026, in an effort to avoid a head-on collision, took immediate evasive action, but too late: According to the debriefing report, the bomber's "right wing went directly through a cluster with absolutely no effect on engines or plane surface." The pilot did add that one of the discs was heard to strike his tail assembly, but that no explosion or damage followed.

Accompanying the discs at a distance of about twenty feet were several clumps of black debris measuring three by four feet in size; this, too, seemed to have no harmful effect on the Flying Fortresses. The debriefing report also noted that two other aircraft flew through the discs with no apparent damage.

Foo Fighters were also seen as nocturnal lights of an orange, red, or white hue. On the night of November 23, 1944, for instance, a three-man crew assigned to the 415th Night Fighter Squadron encountered eight to ten of the mysterious globes over the Rhine River, north of Strasbourg. They looked at first like distant twinkling stars, said intelligence officer Lieutenant Fred Ringwald, but within minutes appeared as orange balls "moving through the air at a terrific speed."

Another B-17 pilot, Charles Odom of Houston, recalled his daytime Foo Fighter experience after the war. The saucers "looked like crystal balls about the size of basketballs," he said. They seemed to "become magnetized to our formation and fly alongside. After a while, they would peel off like a plane and leave."

Crisis Telepathy

Much evidence suggests that telepathy often takes place between people who know each other. But according to a case reported by parapsychologist Lyall Watson, this isn't an irrefutable fact.

The incident studied by Watson concerned a Cajun shipman named Shep, who had just joined a fishing crew off the Hawaiian Islands. At one point during the expedition the crewman decided to go to his quarters. He grabbed the hatch rail and swung himself down the forecastle, but slipped and landed right on his back. Paralyzed by the fall and in intense pain, Shep was convinced he would die. And at 9:12 that evening, his thoughts turned to a friend.

The friend, a woman named Milly, had been visiting the home of the boat's captain that evening, socializing with his wife. The captain's wife, a full-blooded Samoan, kept to her needlework during the visit until she suddenly felt a staggering blow to her head. She fell to the floor in sort of a trance, saying, "Something very bad has happened on the boat." She knew that her impression didn't refer to her husband, but couldn't say anything more. Milly checked the time and saw that it was 9:14 P.M.

It wasn't until the next morning, though, that the women heard from the Coast Guard. They had taken Shep to Kauai with a broken back.

But why did the captain's wife experience the telepathy instead of Milly, Shep's good friend? "The sender was a man from a culture that, at least unconsciously, allows for the existence of telepathy," he explains. "The message was intended for a woman whose upbringing made her less receptive and, when she proved unresponsive, it appeared to have been rerouted to another person nearby, someone who was only indirectly involved but whose cultural background and perceptual set made it easier for her to respond."

Abducted Cop

The morning of December 3, 1967, turned out to be unlike any other in the life of Ashland, Nebraska, police patrolman Herbert Schirmer. Schirmer's logbook for that day contained this bizarre entry: "Saw a FLYING SAUCER at the junction of Highway 6 and 63. Believe it or not!"

At 2:30 A.M., while on routine patrol, Schirmer had seen what looked like a large football encircled by red flashing lights near the intersection of the two highways on Ashland's outskirts. Alone in his patrol car, the trooper watched in silence as the UFO lifted off the ground, trailing a red-orange flame and emitting a shrill sirenlike sound.

Filling out his log report thirty minutes later, Schirmer checked the time and suddenly stopped short. He was sure no more than ten minutes had elapsed before his sighting of the object, but now his watch showed 3 A.M. Where had the missing twenty minutes gone?

Under hypnosis conducted by Dr. Leo Sprinkle, a University of Wyoming psychologist, Schirmer was able to recall the additional details of his seemingly innocent UFO encounter. The experience began, Schirmer said, when "the craft actually pulled me and my car up the hill." The car stopped, he claimed, and two humanoids emerged from the bottom of the UFO. Dressed in uniforms, they had high foreheads, long noses, gray complexions, and round, catlike eyes.

One alien carried a boxlike instrument that flashed a green light around the patrol car, Schirmer said. The other reached in through the open window and touched his neck, inflicting a sharp pain. The humanoid who had touched him asked, "Are you the watchman of this town?" Schirmer replied, "Yes, I am." In a deep voice, without moving his slit of a mouth, the "leader" of the two then intoned, "Watchman, come with me."

Inside the craft, the humanoid showed Schirmer their power source, a spinning contraption that resembled "half of a cocoon, giving off bright colors like the rainbow." He informed Schirmer that the ship employed "reversible electrical-magnetism." They had come to Earth, Schirmer added, "to get electricity."

The guided tour of the craft also included a second level above the power room, where Schirmer saw "all kinds of panels and computers . . . a map on the wall, and . . . this large screen." The map portrayed a sun with six circling planets in a nearby galaxy. Said the patrolman, "They were observing us and *had* been observing us for a long time."

The humanoid leader again said, "Watchman, come with me," and Schirmer was led out of the craft. "What you have seen and what you have heard," he was told, "you will not remember."

Schirmer was eventually interviewed by the University of Colorado Condon Committee, then conducting an Air Force-sponsored UFO investigation. The project staff concluded that "the trooper's reported UFO experience was not physically real." But Sprinkle, who hypnotically regressed Schirmer, disagreed. "The trooper," Sprinkle declared, "believed in the reality of the events he described."

Presidential UFO

"I am convinced that UFOs exist because I have seen one." The speaker? No less a personage than James Earl Carter, a former submarine officer with a degree in nuclear physics and president of the United States.

Carter's sighting took place during his term as governor of Georgia, on January 6, 1969, while in the company of a dozen members of the Leary Lions Club. The group was standing outside, waiting for a speech to begin, when one member noticed a brilliant object low in the western sky.

"It was the darndest thing I've ever seen," said Carter. "It was big; it was very bright; it changed colors; and it was about the size of the moon. We watched it for about ten minutes, but none of us could figure out what it was.

"One thing's for sure," Carter added. "I'll never make fun of people who say they've seen unidentified objects in the sky."

Six months after his election as president, in response to public pressure and a campaign promise, Carter had his science adviser, Dr. Frank Press, ask NASA about the possibility of reevaluating the UFO phenomenon. While declining to open a new investigation, NASA's administrator, Dr. Robert Frosch, did say that "if some new element of hard evidence is brought to our attention in the future, it would be entirely appropriate for a NASA laboratory to analyze and report upon an otherwise unexplained organic or inorganic sample. We stand ready to respond to any bona fide physical evidence from credible sources. We intend to leave the door clearly open for such a possibility."

Underwater Dead Who Seemed Alive

Visitors to the Topkapi Museum in Istanbul, Turkey, are often told of the cruelties and dangers of the times when the Topkapi, built on a cliff high over the Bosphoros, was the imperial palace of the Turkish sultans. The sultans of Turkey, like the Roman emperors, possessed the power of life and death over their subjects. One of the more unnerving legends concerns the disposal of imperial concubines who, through unfaithfulness or petulance, had displeased the sultan.

"Abdul the Damned" was an especially notorious ruler. The penalty for his unhappy concubines was to be sewn, alive, into a weighted sack and dropped down a chute into the waters of the Bosphoros. But they did not quite disappear. Years later divers operating in deep water near the palace sometimes encountered these weighted sacks standing up on the seafloor, swaying back and forth as if alive in the cold waters of the current.

In 1957 an even more frightening underwater incident was experienced by scuba divers in Czechoslovakia in a body of water called Devil's Lake. The divers were searching for the body of a young man presumed drowned while boating on the lake. What they found, however, in deep waters was not one corpse but many, and not all of them were human beings. What they found were soldiers in full combat uniform, some sitting in trucks or on caissons, and many of the horses still standing upright in their harnesses. These were all the remains of a German artillery unit which, while crossing the ice during the fighting German retreat of World War II, had cracked through, probably under bombardment, and settled on the bottom of the lake. The extremely cold and deep water had preserved them for twelve years and would have preserved them for many more, positioned and ready for combat—but dead.

The Nun's Ghost at Borley

The Borley Rectory, in Essex, England, was troubled from the beginning of its existence in the early 1860s. Perhaps its haunting appearance—it was often called a monstrosity and had thirty rooms—had something to do with it. Its first inhabitants, the Reverend Henry Dawson Ellis Bull, his wife, and his fourteen children, told many tales of strange noises and the frequent sighting of the ghost of a nun. After Henry's death, the oldest son, Harry Bull, took over the rectory from 1892 until 1927, and the unusual events continued. So frequently was the nun seen that the area she appeared in was known as the Nun's Walk. Some people even reported a headless coachman driving a coach pulled by fire-breathing horses.

The next inhabitants, the Reverend and Mrs. G. Eric Smith, stayed only a few months, citing the strange events in the house as their reason for leaving.

Finally, the Reverend Lionel Foyster, his wife Marianne, and their daughter arrived. The stories continued, with Marianne insisting a ghost had slapped her in the face and shaken her out of her bed.

In an effort to investigate, the British National Laboratory of Psychical Research intervened. Its founder, Harry Price, advertised in the London *Times* for people to join him in a vigil of the haunted rectory. The ad called for unbiased, critical, and intelligent observers, and Price took forty of them to the house. Again, there were reports of moving objects and unexplained noises. Commander A. B. Campbell said he was hit by a flying piece of soap, for instance, and another man, philosopher C.E.M. Joad, reported seeing a thermometer plummet ten degrees for no apparent reason.

Again controversy ensued. When the Foysters vacated, Price himself moved in and reported a wide variety of phenomena, enough for a book. After his death, however, critics said that Price fabricated some of the phenomena and exaggerated others.

The story becomes more interesting, though, after a fire razed the building in 1939. The Reverend W. J. Phythian-Adams, canon of Carlisle, in Canada, suggested that the nun so often seen was not English, as had always been assumed, but French. A woman named Marie Lurie, it seemed, had left her convent to elope with her lover in the eighteenth century. They went to England, but the scoundrel turned on her and murdered her. In fact, he strangled her and reportedly buried her in the basement of the building that occupied the Borley land before the rectory was built. After the fire, diggers actually uncovered a grave containing only some religious medals and the skull of a woman.

The destruction of the building seems to have eliminated the ghostly walks by the nun, but the story does not end there. A group trying to conduct a recent scientific study of the premises heard strange, inexplicable noises in the night, recorded sudden temperature variations, saw lights of unknown origin, and detected strange smells.

The Battle Heard Ten Years Later

In early August 1951, two English sisters-in-law were vacationing in France when their sleep was disrupted by gunfire. It wasn't long before they realized they were hearing the sounds of war, and the noise continued off and on for the next three hours.

The next day, when the shaken women tried to find out what had happened, they were shocked by the news that no battle had taken place. In fact, no one else had heard a thing.

Upon investigation, however, they learned that they were vacationing in Puys, on the beach near Dieppe, an occupied and heavily fortified area during World War II. There, almost nine years to the day earlier, the Allies had launched an invasion that was to be a rehearsal for the D-Day attack. Sadly, the invasion was a very costly and bloody one. More than half of the 6,086 men who hit the beach on August 19, 1942, were killed, wounded, or captured.

The women soon learned that the sounds they had heard were an almost exact audio reproduction of that battle, as if they had been lodging there the moment it took place. They heard shelling and shouting in the early morning, "about 4 A.M.," and the noise stopped abruptly fifty minutes later. The actual shelling began at 3:47 A.M. and stopped, according to military records, at 4:50 A.M. They heard bombers and the cries of the men, and silence again, and again the military records confirmed the bombing stopped at about that same time, between 5:07 A.M. and 5:40 A.M.

Every sound they had heard matched military records of the battle. Interestingly, the battle had stopped at 6:00 A.M., the same time all the battle noises stopped for the women as well. Yet the sisters-in-law heard the pained cries of wounded and dying men for the next hour, growing fainter and fainter as time passed.

What Happened at Roanoke?

The first British child born in America was named Virginia Dare. Her parents had sailed to the New World with a group of settlers who landed on Roanoke Island, off the coast of North Carolina, and Virginia arrived shortly after, on August 18, 1587.

The vessel that brought the Dares and others to the new land eventually returned to England with all but ten men aboard. Those men were left behind to begin a settlement. But when the next ship arrived, the men could not be found. The second ship, too, returned to England, this time leaving a hundred people to begin the settlement. Some time later, the next ship arrived, and its passengers again found the island empty. There was no trace of violence, struggle, or even a grave, only the word "CRO" carved in one tree and "CROATAN" carved in another. Croatan, another island off North Carolina, was apparently the place the group had settled. But the ship's captain, fearing a lack of food and the approaching winter, decided to set sail for the West Indies and winter there. By the time the next ship reached the island of Croatan, there again was no sign of the abandoned settlers. There was no sign of or story about an Indian massacre.

There were no graves or markers, and save for an occasional tale of an Indian child with "yellow" hair or blue eyes, not a single one of the original 110 was ever found. Although a subject of countless rumors and legends, the mystery has never been explained.

The Long Voyage Home

Whether the homing ability of animals comes from a superior sense of direction or a sixth sense unknown to science, the homing ability of the dog has continually astounded his best friends. In at least three documented cases, dogs have traveled thousands of miles, and there are many instances of dogs finding their way over shorter distances as well.

Doug Simpson's dog Nick, for instance, disappeared during a camping trip they took together in southern Arizona in November 1979. Simpson spent two weeks frantically searching for the German shepherd, but she was not to be found, so he returned to his home in Pennsylvania. Four months later, with cuts still bleeding and fur torn, Nick showed up at the home of Simpson's parents in Selah, Washington. The dog had apparently crossed the Arizona desert, the Grand Canyon, the treacherous mountains of the Rockies, frozen streams, snow-covered mountains, and countless highways. When she arrived in the driveway where Simpson's old car was parked, she promptly collapsed from exhaustion. Simpson's mother found the dog, who was rewarded when her master came to take her back home.

A year later, Jessie, another shepherd, was living at his new home in Aspen, Colorado, where he found himself when his master, Dexter Gardiner, moved from East Greenwich, Rhode Island. The rest of the Gardiner family had remained behind, and so had the dog next door. Jessie, apparently feeling abandoned, left Aspen and showed up at the Gardiners' six months later, only to find his loved ones gone for the summer. After a brief stay in the pound, he was adopted by Mrs. Linda Babcock, but he again took off for his old home, which this time was not nearly so far. This time, the Gardiners were there, and welcomed him back, although they were mystified by his sudden appearance. An investigation of Jessie's long journey eventually led the Gardiners to Mrs. Babcock, who, after friendly negotiations, ended up keeping the dog.

The longest homing effort on record, however, was achieved in 1923 by Bobbie, a collie who belonged to a family in Silverton, Oregon. He was lost on a family vacation in Walcott, Indiana. But six months later, he had made it back home, a distance of more than 2,000 miles. Details of the dog's trek were later supplied by the families that cared for him along the way, and his route was traced through Illinois, Iowa, Nebraska, Colorado, Wyoming, and Idaho. Bobbie had crossed the Rockies in the middle of winter.

JAL Flight 1628

Despite the popularity of the phrase "flying saucers," UFO shapes and sizes actually fall into several categories, including discs hundreds of feet in diameter, and objects that resemble triangles, cigars, and even teapots. UFOs of immense size, frequently accompanied by smaller flying craft, are known as "mother ships."

One such mother ship was reported by the pilot of Japanese

Air Lines flight 1628, a Boeing 747 bound from Iceland to Anchorage, Alaska, on November 17, 1986. Flying over Alaska just after 6 P.M. Captain Kenju Terauchi reported bright white and yellow lights ahead, darting about "like two bear cubs playing with each other." Terauchi radioed Anchorage and the air controller confirmed he had a target on radar. The Japanese pilot switched on his own onboard digital color radar, and though it was designed to pick up weather systems and not solid objects, it also registered a reading.

Then Terauchi noticed his 747 was being shadowed by a single, gigantic walnut-shaped UFO the size of two aircraft carriers. He asked Anchorage for permission to execute a 360-degree turn and descend to 31,000 feet, which was granted. The mother ship remained on his tail throughout the maneuver. Anchorage directed two other aircraft in the area to Terauchi's immediate vicinity, but by the time they arrived the UFO had disappeared, having been in sight and pursuit of the 747 for fifty minutes.

Boy From Nowhere

Caspar Hauser might as well have dropped out of the sky. He appeared on the streets of Nuremberg, Germany, in 1828, barely able to walk and speak his name. According to a crudely scrawled letter on his person, Caspar was sixteen years old. But the letter, addressed to the captain of the Sixth Cavalry Regiment stationed in Nuremberg, offered few other details of the boy's life. "If you do not want to keep him," it offered, "kill him or hang him up a chimney."

The local jailer took pity and installed Caspar in his own quarters, slowly teaching him to talk. All he could remember was that he had been raised in darkness in a room barely larger than a closet, fed on a diet of bread and water. He seemed unfamiliar with the most ordinary items. One observer noted that when confronted with a candle, he kept trying to pick the flame off with his fingers. But his sense of sight was so acute that he could reportedly read in the dark and see stars during the day. Caspar was also ambidextrous, with a marked aversion for meat.

Because of his plight, the whole of Nuremberg adopted Caspar, treating him as its own. He was placed under the personal care of a Professor Daumer, and even attracted the attention of both German and European society.

Then on October 17, 1829, Caspar was found in Daumer's home, his forehead bleeding from a knife wound, delivered by a man in a black mask who had suddenly appeared and stabbed him. In 1831, he was wounded in the forehead again, when a pistol accidentally discharged. On December 14, 1833, Caspar Hauser ran from a park, mortally wounded by yet another knife-stab. A search of the park failed to find the weapon. More mysteriously, only Caspar's footprints could be seen in the fresh snow. He died three days later.

Von Feurbach, one of his biographers, had this to say about the enigma of Nuremberg: "Caspar Hauser showed such an utter deficiency of words and ideas, such perfect ignorance of the commonest things and appearances of nature, and such horror of all customs, conveniences, and necessities of civilized life, and, withal, such extraordinary peculiarities in his social, mental, and physical disposition, that one might feel oneself driven to the alternative of believing him to be a citizen of another planet, transferred by some miracle to our own."

Spring-Heel Jack

Had Charles Dickens a perverted sense of humor he might have created a character the likes of Spring-Heel Jack. That this phantasm apparently sprang full-blown from the bowels of London shows that reality continues to outstrip the artist's imagination.

Spring-Heel Jack first turned up in the 1830s, haunting Barnes Common in southwest London by leaping out at people, physically assaulting them, and bounding away with impossible jumping ability. A typical victim was eighteen-year-old Lucy Sales, attacked on her way home in Green Dragon Alley, Limehouse. The cloaked figure jumped out of the darkness, spat flames that temporarily blinded Lucy, then bounded away.

Another victim was Jane Alsop of Bearhind Lane. Answering a knock at the door, Jane confronted a dark figure cloaked in a cape who said, "I am a policeman. For God's sake bring me a light. We have caught Spring-Heel Jack here in the lane!"

She returned with a candle, but the "policeman" threw back his clothes, revealing a terrible vision dressed in a skin-tight, horned helmet and a form-fitting, white uniform. He immediately grabbed Alsop and began pawing her body. Of her attacker Alsop said, "His face was hideous, his eyes like balls of fire. His hands had icy-cold great claws, and he spewed forth blue and white flames."

Hysteria swept the neighborhood. Vigilante posses were organized, but Spring-Heel Jack stayed a jump ahead of his would-be captors. One of his last known appearances was at the Aldershot Barracks in 1877, where three sentries were attacked and fired rifles at their assailant—to no effect.

One theory said Spring-Heel was actually the wastrel nobleman Henry, Marquis of Waterford, who supposedly managed the athletic agility attributed to Jack by means of carriage-springs strapped to his ankles. Such a hypothesis seems almost as far-fetched as the fire-belching Spring-Heel Jack himself. The Marquis of Waterford would have had to have kept his astounding act up for more than four decades, no mean feat for a man who would have by then been in his sixties.

The above theory seems even less likely in light of the fact that German paratroopers during World War II experimented with similar springs designed to soften their landing. The experiments resulted in a rash of broken ankles instead.

Missie, the Dog That Foretold the Future

When Mildred Probert, a retired pet store manager from Denver, inherited Missie, she hoped to restore the brown Boston terrier puppy to health. It took five years, but finally the extraordinary talents of the little terrier emerged: One day, as Probert was walking down the street with Missie, they passed a woman and her young child. Probert asked the child his age, but the youngster was obviously too shy to respond. The mother answered by saying the boy was three. As she tried to coax the boy into saying "three," Missie spontaneously barked three times. Everyone laughed at the coincidence, but the incident turned out to be more than merely a lark. It turned out that Missie could respond to many questions by barking in response, especially mathematical problems. It also soon appeared that the dog could even predict the future.

But the canine's real breakthrough came on New Year's Eve in 1965, when she was "interviewed" on KTLN radio. New York was undergoing a crippling transit strike at the time, and negotiations were at a standstill, so the talk-show host asked Missie when the strike would be over, phrasing questions that could be answered by the number of times that Missie barked. Missie barked to signify that the critical date would be January 13—which was indeed the exact date the transit strike ended. The little dog also successfully predicted the outcome of that year's World Series.

Sometimes Missie would come up with highly unexpected information. On September 10, 1965, Probert received a visit from a pregnant woman she knew. Since Missie had often predicted delivery dates for babies in the past, the couple decided to consult the dog. Missie responded to the inquiry by signifying September 18. The pregnant woman had to chuckle since, she explained to her hostess, she was scheduled for a Caesarian on October 6. She became even more skeptical when Missie declared that the baby would be born at 9:00 P.M., since her physician didn't work in the evening.

But it all came to pass just as Missie predicted. The visitor went into labor unexpectedly on the 18th and was rushed to the hospital, where her baby was born precisely at 9:00 P.M.

Missie's career as a psychic celebrity didn't last very long. She choked on a piece of candy and died in May 1966. At the time, Walt Disney was planning to make a movie about her extraordinary life.

The Flying Humanoid

At about 8:30 on the quiet evening of July 12, 1977, Adrián de Olmos Ordóñez, forty-two, was resting on the balcony of his home in Quebradillas, Puerto Rico, when he saw something crawl under a barbed-wire fence on a farm not far away. In the dusk De Olmos could see it was a small figure, apparently a child.

A closer look, though, revealed that this was no normal child at all. The creature wore a bulbous green garment and a metallic helmet, at the top of which was an antenna "with a bright light or flame at its tip."

De Olmos called his daughter Irasema to bring him a pencil and paper so that he could sketch the figure as he watched it. As he would tell Puerto Rican ufologist Sebastián Robiou Lamarche, "I told her to turn on the light in the living room, but she made a mistake and she turned on the outside balcony light instead," De Olmos said. The creature took fright and fled.

"The minute the balcony light went on, I saw the creature run back instantly toward the barbed-wire fence. It passed under the wire and then stopped," he explained. "It placed its hands on the front part of its belt and then a thing that it had on its back, resembling a knapsack, lit up and emitted a sound like the noise of an electric drill. And then it rose up into the air and made off toward the trees." At that point the witness's daughter, wife, and two sons came out of the house to see the lights from the flying device on the being's back as it sailed through the air.

For the next ten minutes they watched the lights moving from tree to tree, sometimes descending briefly to ground level. Meanwhile, a group of neighbors joined them and they too saw the strange spectacle. Eventually, a second group of lights, presumably from a second humanoid, joined the first—perhaps, De Olmos thought, to help its companion because "the apparatus on the creature's back was not working quite right."

Soon the lights were out, leaving only a badly frightened collection of people who wasted no time in notifying the police. The police conducted an extensive investigation, as did well-known Puerto Rican ufologist Robiou Lamarche. Reporting on his investigation in Britain's *Flying Saucer Review*, Lamarche wrote, "In the course of our inquiries we ascertained that Sr. Adrián is a serious and well-respected and hard-working person, held in high regard by all the neighbors. He is a businessman, engaged in the distribution of cattle feed throughout the northwestern area of the island. He had never before taken the slightest interest in the UFO phenomenon, or in any related subjects. But, he told us, 'Now I believe in these things.' "

Red Light Over Ithaca

Rita Malley, a young mother of two, was driving home to Ithaca, New York, on the evening of December 12, 1967, when she noticed a red light in pursuit. At first she thought she was being followed by a police car. She was about to pull over to the side of the road when she took another look and this time saw that the light was attached to a strange flying object traveling just above the power lines to her left.

That was startling enough, but nothing compared to her sudden realization that she could no longer control her car. She shouted to her son, who was traveling with her, to brace himself for an accident. But strangely, he did not respond or even move. "It was as if he were in some kind of a trance," she said later.

"The car pulled over to the shoulder of the road by itself, ran over an embankment into an alfafa field, and stopped.

"A white twirling beam of light flashed down from the object," Malley said, "and I heard a humming sound. Then I began to hear voices. The words were broken and jerky, like the way a translator sounds when he is repeating a speech at the United Nations."

As Malley recalls it, she became hysterical when the voices told her a friend was involved in a terrible accident miles away. After a while, though, her car began to move again. She pushed down hard on the accelerator and sped home.

"I knew something was wrong the moment she walked into the house," her husband John told a reporter for the *Syracuse Herald-Journal.* "I thought maybe she had had an accident with the car or something." The next day she learned that a friend indeed had experienced a serious car accident the night before.

For days afterwards, according to reporters and UFO investigators who interviewed her, Mrs. Malley could not discuss the bizarre experience without bursting into tears.

UFOs in Mexico

On May 3, 1975, Carlos Antonio de los Santos Montiel was flying to Mexico City when his Piper PA-24 aircraft began shaking for no apparent reason. Moments later the young pilot spotted a dark gray disc-shaped object, about ten or twelve feet in diameter, just beyond the plane's right wingtip. A similar craft was pacing him on the left.

Most frightening of all, however, was a third object coming straight at him. The UFO passed just under his plane, so close, in fact, that it scraped the underpart of the fuselage.

De los Santos was nearly beside himself with fear, and his terror was intensified when he discovered that the controls seemed frozen. He could not operate them yet, strangely, the plane continued flying at a steady 120 miles per hour.

When the UFOs were no longer visible, de los Santos regained control of the plane. He instantly radioed the airport at Mexico City, and wept as he reported the incident.

The control tower took his report seriously because personnel there had tracked the objects on radar. As air traffic controller Emilio Estañol told reporters, the objects made a 270-degree turn at 518 miles per hour in an arc of only three miles. "Normally a plane moving at that speed needs eight to ten miles to make a turn like that," he said. "In my seventeen years as an air traffic controller I've never seen anything like that."

After he landed safely, de los Santos was given a medical examination and pronounced fit. But as he would soon learn, his ordeal was not over.

His sighting got headline treatment in the Mexican press and two weeks later de los Santos, a retiring twenty-three-year-old man whose ambition in life was to become an airline pilot, was asked to appear on a television talk show to discuss his experience. He reluctantly agreed.

On the day he was to appear, he drove his car down the freeway on the way to the television station. Along the way he saw a large black automobile—he thought it looked like a diplomat's limousine—pull up in front of him. When he looked through the rearview mirror, he saw an identical car behind him. The two cars, which looked so new that to all appearances they were being driven for the first time, were crowding him and soon forced him to the side of the road.

No sooner had he stopped than so did the other cars. De los Santos was about to get out when four tall, broad-shouldered men hopped out of their vehicles. One put his hands on Carlos's door as if to ensure that he would not be able to leave his car. He spoke quickly, speaking an oddly "mechanical" Spanish: "Look, boy, if you value your life and your family's too, don't talk any more about this sighting of yours."

De los Santos, too stunned to respond, watched the four men, who were "Scandinavian" looking, with unusually pale skin and black suits, return to their cars and drive away. For his part Carlos turned around and went back home.

Two days later he told his story to Pedro Ferriz, the host of the television show on which he had been scheduled to appear. Ferriz, a UFO buff, said he had heard other reports of strange "men in black" who threatened UFO witnesses. He assured the young pilot that despite the threats he would not be hurt. In due course he persuaded Carlos to do another interview, which went off without incident.

A month later, Carlos met Dr. J. Allen Hynek, the Northwestern University astronomer who had served as the U.S. Air Force's chief scientific consultant on UFO matters. The two talked and before they parted, Hynek invited him to have breakfast with him the next morning.

At 6:00 A.M. de los Santos left his house and went to the Mexicana Airlines office, where he had applied for a job. Then he went to Hynek's hotel.

As he walked up the steps, he was surprised to see one of the men in black who had forced him off the freeway four weeks earlier. "You were already warned once," the strange man said. "You are not to talk about your experience." As if to underline the seriousness of the threat, he pushed Carlos back several feet.

"Look," he continued, "I don't want you to make problems for yourself. And why did you leave your house at six o'clock this morning? Do you work for Mexicana Airlines? Get out of here—and don't come back!"

De los Santos left immediately without meeting Hynek.

Recalling the bizarre events two years later, de los Santos told two American UFO investigators, "They were very strange. They were huge, taller than Mexicans are, and their skin was deathly white."

Marchers From the Ancient Past

Late one evening in September 1974, writer A. C. McKerracher decided to take a break from work and step outside for a breath of fresh air.

McKerracher and his family had recently moved into a new housing estate on a hill above the small country town of Dunblane in Perthshire, Scotland. It was a clear, frosty night, and the town below was covered in mist. Suddenly, the quiet was disturbed by what sounded like the movement of a large group of people streaming across the fields.

Certain that he was suffering from overwork, McKerracher decided to go inside. But twenty minutes later, puzzled by the occurrence, he went outside again only to find that the sounds were louder, and closer, than ever. This time it sounded as if a mighty legion was marching on the other side of the houses across the street.

"I stood rooted to the spot as the unearthly, unseen cavalcade passed by," he remembered. "The marchers must have numbered in the thousands, for the noise went on and on."

By now fearing for his sanity, he forced himself to go back inside and straight to bed. A week later, however, McKerracher was visiting an older couple who lived nearby when he heard a strange story. Late one night a week earlier, the couple said, their cat and dog had abruptly awakened and stood bolt upright, the hair bristling on their backs. "They seemed to watch something crossing the lounge for about twenty minutes," the couple said. "They were terrified."

McKerracher had said nothing about his own experience. But the animals' curious behavior occurred at exactly the same time he had heard the invisible legion a week before. Seeking an explanation, he soon found that an ancient Roman road ran north directly behind the houses on the other side of the street. Moreover, in A.D. 117 an elite IX Hispania Legion had been dispatched to the area to subdue a tribal uprising in Scotland. It had consisted of four thousand men.

The legion was known as the "Unlucky Ninth" since in A.D. 60 men of the IX had flogged Queen Boadicea of England's Iceni tribe and raped her daughters. Boadicea swore an eternal curse against them and later led a revolt that left the Ninth with severe casualties.

The legion regrouped but was never the same. Its march into Scotland came to a mysterious end: It vanished without a trace shortly after it passed through what centuries later would be Dunblane.

In October 1984 McKerracher, who did not hear the sound again and later moved to the older section of Dunblane, gave a lecture on local history to a ladies' club. Afterwards Cecilia Moore, a member, came up to say she might have heard the ghost of a Roman army herself.

It turned out that she had lived across the street from his former house. "I was putting the cat out one night when I heard what sounded like an army passing right through my back garden," she said. The incident, McKerracher determined, took place the same night and at the same time as his own.

"I am convinced," he wrote, "that what she and I heard—and what my neighbors' animals saw—was the doomed Ninth Legion marching to its terrible unknown fate nearly two thousand years before."

Deathbed Visions

Most of us have heard of the near-death experience in which those who have clinically died report "leaving the body" and journeying to heaven. More rarely discussed, however, are deathbed vision cases in which the patients see welcoming figures, usually friends and relatives, coming to greet them and help them through death. Recently, some important research suggests that these experiences can't be explained away as hallucinations.

For several years now, Dr. Karlis Osis, formerly the director of Research for the American Society for Psychical Research, has been conducting computer studies analyzing hundreds of deathbed vision cases collected from the United States. By checking the pertinent medical records for each patient, Osis has been able to determine that their experiences weren't caused by toxic effects of either their illnesses or medications. Working with psychologist Dr. Erlendur Haraldsson of the University of Reykjavik in Iceland, Osis also traveled to India to conduct an identical study and to see whether these curious visions occurred there as well. The researchers especially wanted to determine if the Indian visions conformed to different cultural patterns, a clear sign that they were psychological in nature instead of real.

The finding? Terminal patients in India describe the same range of experiences the dying report in the West, say Osis and Haraldsson. While psychological reactions to the experiences may differ from East to West, the contents do not. These findings have led Osis and Haraldsson to conclude that deathbed visions really do represent a peek beyond death.

A Big Bird?

It was 10:30 on the evening of January 14, 1976, and Armando Grimaldo was sitting in the backyard of his mother-in-law's house on the north side of Raymondville, Texas. He had come to visit his estranged wife Christina, who was now asleep inside. Grimaldo was about to have an all-too-close encounter with a creature from another world.

"As I was turning to go look over on the other side of the house," he went on, "I felt something grab me, something with big claws. I looked back and saw it and started running. I've never been scared of nothing before but this time I really was. That was the most scared I've ever been in my whole life."

Something had dived out of the sky—and it was something Grimaldo had never seen before or wanted to see again. It was as tall as he—five feet, eight inches—and it had a wingspread of from ten to twelve feet. Its skin was "blackish-brown," leathery and featherless, and its face had huge red eyes.

Grimaldo screamed and tried to run but in his panic tripped over his feet, falling face-first into the dirt. As he struggled back up, he could hear his clothes being ripped by the beast's claws. He managed to dash under a tree as his attacker, now breathing heavily, flew off into the night.

Christina was awakened by his shouting and was on her way downstairs when she heard him crash into the house "in some kind of shock." Unable to speak coherently, he kept muttering *pájaro* (Spanish for "bird") over and over again. He was taken to the Willacy County Hospital and released after half an hour when doctors determined that he had suffered no physical injuries.

Armando Grimaldo may have been luckier than Joe Suárez's goat. Something ripped it to pieces in the early hours of December 26. The animal had been left tied up in a corral behind Suárez's barn in Raymondville. There were no footprints around the body and the police could not explain how it had been killed.

Something had invaded the Rio Grande Valley. Before it was gone a month or so later, local wits had dubbed it "Big Bird" after the "Sesame Street" character. To most people it was an object of amusement. Those who saw it considered it no laughing matter.

A similar creature slammed into Alverico Guajardo's trailer in nearby Brownsville. When Guajardo went outside, he got into his station wagon and turned on the lights to see what he described as "something from another planet." As soon as the lights hit it, the thing rose up and glared at him with blazing red eyes. Guajardo, paralyzed with fear, could only stare back at the creature, whose long, batlike wings were wrapped around its shoulders. All the while it was making a "horrible-sounding noise" in its throat. Finally, after two or three minutes, it backed away to a dirt road three feet behind it and disappeared in the darkness.

Yet another sighting of the creature occurred on February 24, far to the north, in San Antonio, when three elementary schoolteachers driving to work on an isolated road southwest of the city spotted an enormous bird with a wingspan of "fifteen or twenty feet, if not more." It was flying so low that when it swooped over the cars its shadow covered the entire road.

As the three watched this unlikely creature, they saw another flying creature off in the distance circling a herd of cattle. It looked, they thought, like an "oversized seagull."

Later, when the teachers searched through books trying to identify the first bird they had seen, they were able to identify it. The only trouble was that the bird closely resembled the pteranodon, a flying dinosaur that had not existed for 150 million years.

They were not the only south Texans to think they had seen a prehistoric winged reptile. Just a month before, two Brownsville sisters, Libby and Deany Ford, sighted a "big black bird" near a pond. The creature was as tall as they were and had a "face like a bat." Later, when they came upon a picture of a pteranodon in a book, they concluded that was what they had seen.

The Big Bird scare subsided in early 1976, but that was not the last the Rio Grande Valley was to see of the creature. On September 14, 1982, James Thompson, an ambulance technician from Harlingen, saw a "large birdlike object" pass over Highway 100 at a distance of 150 feet. The time was 3:55 A.M.

"I expected him to land like a model airplane," Thompson told the *Valley Morning Star*. "That's what I thought he was, but he flapped his wings enough to get above the grass. It had a black or grayish rough texture. It wasn't feathers. I'm quite sure it was a hide-type covering. I just watched him fly away." It was, he would later realize, a "pterodactyl-like bird."

The International Society of Cryptozoology, a scientific organization that investigates reports of unknown or allegedly extinct animals, noted that the sighting "occurred only 200 miles east—as the pterodactyl flies—of Mexico's Sierra Madre Oriental, one of the least explored regions of North America."

The Persistent Hitchhiker

As he was driving from Mayagüez, Puerto Rico, to his home in Arecibo late in the evening of November 20, 1982, Abel Haiz Rassen, an Arab merchant who lives in Puerto Rico, passed through a section known as "The Chain." A balding man was standing on the side of the road hitchhiking. Haiz Rassen glanced at the man, who was about thirty-five years old and dressed in a gray shirt and brown jeans, and drove on.

But when he stopped for a red light at the next intersection, his car stalled. As Haiz Rassen struggled to start it again, he did not notice that the hitchhiker was opening the passenger door and getting inside.

"I'm Roberto," the man said to the startled Haiz Rassen. "Could you please take me to my home in the housing project, Alturas de Aguarda? I have not seen my son and my wife Esperanza for almost two months."

Haiz Rassen declined the request, saying his wife was waiting for him in Arecibo. But Roberto pleaded with him. The driver went back to trying to start the car, which suddenly began running again.

He agreed to take Roberto as far as the El Nido Restaurant. In the course of the short journey his unwelcome passenger cautioned him to drive carefully and not to drink. He asked that Haiz Rassen pray for him.

It was with some relief that Haiz Rassen pulled up to the restaurant parking lot. Observers nearby saw him talking animatedly, apparently to himself. One asked if he needed help.

"No," Haiz Rassen replied, "but this gentleman wants me to take him home." He turned to his right to indicate his passenger—but there was no one there.

He was so shaken that he nearly became ill. The police were summoned and two officers, Alfredo Vega and Gilberto Castro, took him to a local hospital, where he related his bizarre story.

Skeptical but still intrigued, the officers went to the housing project and knocked at the door with the address the driver said he had gotten from Roberto. A woman carrying a small boy answered. To the officers' questions she replied that her name was Esperanza. She was the widow of Roberto Valentín Carbo.

Her husband, who was partially bald, had been wearing a gray shirt and brown jeans on October 6, 1982, when he was killed in a car accident—at the exact spot along the roadside where six weeks later Abel Haiz Rassen first spotted him.

Out-of-Body Travelers

Parapsychologists have spent a great deal of time studying the phenomenon of out-of-body experiences, or astral projection.

In one case, recorded by a physician, a man named Wilson fell asleep and dreamed that he had visited a woman friend who lived forty miles from him. A maid answered the door and told him she was not at home, but he asked to come in and have a glass of water. The maid obliged. Wilson thought nothing more of it, until another friend of his received a letter from the woman in the dream, and the letter spoke of Wilson's visit, and even mentioned his coming in for water. This caused Wilson to take some friends along to that house to investigate. When he got there, two maids identified Wilson as the man who had been there and had come in.

A more celebrated projector is a man named Blue Haray, who claims the power of leaving his body at will, and has put his claims to the test at the Psychical Research Foundation in Durham, North Carolina. In these experiments, Haray's eye movements, respiration, and other bodily functions were monitored by a maze of instruments, and all monitors showed significant changes when he reported an out-of-body experience. On one occasion, he visited a doctor who was not expecting the visit. The doctor reported seeing a "red orb" flash across his room at 3:15 A.M., exactly the time Haray said he had been there. Pets kept in separate, sealed rooms were used as the targets in another series of experiments. In one test, a cat stopped meowing and sat motionless when Haray reported his visit; in another test, a hostile snake that had been acting normally suddenly tried to strike at something unseen by the cameras, again at the same time Haray said he was "visiting" the target room.

Yet another out-of-body journey was reported by a young lieutenant on duty in Panama in 1943. He was worried about his mother, who had just undergone major surgery in New York. Leave to visit her was not possible. But during a training break at a quarter past one he fell asleep for a few moments and dreamed he was standing in front of the Memorial Hospital near the East River Drive. He entered and asked the receptionist for permission to visit his mother. The receptionist checked a list and signed him in as a visitor. Another nurse told him that she recognized him from the photograph in his mother's room. The picture showed him wearing a winter uniform, the same as he was wearing in the hospital. He got into the elevator and a nurse saw him push the button. On the way up in the elevator the lieutenant felt everything become hazy and dreamlike. He woke up, still in Panama, at 1:15 P.M. Some days later he received a letter from his mother telling about an odd unexplained incident. She had been told that her son had come to visit her, but he never arrived. Although the receptionist and another nurse had seen him enter the elevator, no one saw him get out. The time: 12:15 P.M. in New York and 1:15 P.M. in the Panama time zone. The name of the officer who wanted to visit his mother had been written in the register. It was my own name, Charles Berlitz.

A Massacre in Flight

Something terrifying happened in the air one day in the late summer of 1939—and to this day the incident is shrouded in secrecy.

All that is known is that a military transport plane left the

Marine Naval Air Station in San Diego at 3:30 one afternoon. It and its thirteen-man crew were making a routine flight to Honolulu. Three hours later, as the plane was over the Pacific Ocean, a frantic distress signal was sounded. Then the radio signal died.

A little later the plane limped back to base and made an emergency landing. Ground crew members rushed to the craft and when they boarded, they were horrified to see twelve dead men. The only survivor was the copilot, who, though badly injured, had stayed alive long enough to bring the plane back. A few minutes later he was dead, too.

All of the bodies had large, gaping wounds. Even weirder, the pilot and copilot had emptied their .45 Colt automatic pistols at something. The empty shells were found lying on the floor of the cockpit. A foul, sulfuric odor pervaded the interior of the craft.

The exterior of the airplane was badly damaged, looking as if it had been struck by missiles. The personnel who boarded the craft came down with an odd skin infection.

Strict security measures were quickly put into effect and the emergency ground crew was ordered to leave the plane. The job of removing the bodies and investigating the incident was left to three medical officers.

The incident was successfully hushed up and did not come to light for fifteen years, when investigator Robert Coe Gardner learned of it from someone who was there. The mystery of what the crew encountered in midair that afternoon in 1939 has never been solved.

Lightning Strikes More Than Twice

In 1899 a bolt of lightning killed a man as he stood in his backyard in Taranto, Italy. Thirty years later his son was killed in the same way and in the same place. On October 8, 1949, Rolla Primarda, the grandson of the first victim and the son of the second, became the third.

Just as strange was the fate of a British officer, Major Summerford, who while fighting in the fields of Flanders in February 1918 was knocked off his horse by a flash of lightning and paralyzed from the waist down.

Summerford retired and moved to Vancouver. One day in 1924, as he fished alongside a river, lightning hit the tree he was sitting under and paralyzed his right side.

Two years later Summerford was sufficiently recovered that he was able to take walks in a local park. He was walking there one summer day in 1930 when a lightning bolt smashed into him, permanently paralyzing him. He died two years later.

But lightning sought him out one more time. Four years later, during a storm, lightning struck a cemetery and destroyed a tombstone. It was Major Summerford's.

K-19

For years Thomas Wolfe, the famous American writer, had an idea for a novel. It was to be titled *K-19* and it would be about a Pullman car bearing that designation. The lives of all the characters in the story would in some way be affected by that car. He discussed *K-19* with his editor, Maxwell Perkins, but he could never put the story together in a satisfactory manner. Perkins suggested he concentrate on other writings until he was sure he had a plot that worked. Wolfe agreed, but as fate would have it, he was unable to return to his *K-19* idea. He died suddenly of a heart attack in 1938.

Perkins took responsibility for shipping Wolfe's body back to his native Asheville, North Carolina, where it would be buried. As the train was pulling out of the station, Perkins was watching the car bearing Wolfe's casket. As it passed out of sight, he suddenly realized what its number was: K-19.

The Crash That Never Happened

On October 10, 1931, America's newest dirigible, the U.S.S. *Akron*, was scheduled to circle the Fairfield Stadium in honor of the Washington and Jefferson-Marshall football game in Huntington, West Virginia.

The first person to see the dirigible en route was Harold MacKenzie, who watched it making its way over the nearby town of Gallipolis, Ohio. He called to friends at the Foster Dairy plant to come watch it with him.

Two of them, Mr. and Mrs. Robert Henke, went to First Avenue with their friend Mrs. Claude Parker. The three watched the craft through binoculars and were soon joined by other observers, who saw the *Akron* sail over the river.

On the other side, in Point Pleasant, West Virginia, other watchers followed the ship's progress. The ship, about 100 to 150 feet long, was flying at the altitude of about 300 feet when, at 2:50 P.M., something unexpected and terrifying happened.

As Mrs. Henke told the *Gallipolis Daily Tribune* on October 12, "When we caught sight of the ship, it seemed to buckle and fall. Some who saw it said that four persons jumped with parachutes. There seemed to be smoke surrounding the object but it may have been clouds that we saw."

Horrified observers saw the blimp erupt into flames and crash into the hills south of Gallipolis Ferry, West Virginia.

Half a dozen witnesses reported the incident to Dr. Holzer, owner of the Gallipolis Airport. At dawn the next day searchers set out for the site. All that day they went over the site from both ground and air—and found no trace of the ship or its doomed crew.

There was a simple reason: They did not exist.

By evening the day of the alleged disaster, spokesmen from the Akron Airport were denying that any such tradegy had occurred. The *Akron* was safe in its hangar, as were the three blimps of the Goodyear Zeppelin Company. The *Akron* had flown over northern Ohio earlier that day but had not gone south to the Huntington stadium because the navy had turned down Senator H. D. Hatfield's request that it do so.

All eastern and midwestern airports asserted that none of their craft were missing. Nor were there any foreign dirigibles operating in that area of the United States.

The witnesses, however, adamantly rejected theories that they had seen a flock of birds or simply dreamed the sighting. To this day this peculiar episode remains unexplained.

Psychic Control of the Weather?

The place was the Indian city of Dharamsala, home to many Tibetan refugees. The date was March 10, 1973, time for the refugees to mourn the flight of the Dalai Lama from Tibet. But with storms rolling down the Himalayan slopes for weeks, the proceedings seemed doomed. With no letup in sight, the local residents finally sought help from Gunsang Rinzing, an elderly lama both feared and renowned for his power to control the weather. The lama's work was later described by David Read Barker, an anthropologist conducting fieldwork in India at the time. It was 8:00 P.M., Dr. Barker explains, and Rinzing began by building a fire in the rain.

"He was in a state of concentration," reported Barker, "and recited mantras and a sadhana, frequently blowing on a trumpet fashioned from a human thighbone and beating the two-headed drum of a shaman. After several hours of watching him from a respectful distance, we retired to bed, certain that the weather would be as miserable the next day as it had been for the preceding days. Early the following morning the rain had diminished to a drizzle, and by ten o'clock it had become only a cold fog over a circle with a radius of about one-hundred and fifty meters. Everywhere else in the area it continued to pour, but the several thousand refugees were never rained on during the six hours they were assembled. At one point during the Dalai Lama's speech, a huge hailstorm swept past, causing a tremendous clatter on the tin-roofed houses adjoining the festival grounds, but only a few dozen hailstones fell on the crowd."

Fourteen years before, at the time of the Chinese Communist invasion of Tibet and the Dalai Lama's escape to India, unexpected atmospheric conditions assured his safe arrival across the Himalayas into India. While Chinese aircraft tried to find him and his party, a thick fog providentially cloaked the area he was traversing, making the travelers completely invisible from the air. To Tibetans, of course, this sudden zero visibility was simply a proof of the Dalai Lama's divine power over the weather.

Saved by a Dead Boy

At 10 o'clock one night early in 1978, seventy-two-year-old retired farmer Henry Sims returned from a Florida hospital, where his eighteen-year-old daughter was staying. His wife Idellar remained at the hospital. Another daughter, five grandchildren, and a family friend were sleeping in the house when Sims returned. He went to bed and soon fell asleep.

"The next thing I remember," he would recall, "is the dream. I could see my brother-in-law's two children—Paul and his eight-month-old baby sister—coming toward me. They were both burned to death in 1932 when fire swept through their home in Live Oak, Florida. In my dream Paul, whom I remember clearly, was walking toward me saying, 'Uncle Henry, Uncle Henry.' I had never had a dream like this before and I awoke suddenly with the smell of smoke in my nostrils. My first thought was my grandchildren—to get those kids out of the place. So I began shouting and yelling."

His cries awoke the other sleepers, who fled the burning house just in time to save their lives.

Fire inspector Lieutenant Frederick Lowe of Hialeah Heights, Florida, said, "Miraculously, this man managed to wake up at the vital moment. Another two minutes and everyone would have been dead."

"God wasn't ready for me to die," Henry Sims concluded. "It was He who sent young Paul to warn of the danger and to pluck us all from that burning building."

The Deadly Number—191

In May 1979 an American Airlines DC-10 crashed near O'Hare Airport in Chicago shortly after taking off for a flight to California. Among the victims was author Judy Wax, whose book, *Starting in the Middle*, had just been published.

The flight number of the doomed plane was 191. On page 191 of her book Mrs. Wax had discussed her fear of flying.

The May 1979 issue of *Chicago* reviewed her book and ran a picture of her with it. Readers who held up the page to the light could see on the reverse side a full-page advertisement for an American Airlines DC-10 flight to California.

Disappearance of the S.S. *Iron Mountain*

Nothing seemed out of the ordinary in June 1872 when the steamship *Iron Mountain* chugged off from Vicksburg, its crew intact, its cargo of baled cotton and barrels of molasses stacked on the deck and a line of barges in tow.

A few minutes later it rounded a bend, making its way northward toward the steel town of Pittsburgh. The ship was never seen again.

The *Iroquois Chief*, another steamer, was traveling on the river late that morning when its crew spotted a line of barges churning downriver. The ship managed to steer clear of the barges and then, assuming they had been separated from their towship, caught up to the barges, secured them, and waited for the towing steamer. It never came.

The tow line for the barges had been cut, indicating that the crew of *Iron Mountain* had sensed a problem: Perhaps the boilers were about to explode, perhaps the ship was about to sink. But there was, however, no trace of the ship anywhere along the river, nor was there any trace of its cargo, which would have dotted the river for miles had the steamer gone down.

The mystery of the *Iron Mountain* has never been solved.

Annemarie's Poltergeist

It was a paranormal version of the bull in the china shop when the events struck a lawyer's office in Rosenheim, Germany, in 1967. While the town is usually quiet and uneventful, something began running amok in the office by making phones go haywire, blowing fuses, and causing other electrical malfunctions. Soon the phenomenon accelerated: Lights began to flash on and off; light bulbs exploded for absolutely no reason; and the phones rang without apparent cause.

The staff didn't know what to do, so they began with the obvious: They called in experts from the local power company. The investigators who came checked every conceivable fuse, wire, and power source, but failed to find any natural cause for the problem. They even cut off the building's power supply and hooked up an emergency unit to feed juice into the office. These procedures didn't faze the spook and the disturbances went on.

Finally, renowned German parapsychologist Hans Bender was called in. The country's chief ghost-hunter, he quickly diagnosed the problem as a poltergeist—a type of ghost likely to throw household items, move furniture, pelt houses with stones, and start fires. Unlike conventional ghosts, who infest a particular place, poltergeists usually focus on a person. And it didn't take long for Bender to find the individual human target: Annemarie Schnabel, a teenager who worked in the office. Sometimes the disturbances would occur as soon as she showed up.

"When this young girl walked through the gangways [halls],

the lamps behind her began to swing,'' reported Bender. ''If bulbs exploded, the fragments flew towards her. Soon,'' he added, ''paintings began to swing and to turn, drawers came out by themselves, documents were displaced. But when Annemarie was sent on leave, nothing happened. And when she left the offices for a new position, no more disturbances occurred, though similar, less obvious events happened for some time in the new office where she was working.''

Once Schnabel left, the lawyer's office seemed to be haunted by more conventional ghosts. When a news team arrived at the office, for instance, several witnesses saw a vapory materialization, resembling a human arm, appear by a floor vent. The materialization flew to a nearby wall, where it crashed into a painting, which reeled on its wire. Luckily, the shouts of the bystanders alerted the crew, and they successfully filmed the movements of the painting.

What was the cause of the Rosenheim poltergeist? According to Bender, it was Annemarie herself. She was an unhappy girl possessed by pent-up frustrations over her job and romantic life, he said. No doubt, he added, her repressed hostility seethed within her unconscious mind until it erupted in the form of the poltergeist.

A Hymn for the *Titanic*

One Sunday morning the Reverend Charles Morgan, minister of the Rosedale Methodist Church in Winnipeg, Manitoba, Canada, arrived early to prepare for the evening service. Before entering his study, he posted on the hymn board the choirmaster's choice of hymns, then went on to other preparations.

This done, he retired to his office and decided to nap until it was time for the service. Soon he fell asleep, and no sooner had he begun to doze than he had a vivid dream of darkness and the sounds of huge, crashing waves. Above the din a choir sang an old hymn Reverend Morgan hadn't thought of in years.

The dream was so disturbing that the minister awoke, the hymn still ringing in his ears. He checked his watch and saw that he had time to resume his nap, which he did—assuming, incorrectly, that his brief waking period had cleared his mind of the unsettling vision.

As soon as he fell back asleep, the dream returned: the crashing waters, the deep darkness, the old hymn. He woke up with a start, strangely upset. Finally he got up, walked out into the empty church, and posted a new hymn number on the board.

When the service began, the congregation sang the hymn that had haunted Morgan's dreams—an odd hymn to sing in a church thousands of miles from the ocean: "Hear, Father, while we pray to Thee, for those in peril on the sea." Hearing the words, Morgan felt tears fill his eyes.

Not long afterward the minister was to learn that at the time he and his flock were singing the hymn, a great tragedy was occurring on the ocean. It was April 14, 1912, and far out on the North Atlantic the *Titantic* was sinking.

The Fourth Death of Musyoka Mututa

Musyoka Mututa of Kitui, Kenya, was lowered into the ground in September 1985. His brother Timothy said the body had been left out for two days—just in case, even though "we had no expectation of another miracle. He told me the fourth time would be for good."

Although only a humble shepherd, Mututa was a legend in Kenya. He was known as the "man who cheated death."

His first "death" occurred when he was three years old. As he was being lowered into the ground, he cried out and was quickly brought back to the surface.

When he was nineteen, he disappeared. Six days later searchers found his apparently lifeless body in a field. A funeral was held and as his coffin was being lowered, mourners were startled to see the lid start to rise. Mututa had "come back to life."

He "died" again in May 1985 after a short illness. A surgeon pronounced him dead. His body lay in state for a day, at the end of which he rose and demanded a glass of water.

Mututa claimed that during each of his three "deaths" his soul left his body and ascended to heaven, where angels explained it was a "case of mistaken identity" and returned him to earth.

Apparently on the fourth try they got the right man.

Dowsing With a Peach Tree Stick

Officials at Gates Rubber Company in Jefferson, North Carolina, were frantic when they learned that leaks in the town's water system threatened to drain the plant's water supply. Desperately seeking new water sources, they hired professional well-drillers, who brought $350,000 worth of equipment to the search. They couldn't find water.

Then in September 1983, an eighty-year-old retired stonemason named Don Witherspoon came on the scene, a Y-shaped peach tree branch in hand. He said he had been dowsing for thirty-eight years and was sure he could find what everyone was looking for.

He walked up and down the company's grounds until his branch suddenly tugged and pointed to the ground. Some distance away the branch repeated this strange performance.

The company found water at both sites—so much, in fact, that soon it was drawing up to seventy gallons a minute, nearly eliminating the plant's need to draw on the town's water supply.

"It may be 'witching' but it apparently works," plant manager Richard Thurston said. "All I know is we've got water and we're thankful."

Witherspoon said he could not explain his ability. He called it a "gift. To tell you the truth," he said, "I didn't believe in the water fork myself until I tried it."

A Temporal Lobe Apparition

Brain dysfunctions can cause people to report all sorts of strange experiences. Small seizures in the brain's temporal lobes, for instance, can cause a person to smell strange odors, hear bizarre sounds, be overwhelmed by mystical feelings, and even see phantoms.

A fascinating temporal lobe apparition was reported by Scottish psychiatrist James McHarg in 1976. He reported that a patient suffering from temporal lobe epilepsy was visiting a friend in 1969 when she experienced a sudden attack. First she smelled a foul milky odor, then her surroundings seemed to become "unreal," and finally she saw a phantom. The figure appeared to be a woman with soft brown hair standing by a cooker on the far side of the kitchen. The figure lingered only temporarily and faded from view when the seizure subsided.

The patient reported what she had seen to her hostess, who was fascinated by the story. Though the friend's kitchen currently lacked a cooker, there once *had* been one placed in the kitchen exactly where the patient reported seeing it. By researching the history of the house, moreover, the hostess discovered that the figure probably represented one of two sisters who had previously lived there. When the patient was shown a photograph of the sisters, she immediately recognized the lady she had seen.

So did this patient see a genuine ghost? Not likely, according to Dr. McHarg, since the woman in the vision was still alive. Nonetheless, he concluded, the seizure probably rendered his patient open to extrasensory influences, which came into play and influenced what she saw.

"Come Find Me"

Mary L. Cousett, twenty-seven, of Peoria, Illinois, vanished one day in April 1983. The police soon concluded that she had been murdered and they arrested her boyfriend, Stanley Holliday, Jr. But because her body was nowhere to be found, they feared they would be unable to mount a successful prosecution.

Finally, all other means having failed, Madison County authorities took their problem to Greta Alexander of Delavan, Illinois. Alexander, a psychic, provided a detailed description of where the body lay. It would be found, she said, near an embankment, a river, and a bridge. A church and salt would have something to do with the discovery. The body would have leaves around it. Part of a leg would be missing. The head would be recovered some distance away.

A man "with a bad hand" would find the body. The initial "S" would be involved. The body would be found near a main road.

On November 12 auxilary policeman Steve Trew, who had an injured hand, uncovered Cousett's remains near an embankment close to a bridge over the Mackinaw River, half a mile from a church camp and across the river from a highway salt-storage area. The body lay in a shallow grave covered by leaves. The left foot was missing and the skull, apparently removed by animals, lay five or ten feet from the rest of the body.

Detective William Fitzgerald of Alton told reporters that twenty-two of Alexander's psychic impressions had hit the mark.

"This young woman was really wanting to be found," Alexander said. "The spirit never dies; it lives on. She was saying, 'Here I am. Come find me.' "

Two Snowbanks

Warren Felty and William Miller of Harrisburg, Pennsylvania, got together on Veterans Day 1986 to celebrate an unlikely series of events that had taken place more than four decades before.

One night in February 1940 Felty was driving home to Middletown, Pennsylvania, when he saw the taillights of the car in front of him begin to sway. The car was skidding into an embankment near Camp Hill.

Felty pulled over and ran to the scene of the accident. When he got to the car, he saw that the driver had been thrown through the windshield into a four-foot snowbank and was now unconscious and covered with blood. Felty lifted him up, carried him back to his own car, and drove him to the Harrisburg Hospital.

Four days later the accident victim, William Miller, recovered consciousness. Later he learned the name of the man who saved him. After he left the hospital, his path crossed Felty's a few times but the two men did not really become acquainted.

They could not know, when America entered World War II, that each had signed on with the Army Air Force and become a B-17 pilot. They did not know, either, that the other had been shot down over Germany and herded with four thousand other prisoners toward Nuremberg, just ahead of the advancing Russian army.

The prisoners were weak from hunger and ill-clad for marching in the bitter winter of 1944, the coldest Germany had experienced in eighty years. Many didn't make it, falling to the ground and freezing to death in the snow.

As Warren Felty was marching along, he saw a body in the snowbank along the road. Hoping to revive the fallen fellow marcher, he kicked the man and, as Felty would recall years later, "there he was, Bill Miller. Unbelievable."

Miller, who was only barely conscious, had to be dragged and tugged all the way to the march's destination. Felty, Miller, and the other prisoners eventually ended up at a detention camp at Moosburg, from which Patton's Third Army freed them on April 29, 1945.

The two men still remember how on two occasions, in places five years and four thousand miles apart, one carried the other to safety by lifting him out of a snowbank.

Blue Man on Studham Common

At 1:45 in the afternoon of a rainy day, January 28, 1967, on Studham Common in England's Chiltern Hills, seven boys were walking to school through a shallow valley called the Dell. One of them, ten-year-old Alex Butler, happened to be looking south over the Dell when he saw what he later described as a "little blue man with a tall hat and a beard."

He quickly pointed it out to a friend who was walking next to him, and the two decided to get a better look at the curious looking figure. They ran toward it but when they were about twenty yards from it, it "disappeared in a puff of smoke."

The boys alerted their companions, who began looking for the little man, hoping he would reappear. Soon he was back, this time on the opposite side of the bush from where he had been when first observed. As the boys approached him, he vanished again, then reappeared at the bottom of the Dell. About this time the boys heard "voices" speaking in a "foreign-sounding babble" in nearby bushes and for the first time they felt slightly afraid.

When they got to school that rainy afternoon of January 28, 1967, their teacher, Miss Newcomb, could tell they were excited about *something*. At first they wouldn't give her the reason. All they would say was, "You'll never believe us." Finally she separated all seven and got each to write his own independent account of the strange event. The accounts were remarkably similar, enough so that Miss Newcomb was persuaded that something decidedly out of the ordinary had taken place that afternoon.

The accounts were eventually published in a booklet called *The Little Blue Man on Studham Common.*

In due course the report came to the attention of British investigators Bryan Winder and Charles Bowen, who learned that in recent months a number of local people had reported seeing UFOs. Two landings had been reported at the spot where the little blue man was seen. The connection with UFOs, however, remained conjectural, since the boys had claimed no sighting of one.

The investigators interviewed the boys in the presence of their teacher. As Winder wrote, "They estimate the little man as three feet tall, with an additional two feet accounted for by a hat or helmet best described as a tall brimless bowler. They could discern a line that was either a fringe of hair or the lower edge of the hat, two round eyes, a small seemingly flat triangle in place of a nose, and a one-piece vestment extending down to a broad black belt carrying a black box at the front about six inches square."

The Teleported Coin

Raymond Bayless has confronted the paranormal many times during his career as a psychic investigator. His strangest encounter, however, involves a phenomenon known as teleportation in which matter travels mysteriously from one location to the next.

The incident took place in 1957, when Bayless was walking down Hollywood Boulevard with psychic Attila von Szalay. The two men entered a leather-goods store and Bayless, an enthusiastic coin collector, saw a curious British coin on the proprietor's desk. One side depicted one of England's royal princesses, and the reverse side was marred by a long scratch. Intrigued, Bayless asked to buy the coin, but his offer was refused.

As the two men walked from the store, Bayless glanced at the coin one last time and continued on his way. "We had walked perhaps one hundred feet down the block," he said, "when I suddenly felt something strike my elbow and then my pants leg. I looked down in surprise and found on the sidewalk by my feet the identical penny. To make sure it was indeed the same coin, I looked on the reverse side, and there was the scratch I had noticed on its surface in the leather store.

"Mr. von Szalay was on my other side and was surprised when I picked up the penny and showed it to him, explaining that the last time I had seen it, it was lying on the storekeeper's desk. Without going into any more details and lengthy explanations, I will rest content in stating that there was no way that the coin could have reach me normally, and its strange transportation provided a remarkable mystery."

It probably didn't seem too mysterious to the shop owner, who no doubt figured his customer had pocketed the coin.

Mr. Wilson's 1897 Airship

The deepest mystery of American aviation is a mostly forgotten but still unexplained episode that began in November 1896 and ended in May of the following year.

From California to Maine thousands of Americans reported seeing large, piloted "airships" unlike anything that could have flown in those years, several years before the Wright Brothers invented heavier-than-air flight and forever changed history. The "airships" sparked wonder and speculation about who their inventor or inventors were, but to this day nobody knows. All we have are some tantalizing clues, none more intriguing than those concerning a very strange man named Mr. Wilson.

On April 19, 1897, Mr. Wilson made his presence known. A young man from Lake Charles, Louisiana, was driving a team of horses when he saw an enormous airship pass overhead, frightening the animals so badly that they bolted and threw the driver to the ground. At that point the airship stopped and hovered nearby—the ability to hover was just one of the unlikely capabilities of these mysterious craft—while a rope ladder dropped down. Two of the airship occupants climbed down and helped the witness to his feet. "It was decidedly gratifying to find that they were plain, everyday Americans like myself," the young man would report. The aeronauts apologized for the trouble they had caused. To make up for it, they invited him aboard the ship, introducing themselves as Scott Warren and "Mr. Wilson." Wilson said he was the ship's owner. Aboard the craft Wilson and Warren explained the vehicle's propulsion system, but the account was so technical that the young man did not understand what they were talking about.

A day later, near Uvalde, Texas, an airship landed and was discovered by Sheriff H. W. Bayler, who conversed with members of the crew. One identified himself as Wilson and said he was a native of Goshen, New York. Wilson then asked about Captain C. C. Akers, a local man.

Later, when asked about Wilson, Akers told a reporter, "I can say that while living in Fort Worth in seventy-six and seventy-seven I was well acquainted with a man by the name of Wilson from New York State and was on very friendly terms with him. He was of a mechanical turn of mind and was then working on aerial navigation and something that would astonish the world. He was a finely educated man, then twenty-four years of age, and seemed to have money with which to pursue his inventions, devoting his whole time to them. From conversations we had while in Fort Worth, I think that Mr. Wilson, having succeeded in constructing a practical airship, would probably hunt me up to show me that he was not so wild in his claims as I then supposed."

The airship next appeared a day or two later, when it came down for repairs at Kountze, Texas. Witnesses talked with the pilots, who said their names were "Wilson and Jackson." On the twenty-fifth, between midnight and 1:00 A.M., the *San Antonio Daily Express* reported the next day, "The sky was heavily clouded and not a star was visible. This brought out all the stronger the keen white light of the airship headlights together with the shimmer that the strong illumination cast about it. It prevented, however, anything like a view of the structure itself, but as the strange object wheeled about and came nearer, a dozen or more dim lights, among them a cluster of green lights on the side of the ship toward the city, and another immense cluster of red lights at the stern, plainly indicated its artificial nature."

The paper goes on to say, without explaining how it knows this, that the "inventors were Hiram Wilson, a native of New York and son of Willard B. Wilson, assistant master mechanic of the New York Central Railroad, and electrical engineer C. J. Walsh of San Francisco. The men had labored on their project several years, and when their plans had matured they had the parts of the ship constructed to order in different sections of the country, whence they were shipped to the rendezvous at San Francisco and put together on the island."

The Daily Express claimed that after being tested in California, the ship flew to Utah and was hidden "in some out-of-the-way section of the West" while defects were corrected. Then it resumed its eastward flight across the United States.

And then no more was heard of Wilson and his remarkable machine.

Who was he? Inquiries in recent years have come up with a blank. And a study of airship reports from 1897 gives us reason to suspect Mr. Wilson was even more mysterious than first appearances suggest. According to writer Daniel Cohen, author of *The Great Airship Mystery*, "There is a great deal about this Wilson episode that is confusing and contradictory. Any attempt to trace the path of 'Wilson's airship' across south Texas during the last week or two of April 1897 is hopeless. Airships seemed to pop up all over the place. There would have to be at least two or perhaps three different airships all pursuing highly erratic paths in order to account for all of the sightings and encounters. Aside from the name *Wilson*, which appears in at least five separate accounts, the names of the other crewmen vary. So does the size of the crew, from two to eight. And though many stories quote the inventor as saying that he soon will make his airship public, he never did."

Another researcher, Jerome Clark, noticed something even odder: "We have one simple 'impossible' fact, which by itself is sufficient to raise some profound questions about Wilson's purported role," Clark said. "Namely, Captain Akers says that twenty years prior to Wilson's appearance at Uvalde, he was twenty-four years old. At Lake Charles in 1897, he is described as 'apparently a young man.' Even today, with our longer life spans, a forty-five-year-old man is never called young except in the most relative sense; eighty years ago he would have been well into middle age."

Some researchers have speculated that the episode was not what it seemed. The airships and their mostly human-looking occupants were not American inventors who inexplicably never came forward to claim the rewards their creations would have brought them, but instead the products of an enigmatic alien intelligence, that sought to disguise itself by donning a garb that American culture of that period could accept.

That is a fantastic explanation and there is no way for us, nearly a century later, to know whether it is true or not. We can only be certain that the mysterious Mr. Wilson—and the strange airships associated with his appearance—will remain an enigma.

Teleported Through the Fourth Dimension

The strange story began routinely enough on June 3, 1968.

Dr. and Mrs. Gerardo Vidal of Maipú, Argentina, had gone to Chascomus to attend a family reunion. Another couple from Maipú, also relatives of the family, went as well.

The neighbors traveled in separate cars and later that evening, both couples set out toward home. When the Vidals did not arrive, however, their neighbors got back into their car and retraced the route, fearing an accident had occurred. They drove eighty miles back to Chascomus but saw no sign of the Vidals or their car. Back in Maipú they began calling hospitals and still no information emerged.

Forty-eight hours later Señor Rapallini, at whose home the reunion had been held, got a long-distance call from Mexico City. The caller was Dr. Vidal, who said he and his wife were well and would be flying back to Buenos Aires. He asked his relative to pick them up at the airport.

Friends and relatives were waiting when the couple got off the plane, wearing the same clothes they had on when they left the party. Mrs. Vidal, who appeared greatly shaken, was immediately taken to a private hospital, suffering from what a press account called a "violent nervous crisis."

Dr. Vidal told an incredible story about what had happened to him and his wife in the previous two days. He said that on their drive home they had entered a bank of fog. The fog was so intense that everything went black. And then, suddenly, it was daylight.

They were on an unfamiliar road. And when the doctor got out of his car, he discovered that all the paint had been scorched off the automobile's surface.

When he flagged down a motorist to ask where they were, the man told him they were outside Mexico City. Later, when the couple went to the Argentine consulate, they learned two days had passed since they had entered the fog.

The incident caused a sensation in Argentina.

"In spite of the halo of fantasy that the story of the Vidals seems to wear," the publication *La Razón* remarked, "there are certain details that do not cease to preoccupy even the most unbelieving: The entrance of Vidal's wife into a Buenos Aires clinic; the proved arrival of the couple on an airplane that arrived nonstop from Mexico; the disappearance of the car; the intervention of the consulate; the serious attitude of the police in Maipú in regard to the event; and the telephone call from Mexico to the Rapallini family." All this makes the account one people must strive to understand.

Death of an Alien

One of the most peculiar—and tragic—close encounters ever reported occurred in May 1913, on a Farmersville, Texas, farm.

Three brothers, Silbie, Sid, and Clyde Latham, were chopping cotton when they heard their two dogs, Bob and Fox, barking, Silbie would recall, "just like they was in terrible distress." When the "deathly howl" continued, Clyde, the oldest, said,

"Let's go up and see what them dogs treed. Must be somethin' pretty bad."

The dogs were about fifty to seventy-five feet away on the other side of a picket fence. Clyde, the first to get there, would be the first to see what had upset the dogs. "It's a little man!" he shouted.

According to Silbie Latham, who related the story to Larry Sessions of the Fort Worth Museum of Science and History, "He looked like he was resting on something. He was looking toward the north. He was no more than eighteen inches high and kind of dark green. He didn't have on any clothes. Everything looked like a rubber suit including the hat."

Right after the brothers arrived, Silbie said, the dogs jumped the entity and tore him to bits, leaving red blood and human-looking internal organs on the grass.

"We were all just country as hell and didn't know what to do about it," Silbie Latham would say to explain why he and his brothers had done nothing to stop the slaughter. "I guess we were just too dumb."

The boys went back to their hoeing, occasionally returning to the spot to view the remains. The dogs huddled by them, as if afraid. The next day when the three returned to the site, there were no traces of any kind. All evidence of the little man was gone.

"My grandfather has a most solid reputation for truth and honesty but has never told this story outside the family for fear of ridicule," Lawrence Jones, Silbie Latham's grandson, recently told the Center for UFO Studies in Chicago. "He has agreed to tell this only after much prompting and encouragement from me, his history-oriented grandson. He would take a polygraph or be hypnotized or whatever you need. There is no question in my mind that he is telling the truth."

Gilbert Murray's Games

Gilbert Murray, an esteemed professor of Greek at Oxford University, was also a psychic and a keen student of the paranormal. Most of his experiments weren't conducted in a laboratory, but in a gamelike setting at his home. In a typical demonstration, one of his two daughters, Agnes Murray and Mrs. Arnold Toynbee, would choose a subject and sometimes communicate it to the other guests after their father had left the room. He would then return, concentrate for a moment, and reveal his impressions. Dozens of these tests were completed with outstanding success.

For example, in one session Mrs. Toynbee thought of a scene from a play by Gustav Strindberg: A gentleman sitting by a tower has fainted and his wife wishes he were dead.

When Professor Murray came back into the room, he immediately sensed the literary theme of the target. "This is a book and a book I haven't read," he began. "No, not Russian, not Italian. It's somebody lying in a faint. It's very horrible. I think somebody is fainting and his wife or some woman is hoping he is dead. It can't be Maeterlinck—I think I have read them all. Oh, it's Strindberg!"

During the course of another experiment, Mrs. Toynbee thought of two mutual friends drinking beer in a Berlin cafe. Professor Murray not only immediately felt that the target concerned a public house, but eventually named both people chosen by his daughter.

These informal but impressive experiments were conducted

in the Murray household for many years, from 1910 through 1946. Some skeptics believe that Professor Murray probably had an acute sense of hearing and simply overheard his daughters talking about the targets to the other guests. But this theory can't explain Professor Murray's success when the targets were mentally created and never explained to the other spectators at all.

Exorcising the Loch Ness Demon

The late Reverend Dr. Donald Omand, an Anglican priest and exorcist, had no doubt that the fabled monster of Loch Ness, known affectionately to some as "Nessie," existed. But he had serious reservations about the notion that it was some kind of prehistoric animal or, for that matter, any living creature at all.

Writer F. W. (Ted) Holiday, who had spent years on the shores of Loch Ness, tended to agree. In a 1973 book, *The Dragon and the Disc*, he rejected biological theories about the creature and urged investigators to consider the notion of visitors from the paranormal realm.

So when Holiday heard of Dr. Omand's belief, he wrote a letter, and in due course the two men met. One thing they talked about was the strange tale of Swedish writer Jan-Ove Sundberg, who had been at Ness on August 16, 1971. That evening Sundberg had tried to take a shortcut through the woods near the lake and somehow got lost. As he wandered through the trees, he came upon an "extremely strange machine": a 35-foot-long gray-black cigar resting on the ground about 200 or 250 feet away from where he stood.

Sundberg claimed to have seen three figures come out of the bushes each wearing a diving suit and a helmet over his head. At first Sundberg thought they were technical workers from a nearby power plant. After a while the figures entered the craft through a hatch in the top. The craft then rose forty or fifty feet into the air, then shot off.

When Sundberg returned to Sweden, he was, he said, trailed by mysterious figures in dark suits—the fabled "men in black" who are reported to intimidate some UFO witnesses—and eventually suffered a nervous collapse.

Holiday would normally have dismissed the story as "psychotic bunk" (his words), if he had not heard of other UFO sightings at the loch that same week in August 1971. But there was one problem: At the site of the incident, investigators found a forest so dense that "nowhere could a UFO bigger than a matchbox land." Sundberg's photograph had shown only trees.

Sundberg believed he had had a UFO encounter. But there also seemed no question that it had not happened as he thought it did. Had he been swept up in some kind of supernatural event?

Acting on that theory, Omand, accompanied by Holiday, went to Loch Ness to exorcise its demon on June 2, 1973. Omand performed the rite of exorcism at five locations around the lake.

"Grant that by the power entrusted to Thy unworthy servant," he prayed at each site, "this highland loch and the land adjoining it may be delivered from all evil spirits; all vain imaginations; projections and phantasms; and all deceits of the Evil One. O Lord, subject them to Thy servant's commands that, at his bidding, they will harm neither man nor beast, but depart to the place appointed them, there to remain forever."

"I am not formally religious," Holiday would write of the experience, "yet I felt a distinct tension creep into the atmosphere at this point. It was as if we had shifted some invisible levers, and were awaiting the result."

The following Monday, Omand reenacted the exorcism for a crew from the BBC. On Tuesday, Holiday set out to investigate the Sundberg UFO report. First, however, he called on Winifred Cary, a psychic who lived nearby. When he told her about Sundberg's reported encounter, she replied that she and her husband, a Royal Air Force commander, had seen UFOs in the area as well. She urged Holiday not to go to the site. "One reads of people being whisked away," she said. "It may be nonsense but I shouldn't go." Dr. Omand had told Holiday the same thing.

"At that precise moment," Holiday wrote in his book *The Goblin Universe*, "there was a tremendous rushing sound like a tornado outside the window, and the garden seemed to be filled with indefinable frantic movement. A series of violent thuds sounded as if from a heavy object striking either the wall or the sun-lounge door. Through the window behind Mrs. Cary I suddenly saw what looked like a pyramid-shaped column of blackish smoke about eight feet high revolving in a frenzy. Part of it was involved in a rosebush, which looked as if it were being ripped out of the ground. Mrs. Cary shrieked and turned her face to the window. The episode lasted ten or fifteen seconds, and then was instantly finished."

Cary also heard the sound. "I saw a beam of white light that shot across the room from the window on my left," she said. "I saw a white circle of light on Ted Holiday's forehead. I got a terrible fright."

Holiday decided not to go to the site of the Sundberg sighting. But early the next morning, as he stepped outside on a small errand, he was surprised to see an odd-looking figure standing thirty yards away. It was a man dressed entirely in black.

He recalls, "I felt a strange sensation of malevolence, cold and passionless. He was about six feet tall and appeared to be dressed in black leather or plastic. He wore a helmet and gloves and was masked, even to the nose, mouth and chin."

Holiday approached the figure and walked a few feet beyond him, then gazed at the lake for several seconds. He then turned his head in the direction of the mysterious man in black. At that moment he heard a "curious whispering or whistling sound." He turned to see nothing at all.

Holiday immediately dashed to the nearby road. "There was about half a mile of empty road visible to the right and about a hundred yards to the left," he wrote. "No living person could have gotten out of sight so quickly. Yet he had undoubtedly gone."

The next day Dr. Omand left, saying he would try to exorcise the long-lived phantom when he visited the loch again.

Holiday, meanwhile, returned to Loch Ness in 1974. A few days into his trip, he was felled by a nonfatal heart attack while on the lake shore. As a stretcher carried him up the side of the loch, it passed directly over the spot where the man in black had stood.

A second heart attack killed Ted Holiday in 1979.

Visions of Aberfan

One of the worst disasters in British history struck in Wales on October 21, 1966, when a huge stockpile of coal refuse collapsed and buried a school in the small mining town of Aberfan. More than 140 people, including 128 school children, were killed.

During the weeks that followed, it became increasingly clear that some of the children, as well as other people throughout England, had foreseen the tragedy. Thirty-five such cases, in fact, were collected by British psychiatrist J. C. Barker. One of his informants was the mother of a child killed in the slide. She told Barker that the day before the disaster, her daughter suddenly started talking about death, explaining that she wasn't afraid to die. Her mother was perplexed by the strange conversation, but didn't realize the significance of the child's subsequent remarks, which concerned an odd dream she'd just had.

"I dreamt I went to school," she told her mother, "and there was no school there. Something black had come down all over it."

Even the child failed to recognize that the dream was a warning, and skipped off to school the next day, only to be killed two hours later.

A middle-aged woman from Plymouth, England, had experienced precognitions of the tragedy, too.

"I actually 'saw' the disaster the night before it happened," she related, "and the next day I had already told my next-door neighbor about it before the news was broadcast. First, I 'saw' an old schoolhouse nestling in a valley, then a Welsh miner, then an avalanche of coal hurtling down a mountainside. At the bottom of this mountain of hurtling coal was a little boy with a long fringe looking absolutely terrified to death. Then for a while I 'saw' rescue operations taking place. I had an impression that the little boy was left behind and saved."

Of the many cases collected by Dr. Barker, the majority were symbolic dreams that tended to occur the week before the slide.

Falling Alligators

Accounts of living things falling from clear skies are as old as recorded history and have never been explained in any satisfactory way. Most reports describe falls of small animals—frogs, fish, and insects—but sometimes larger creatures come plummeting out of nowhere, too. Alligators, for instance.

On December 26, 1877, no less than *The New York Times* reported the following: "Dr. J. L. Smith of Silverton Township, South Carolina, while opening up a new turpentine farm, noticed something fall to the ground and commence to crawl toward the tent where he was sitting. On examining the object he found it to be an alligator. In the course of a few moments a second one made its appearance. This so excited the curiosity of the doctor that he looked around to see if he could discover any more, and found six others within a space of two hundred yards. The animals were all quite lively, and about twelve inches in length. The place whereon they fell is situated on high sandy ground about six miles north of the Savannah River."

A similar story emerged in 1957, courtesy of writer John Toland, who told the story of the U.S. Navy airship *Macon*. In 1934 the *Macon* had participated in maneuvers in the Caribbean and was sailing westward on its return trip. As it was entering the sky over California on the afternoon of May 17, the commander, Robert Davis, heard a loud splashing over his head from one of the ballast bags.

Concerned, he climbed into the rigging as the splashing grew louder and louder. He opened the ballast bag and looked in. Swimming around excitedly was a two-foot alligator.

No one had any idea where it came from. They had been in the air for several days and it seemed highly improbable that this big, noisy creature could have been with them all that time without making its presence known. Moreover, Davis, a restless fellow by nature, had been up and around the ship ever since their departure and he had seen nothing so out of the ordinary as an alligator.

The only possible explanation—though it made no sense at all—was that the reptile had fallen on the ballast bag from above.

Yet another tale comes from Mr. and Mrs. Tucker of Long Beach, California, who heard a loud thump in their backyard in 1960. Immediately following that, they heard a loud grunt. When the couple stepped outside, they were astonished to encounter a five-foot alligator. They could only conclude it had dropped from the sky.

The Man Who Shot a UFO Traveler

One of the strangest close encounters ever took place on a cold November night in 1961. The witnesses were four North Dakota men driving home from a hunting trip as freezing rain beat down on the windshield of their car. The heating system had nearly given out and the rain turned to ice on the windows. Three of the travelers were asleep when the only one who was awake, the driver, saw a blazing object descending out of the sky.

It came down half a mile away, on the right side of the highway. The driver, alarmed, nudged the sleeping man on the passenger side and he revived quickly enough to see the object, too. So did one of the sleepers in the backseat. All were certain they were witnessing a plane crash.

They sped to the scene, where they found a silo-shaped object sticking at about an eighty-five-degree angle from the ground and 150 yards away. Four figures stood around it. Trying to make all this out on a dark night and at some distance made for serious eyestrain, so the men in the car plugged a hand spotlight into the cigarette lighter and shined it on the craft and its occupants. At this point, as one of the hunters later told an investigator for the National Investigations Committee on Aerial Phenomena, "there was an explosion and everything went out."

The men were horrified. They thought the plane had blown up and began driving into the field. But as they approached the site, the craft was nowhere to be found.

Now they awoke the fourth man, a medic at a local Air Force

base, and told him that once they found the "accident" site they would need his help. The medic urged them to go back to where they had been when they first saw the object. That way, he said, they could retrace their steps and make another guess as to where the plane had gone down.

Soon after they returned to the highway, they saw the object and its occupants again. The medic turned on the spotlight and ran it up and down the silvery, silo-shaped vehicle. Then his light hit one of the figures, a human-shaped form about 5½ feet tall and dressed in white coveralls. Strangely, he was waving his arm in a get-out-of-here gesture. If there had been a plane crash, the witnesses wondered, why was this man signaling them to leave?

The hunters drove a short distance, arguing all the while about what they should do next. Someone thought the object was an Air Force test device that they weren't supposed to see. One argued that the figure was a farmer and the "plane" was a silo. Eventually they resumed their journey home. They drove two more miles when the object returned and gently landed less than 150 yards away. Suddenly two figures were visible in front of the ship.

One of the hunters got down to a prone position with a rifle and squeezed off a shot. The closer figure was hit in the shoulder. He spun around and fell to his knees. As his companion helped him up, he hollered, "Now what the hell did you do that for?"

The four men later tried to reconstruct what happened next, and realized their memories were hazy at best. Two of them would deny that a rifle had been taken out of the car at all. The man who remembered shooting the figure said his behavior seemed irrational and bizarre. The only clear memory they had was that of arriving home just as it was becoming daylight, their worried wives sitting in wait.

The next day the medic—the man who had fired the shot—was surprised to find some strange men waiting for him at work. Addressing him by name, they said they had "received a report" about his experience the night before. They asked if he had gotten out of the car during the first part of the experience, and they also wanted to know what he had been wearing. When he answered hunting gear and boots, they asked him to take them to his home to examine the clothes.

After examining the gear, they got up to leave. The one who had done most of the talking thanked him for his cooperation, then warned, "You'd better not say anything about this to anyone from now on." The men got into their car and drove off, leaving the medic stranded. He had to call a cab to get back to the base.

"They never asked anything about the shooting and all their questions were concerned entirely with the first part of the sighting," the medic remembered. "I think they probably knew more than they said, but I don't know."

He never saw them again and to this day he has no idea who they were and exactly what they wanted from him.

The Little People of Iceland

There is hardly a place in the world where people did not at one time believe in the existence of a hidden race of little people with supernatural powers. As it happens, belief in a hidden race of little people persists even in modern Europe, especially in Iceland, a nation with an excellent educational system and a high literacy rate.

"Those who tell me these stories," says Helgi Hallgrimsson, manager of the Museum of Natural History in Akureyri, "are honest people and many of them did not believe in such creatures until they saw them themselves."

The fairies are supposed to be protective of their territory and no end of trouble to those who try to invade it. In 1962, when the new harbor at Akureyri was being constructed, for instance, workers tried to blast some rocks with no success. No matter what they did, the equipment would not function at the critical moment. Workers were continually suffering injuries or falling suddenly ill.

Finally a young man named Olafur Baldursson stepped forward to declare that the fairies were unhappy because they lived at the site of the blasts. He offered his services as a mediator, saying that if the city authorities wanted, he would work things out with the little people. The magistrates agreed and in due course the fairies were satisfied. At least it was so assumed, because after Baldursson reported as much the work went ahead with no further problem.

This wasn't the last time the fairies apparently acted to protect their land. In 1984, when the Icelandic Road Department tried to build a new road near Akureyri, construction workers suffered strange illnesses and excavators broke down without apparent reason.

Not all Icelanders are prepared to believe in the hidden folk, of course. The Custodian of Antiquities, Thor Magnusson, dismisses the many sightings, saying, "Personally, I think that those who see fairies and little people should have their eyes examined."

But believers disagree. Helgi Hallgrimsson retorts, "There are many things in nature that science cannot yet explain."

Phantom Landscape

Is time travel possible? Incredible as it may seem, a number of seemingly sane, reputable individuals have reported traversing the years to visit centuries before.

One such case was investigated by Mary Rose Barrington of London's Society for Psychical Research. According to Barrington, the participants, who went by the names of Mr. and Mrs. George Benson, took a trip to the hills of Surrey one Sunday in July 1954. The day had begun oddly when the two woke up feeling inexplicably depressed. Neither told the other about this feeling, which seemed irrational in view of the pleasant diversion of the day.

Arriving in Surrey by bus, the couple decided to visit the Evelyn family church at Wotton. They had a long-standing interest in John Evelyn, a seventeenth-century diarist, and were curious to see which of his relatives were buried in the graveyard. The visit proved so interesting that the Bensons spent more time there than they had intended.

When they finally left the churchyard, they turned right and discovered an overgrown path with high bushes on either side. Climbing up the path, they soon came to a wide clearing with a wooden bench. An expanse of grass stretched from the left of the bench to trees about twenty-five yards away. To the right of the bench the land fell sharply down into a valley, from which they could hear the sounds of chopping wood and a dog's steady bark.

At that point Mr. Benson looked at his watch, saw it was noon, and unpacked the sandwiches the couple had brought along. Too depressed to eat, however, Mrs. Benson crumbled up the bread for the birds. Suddenly everything became silent, and no birds could be heard.

A feeling of sheer terror overcame Mrs. Benson, she reported, as she literally sensed three menacing figures in black clerical garb standing behind her. When she attempted to turn around, she couldn't.

Mr. Benson saw nothing, but he touched his wife. Her body was so icy that it could have been a corpse. Eventually Mrs. Benson felt better and the two agreed to move on.

They walked down the hill and a short time later crossed a railway line. Then, though they had planned to take a walk, they suddenly lay down and fell asleep. Everything after that was a blur, and the next thing they knew they were in Dorking getting on the train that would take them home to Battersea.

For the next two years Mrs. Benson lived in almost constant fear. She remembered vividly the terror that had gripped her when the three oddly garbed strangers appeared. Finally, feeling that only by confronting the experience head-on could she leave it behind, she went off by herself to retrace the path she and her husband had taken that fateful day.

But as soon as she got to the church, she realized something was wrong. First of all, there was no path to the hill—because there was no hill. In fact, the area was flat. There was no abundance of overgrown bushes and there were no woods for half a mile.

She talked with a local man who said he knew the area well and knew of nothing in any way comparable to what she was describing. He also said that there was no wooden bench along any local path of which he was aware.

On her return to Battersea Mrs. Benson told her husband what she had learned. He did not believe her, but when he came to the church the following Sunday, he quickly discovered that she was speaking the truth.

Some years later Mary Rose Barrington and John Stiles of the Society for Psychical Research went to the area hoping to find the landscape the Bensons had entered. They found nothing, to Mrs. Benson's disappointment, that could provide a conventional explanation, and they concluded that some kind of extraordinary psychic experience had taken place.

Barrington read through John Evelyn's diaries hoping to find some clues. She noticed that Evelyn's description of the landscape of his youth was very similar to the one the Bensons observed. In a later entry, dated March 16, 1696, Evelyn mentioned the execution of "three unhappy wretches, whereof one a priest," who were part of a Catholic plot to assassinate King William.

Barrington theorized that in some way the Bensons had entered a "deviant reality" and that their fascination with John Evelyn had caused them in some unknown fashion to enter his world—a world that had not existed for 250 years.

UFOs Over the White House

One criticism leveled at UFOs asks why, if they exist, haven't they landed on the White House lawn and made themselves known? Aside from the fact that their occupants might not have found a presidential administration to their liking, UFOs *have* appeared in close proximity to Pennsylvania Avenue on more than one instance.

Late on the night of July 26, 1952, for example, unidentified flying objects peppered radar screens in the nation's capital. At one point as many as twelve separate targets were picked up: four, spaced a mile and a half apart, proceeded in an orderly pace at a speed of a hundred miles per hour, while eight others moved randomly about at higher speeds. At least two military personnel and a commercial pilot bound for Washington National Airport reported visual contact with white and orange-white lights in the night sky.

On January 11, 1965, UFOs were again reported over the White House by both military and civilian personnel. Immediately prior to that, on December 29, 1964, three unknown targets had been tracked on radar at speeds established at almost five thousand miles per hour. The Air Force later discounted the incident as due to mechanical malfunction.

Eight days before, one Horace Burns said his car stalled on U.S. Highway 150 while in the presence of a large, cone-shaped UFO. Measuring 125 feet wide and 75 feet high, the UFO sat in an adjoining field for more than a minute and a half before leaving "at a square angle." Professor Ernest Gehman and two DuPont engineers subsequently examined the site for radiation and found levels much above normal.

In fact, five other sightings of UFOs over or near Washington were reported between October 1964 and January 1965 alone. On January 25, policemen in Marion, Virginia, saw a glowing, hovering object that departed in a shower of sparks. Twenty minutes later, nine people in Fredericksburg, 300 miles away, also reported a bright light trailing sparks.

Sea Serpent Sunk

May 1917 found the *Hilary*, a 6,000-ton, armed merchantman, traversing calm waters near Iceland, when the lookout spotted "something large on the surface." Fearing a sneak attack by a German submarine, Captain F. W. Dean alerted his gun crews and sailed straight for the target.

But Dean and crew encountered no enemy U-boat. What they found instead was a marine mystery. From a distance of thirty yards, the captain stared in wonder as a "head . . . about the shape but somewhat larger than that of a cow" broke surface. No visible protrusions, such as horns or ears, were evident. The head itself was described as "black, except for the front of the face, which could clearly be seen to have a strip of whitish flesh very like a cow has between its nostrils." A four-foot high "thin and flabby" dorsal fin was also visible. The entire creature was estimated to be some sixty feet long, twenty feet of which consisted of a sinewy neck.

Then in one of the more unfortunate bungles of maritime and zoological history, Dean decided his gun crews could use practice. Withdrawing to a distance of 1,200 yards he ordered them to open fire. A direct hit struck the creature. Its death throes roiling the water, the living submarine sank from view.

Two days later, on May 25, 1917, the *Hilary* itself sailed into the sights of a real U-boat. Still, she fared better than the sea serpent she had sunk: Most of her crew survived to fight again.

Vanishing Regiment

War not only tries the soul, it tries the senses as well. Who knows what can happen in the crash of conflict. Perhaps one world can open and swallow another, as seems to have happened with an entire British regiment during the Turkish campaign of World War I.

The date was August 28, 1915. The Turks occupied high ground near Sulva Bay, and the fighting between them and attacking British, New Zealand, and Australian troops was fierce, with many casualties suffered on both sides.

Weather that morning was clear and sunny, marred only by six to eight bread-loaf-shaped clouds surrounding a contested mound of earth known as Hill 60, from which the Turkish forces unleashed a withering fire. Curiously, despite a five-mile-an-hour breeze from the south, the strange clouds held their ground.

The First Fourth Norfolk regiment drew the dirty job of mounting a charge on the Turkish position. They moved forward and straight into one of the clouds straddling a dry creek, Kaiajak Dere. It took almost an hour for the file of one to four thousand men to disappear into the cloud, according to New Zealand sappers dug in 2,500 yards away.

Then the incredible happened. The low-lying cloud, described as eight hundred feet long and two hundred feet wide, rose slowly in the sky and disappeared in the direction of Bulgaria.

With the cloud went the men of the British First Fourth regiment. No earthly crosses mark their graves today. If they were annihilated in battle, then their obliteration was more abrupt and complete than any in military history. But if they were lifted in the clouds and carried away, as the New Zealand sappers said, they could well be anywhere, perhaps even in a world without war.

Doorway to the Beyond

Suspected, but never seen, black holes may be the gateway to universes beyond our own. Such sinkholes in the fabric of space were first postulated by the German astronomer Karl Schwarzschild in 1916. Schwarzschild suggested the existence of a mass so dense that nothing, not even light, would be able to escape its gravity.

Everything within the black hole's immediate vicinity is inexorably sucked toward its center, what physicists call a "singularity," the point of infinite density where the laws of space and time as we know them break down and fall apart. The point of no return for energy and objects being drawn toward the singularity is known as the "event horizon."

Although a black hole has never been directly detected, astronomers think they are formed when the matter in immense stars suddenly collapses on itself. Black holes may lie at the center of our own galaxy, at the heart of quasars (highly active, quasi-stellar energy sources) and even in some binary star systems.

Theoreticians like Cambridge mathematician Roger Penrose have formulated a potentially unique use for black holes. An astronaut, for example, might be able to plunge below the event horizon of a particularly massive, rotating black hole and emerge in another universe altogether, or reemerge in our own universe, vast distances away, at the same instant. A third alternative is that our adventurous astronaut could enter into a negative universe where nature is upside down. Gravity, for instance, might appear more like a repelling than an attracting force.

To accomplish such a feat requires the existence of the black hole's opposite, the "white hole," which spews matter and energy *out* of its singularity and beyond the event horizon.

Presently the search for both supermassive objects goes on, especially for possible black holes among the star clusters. One of the leading candidates in the search is the Star Cygnus X-1 in the constellation Cygnus. The search is of considerable import, since if our earth or solar system came too close to a large enough black hole, it could theoretically be sucked into it, totally modifying, compressing, or destroying all matter with which we are familiar and perhaps spewing it out again in a different form.

It seems incredible that the astronomy of our time, after only several hundred years of practice and research, has been able to identify the secrets—and dangers—present in the distant stars. But has our cosmic knowledge been so recent? Clay tablets kept by the Sumerians 5,000 years ago refer to a danger star, called by them the "demon bird of Nergal." Nergal was the powerful and sinister lord of the underworld. And the dangerous "demon bird," when translated and located on their star-charts, turns out to be *our* Cygnus X-1.

Pierced Brain

On September 11, 1874, Phineas P. Gage, twenty-five, was using an iron tamping rod three feet seven inches long to pack explosives in holes prior to their detonation. For some reason, one of the loads exploded prematurely, blasting the rod back in Gage's face. The thirteen-pound tamping tool, one and a quarter inches in diameter, penetrated his left cheek just above the jaw line. The force of the explosion drove the rod completely through and out his brain, disloding a large frontal chunk of his skull in the process.

A few hours after the accident Gage was said to have asked about his work! For the next several days he spat out bits of bone and brain through his mouth. Then he fell into a delirium and eventually lost sight in his left eye. After that, Gage recovered physically, though acquaintances said he had deteriorated into an untrustworthy brute.

Gage's miraculous survival was written up at length in both the *American Journal of Medical Science* and the *British Medical Journal* of the day. His story, sad as its outcome was, causes us to ponder how much of our brain is really necessary for survival? A 1982 Swedish TV documentary on the subject showed several patients functioning normally with just a fraction of their gray matter. One subject, a young man named Roger, had only 5 percent of his brain intact yet managed to earn a degree in mathematics.

Curse of the Hope Diamond

According to legend, the fabulous jewel now known as the Hope Diamond once decorated the forehead of an Indian idol, from whence it was stolen by a Hindu priest. The poor priest, so the story goes, was captured and tortured for his troubles.

The remarkable gem, said to carry a deadly curse, first surfaced in Europe in 1642, in the possession of French trader and smuggler Jean Baptiste Tefernier. He reaped a sizable profit from its sale, but allowed his wastrel son to squander much of the money. Traveling to India to recoup his fortune, Tefernier was attacked by a pack of rabid dogs and torn to pieces.

The gem passed next to France's fabled King Louis XIV, who reduced its staggering size from 112.5 carats to 67.5. This reduction, however, did not affect the curse. After Nicholas Fouquet, a government official, borrowed the diamond for a state ball, he was convicted of embezzlement and sentenced to life in prison, where he died. Princess de Lambelle, who wore the diamond regularly, was beaten to death by a Parisian mob. The King himself died broke and scorned, his empire in ruins. Louis XVI and Queen Marie Antoinette died beneath the blade of the guillotine.

In 1830, the now historic treasure was purchased by London banker Henry Thomas Hope for $150,000. It proved a mixed blessing. Family fortunes declined rapidly, and one grandson died penniless before another heir finally sold the tainted stone. Over the next sixteen years, the Hope Diamond went from owner to owner, including Frenchman Jacques Colet, who committed suicide, and Russian Prince Ivan Kanitovitsky, a murder victim. In 1908, Turkish Sultan Abdul Hamid paid $400,000 for the Hope and promptly bestowed it on his favorite concubine, Subaya. But within a year Hamid had stabbed Subaya to death and had been dethroned himself. Simon Montharides had it next, until his carriage overturned, killing him, along with his wife and infant daughter.

Diamond and accompanying curse next made their way to American financial tycoon Ned McLean, who payed the bargain price of $154,000. Vincent, his son, soon succumbed in a car crash, and a daughter died from a drug overdose. McLean's wife became addicted to morphine, and McLean himself died in an insane asylum. Mrs. McLean passed away in 1947, leaving the hazardous heritage to six grandchildren, including then five-year-old Miss Evalyn.

Two years later, the McLean family sold the diamond to Harry Winston, a dealer in precious stones. Winston, in turn, deeded it to the Smithsonian Institution, where it now remains. Perhaps the curse can't work its misery on institutions the way it did on individuals. Or perhaps the terrible disenchantment finally died with Evalyn McLean, one of the six McLean grandchildren, found dead of unapparent cause in her Dallas apartment on December 13, 1967, at the age of twenty-five.

Sailing to Oblivion

She was a fine brig she was, firm of timber and square of sail, when first christened the *Amazon* at Spencer Island, Nova Scotia, in 1861. But there were forebodings even then when her first captain died within forty-eight hours of taking command.

A series of smaller disasters ensued. On her maiden voyage the *Amazon* struck a fishing weir, gashing her hull. A fire broke out during repairs, resulting in the firing of her second captain. Under her third master she undertook her third Atlantic crossing—and collided with another ship in the straits of Dover.

Then in 1867, the *Amazon* was wrecked in Glace Bay, Newfoundland, where she was left for the salvagers. A company of Americans eventually raised her, restored her, and sailed her south. There they registered the ship under the U.S. flag and rechristened her the *Marie Celeste*.

Captain Benjamin S. Briggs bought the *Celeste* in 1872. On November 7 of that year he set sail from New York for the Mediterranean with his wife, daughter, a crew of seven, and seventeen hundred barrels of commercial alcohol valued at $38,000.

On December 4, a British brigantine found the *Celeste* 600 miles west of Portugal. Crewmen boarded her, but found no one alive above or below decks. The cargo was in good order with one exception—a single cask of alcohol had been opened. The crew's sea chests, still packed with their belongings, including pipes and tobacco pouches, remained behind. The last entry in the log, dated November 24, gave no hint of impending disaster. The only clue was a section of railing, which lay on the deck where the lifeboat had been.

The fate of Captain Briggs, his family and crew, remains one of the more endurable of the open sea's many mysteries. What seems clear is that everyone abandoned ship in the single lifeboat in great hurry. Perhaps they feared an immediate explosion. The alcohol, loaded under cold conditions, *could* have begun giving off fumes in the heat of the tropics. Briggs, unfamiliar with his cargo, *could* have sounded the alarm to abandon ship. A wind *may* have come up and blown the *Celeste* away.

The one thing for certain is that we will never know.

Fire From Above

Furnacelike blasts of heat from the heavens have occurred on several occasions. Ask anyone near Lake Whitney, Texas, on the otherwise uneventful night of June 15, 1960.

At first, witnesses report, the sky overhead was clear, stars sparkled and temperatures hovered around seventy-five degrees Fahrenheit. Then lightning flickered on the horizon and a light breeze blew off the lake. Without warning a roaring wind tore away the roof of the Mooney Village Store, sprawling bread and canned goods in the aisles.

And with the winds came a lung-searing heat. The thermometer outside the Charley Riddle Bait and Tackle Shop shot from a midnight reading of near 70 degrees to 100 in a matter of minutes, then peaked at 140 degrees Fahrenheit.

Car radiators boiled over, sprinkler systems went off, and frightened mothers in the small town of Kopperl literally swathed their babies in wet sheets. When rancher Pete Burns turned in earlier that night, his newly plowed cotton crop had been in the best of health. The morning found it charred black. Cornfields in the same area were wilted and scorched.

Even so, the strangest storm ever to hit Texas probably would have gone unrecorded if veteran TV cameraman Floyd Bright had not photographed evidence of the destruction the following day. Weather forecaster Harold Taft of Channel Five in Forth Worth theorized that the downdraft from a roaming thunderstorm might have been responsible. "Descending air heats at the rate of five point five degrees Fahrenheit for every one thousand feet of fall," Taft said. If the downdraft began at the top of a 20,000-foot tall thunderhead, at 25 degrees temperature, it would have heated an additional 110 degrees by the time it reached ground level.

But hot air also tends to rise. Taft admitted "the downward force must have been fierce," which would help explain the eighty to one-hundred-mile-an-hour winds recorded that night.

One is still left in awe at the force and fury of the heavens, wondering if what incinerated a cotton field in central Texas might not have caused, on other nights, some of the great unexplained fires that occasionally appear around the world.

Bligh Bond's Amazing Archaeology

The site of Glastonbury in Somerset, England, figures prominently in ancient traditions and lore. Arthurians hold that King Arthur was buried beneath the Glastonbury Abbey. Christian legend says that Saint Joseph of Arimathea brought the Holy Grail to Glastonbury and planted a thorn tree that can still be seen on the grounds. Moreover, Glastonbury is said to be the site where those in the field of "psychic archaeology" made perhaps their strongest mark.

In 1907, Glastonbury Abbey, a pile of neglected and overgrown ruins, was bought by the state and placed in the care of a Diocesan Trust anxious to excavate the site. The trust handed the work over to the Somerset Archaeological Society, which selected as its director of excavations a promising ecclesiastical architect from Bristol named Frederick Bligh Bond.

Unbeknown to the clerics and other officials involved, Bond was a member of the Society for Psychical Research, as was his friend, Captain John Bartlett. The two agreed to employ Bartlett's automatic writing ability, in which spirits supposedly communicated through the captain's pen, to excavate Glastonbury.

At 4:30 P.M., on November 7, 1907, the experiment began. "Can you tell us anything about Glastonbury?" Bond asked. Bartlett responded by tracing out plan drawings of the abbey, including measurements, followed by messages in a mixture of bad Latin and what appeared to be early English, seemingly dictated by long departed monks. Much of what he learned went against Bond's educated knowledge, but he pressed ahead.

The discoveries began pouring in, first an unsuspected chapel at the eastern end of the abbey, next an unknown doorway, then a polygonal apse and a crypt. Bond's genius was celebrated in both archaeological and ecclesiastical circles—until 1918, when he revealed in *The Gate of Remembrance* how monkish spirits had led him to his finds. The horrified authorities began a movement to strip Bond of his position, and they succeeded. They then removed or altered many of the archaeological inscriptions he had erected at the site, and even forbade the sale of his scholarly books at the abbey.

Despite Bligh Bond's record of amazing psychic discoveries at the abbey, and his personal love for the site, he was hounded from Glastonbury by narrow minds solely because he employed unconventional techniques to reveal its wonders.

Ghost of the *Great Eastern*

The *Great Eastern* was undoubtedly one of the grandest ships ever to sail the seven seas. She was also one of the most ill-starred, cursed from the start by the ghost of a worker walled up in her double hull.

Her creator, Isambard Kingdom Brunel, was already a successful bridge and railroad contractor when he conceived the idea of a floating city connecting London and the rest of the world. Naval architects had already designed and built transatlantic passenger liners that displaced nearly three thousand tons. But Brunel's *Great Eastern* dwarfed all ships that had come before. In fact, with an estimated displacement of one hundred thousand tons, it shamed anything afloat. Ten big boilers driven by 115 furnaces powered her two 58-foot paddle wheels and a backup 28-foot propeller. Five funnels shoveled her coal smoke skyward. The *Great Eastern* had enough auxiliary systems to support a small navy, including ten anchors of five tons each, six towering masts and sails, and her own gas plant for lighting.

Yet the ship proved haunted from the start. For the world's largest boat launch, Brunel invited the army of workers who had built her. One who failed to show was a quiet master shipwright who had labored on the double hull.

The christening ceremony didn't quite go according to plan as the *Great Eastern*'s bulk and weight caused the launching mechanism to jam. She probably wouldn't have been launched at all, if record high tides hadn't floated her into the Thames. But soon after that small success Brunel's Great Eastern Steam Navigation Company went broke—and Brunel himself was dead. On the day of his death, in fact, the captain complained to his chief engineer that his sleep had been "rudely disturbed by constant hammering from below."

On the heels of that ghostly incident, one of the *Great Eastern*'s stacks exploded, killing six and wrecking the grand saloon. Though her fortunes improved momentarily, on the luxury liner's fourth Atlantic crossing a vicious gale wrecked her paddle wheels and blew her lifeboats overboard. Again, even in the high winds, a phantom hammering was heard below decks.

The *Great Eastern* was able to make port, but as a passenger ship she was finished. Her last owners even had a difficult time selling her for scrap. In 1885, as she was finally being broken up, the welders made a ghastly find. Beside a carpetbag of rusting tools lay the skeleton of the missing shipwright, lodged between the iron walls of the *Great Eastern*'s double hull.

Spacebase Baalbek?

Near the devastated plains where Sodom and Gomorrah once stood lie the magnificent ruins of Baalbek, named after the god worshipped by the ancient Phoenicians. Baalbek's most prominent remnant of times past is a gigantic stone acropolis unmatched in antiquity for the massive building blocks used in its construction.

In fact, the Baalbek blocks are unmatched in modern times as well, leaving some to speculate that they may have served as a platform for visiting spaceships. What else could blocks of stone sixty-four feet long, thirteen feet high, ten feet thick, and weighing as much as 2 *million* pounds be expected to support? The huge monoliths of Baalbek were hand-quarried, laboriously transported a half mile, and then raised twenty feet off the ground to provide a virtually immovable base for—what?

A clue may be found in the biblical account of the former inhabitants of Baalbek rendered in Numbers. While wandering in the wilderness, it was written, Moses sent spies into Canaan to determine the odds of an invasion.

''We be not able to go up against the people,'' they reported, ''for they are stronger than we. . . . The land, through which we have gone . . . is [one] that eateth up the inhabitants thereof; and all the people that we saw in it are men of a great stature. And there we saw the giants, the sons of Anak . . . and we were in our own sight as grasshoppers, and so were we in their sight.''

It boggles the mind to ponder the posssibilities of ancient giants working to colossal ends at which we can only guess. But the fact that the monumental stones of Baalbek rose so near to the obliterated cities of Sodom and Gomorrah may be more than just a curious coincidence.

Tektites From Above

No scientist has ever sufficiently explained the existence of tektites, strange globules of glasslike, radioactive rocks found in, among other places, Lebanon. According to a theory put forward by Dr. Ralph Stair of the U.S. National Bureau of Standards, tektites might have come from a destroyed planet, fragments of which now orbit between Mars and Jupiter as the asteroid belt.

Another even more startling proposal has been put forth by a Soviet mathematician known as Professor Agrest. Agrest reasoned that tektite composition called for high temperature as well as nuclear radiation. He knew that no nuclear devices had *recently* been exploded in Lebanon, but what about during Biblical times? There was, after all, *this* curious account of the destruction of Sodom and Gomorrah recorded in the *Dead Sea Scrolls*:

"A column of smoke and dust rose into the air like a column of smoke issuing from the bowels of the Earth. It rained sulphur and fire on Sodom and Gomorrah, and destroyed the town and the whole plain and all the inhabitants and every growing plant. And Lot's wife looked back and was turned into a pillar of salt."

The column of smoke and soot sounds suspiciously like an atomic mushroom cloud, Agrest says. But who in Biblical times could possibly have possessed nuclear weapons? For Agrest there was only one inescapable conclusion: Weapons capable of wreaking such havoc could only have come from above. Perhaps we have been visited by extraterrestrials in the remote past, he suggests, though we will never know for sure until the violent secrets of tektite structure have been revealed.

The Ship With a Mind of Its Own

Even while she was under construction, the Nazi dreadnought *Scharnhorst* had a mind of her own. When she was only half-built, she suddenly groaned and rolled over, crushing 60 men to death and seriously injuring 110 more.

On the night before her scheduled launching, the *Scharnhorst* broke from her bounds and ground up a pair of huge barges as she proceeded, unmanned, from the docks into the water. Then, in one of her first engagements, a turret exploded, killing twelve.

Near war's end the battle cruiser was dispatched to destroy British convoys off the northern tip of Norway. One British commander, sensing a Nazi ship nearby, ordered a salvo fired at random. The *Scharnhorst* sailed squarely into it, and was subsequently ripped apart by explosions. She rolled over and plunged to the bottom of the sea, about sixty miles off the coast of Norway.

Most of her crewmen died immediately, but a few survivors were picked up by the British. Two others managed to reach a tiny island on a life raft. Their bodies were only found years later, when the war was just a cruel memory. Apparently their emergency oil stove had exploded, killing them instantly.

The curse of the deadly *Scharnhorst* had reached out again.

Trans-en-Provence Case

These days, France is the only country with a government-sponsored UFO agency. GEPAN, the unidentified aerial phenomena research group, is a separate department within the French national space agency. All UFO reports originating in France go directly to GEPAN, which then determines the merits of the case.

Because of the transient nature of UFO phenomena, GEPAN has come up with few extraordinary or even conclusive results. But one French case stands out. On January 8, 1981, at about 5 P.M., a Monsieur Renato Nicolai, age fifty-five, was working in his garden in Trans-en-Provence when he heard a whistling noise. He turned around, he claimed, to see a spacecraft descending toward the ground.

Nicolai said the craft "was in the form of two saucers upside down, one against the other. It must have been just about 1.5 meters high and the color of lead." According to Nicolai, the craft remained on the ground for about a minute. Then, he said, "it took off rapidly in the direction of the forest, which is to say toward the northeast."

GEPAN investigators took soil and plant samples at the landing site the following day, and again three days later. The agency also collected samples thirty-nine days after the incident, and once more two years later.

According to GEPAN, physical traces of a landing were found. The soil, the agency says, included small quantities of phosphate and zinc, and seemed to have been heated to a temperature between three and six hundred degrees Centigrade. But perhaps the most important finding was a subsequent 30- to 50-percent decrease in the amount of chlorophyll and carotenoid pigments produced by plants in the immediate vicinity of the landed craft. Moreover, according to GEPAN, "there was a significant correlation between the disturbances observed and the distance from the center of the phenomenon." The trauma, GEPAN noted, *might* have been induced by an electromagnetic field.

Although hesitant to conclude that an actual extraterrestrial spaceship had touched down in Nicolai's garden, French scientist Alain Esterle, former head of GEPAN, concluded that "for the first time we have found a combination of factors suggesting that something similar to what the eyewitness has described actually did take place."

No Hand at the Helm

Ships sometimes do the strangest things, even without a human hand at the helm. In 1884, while on the return run to Rouen from Spain, for instance, the French boat *Frigorifique* collided in dense fog with another steamer, the British-registered *Rumney*. When the *Frigorifique*'s sides split open, the French captain gave the order to abandon ship. Fortunately, the crew and passengers were picked up by the *Rumney*, whose captain called for a course that steered her away from the sinking *Frigorifique*.

The soaking French sailors and their rescuers were celebrating their success when the watch again cried out. Looming momentarily out of the fog was the ghost of the *Frigorifique*, which just as quickly vanished from view. The two crews heaved a sigh of relief.

But the damaged *Frigorifique* hove into sight once more. This time she rammed the *Rumney*, forcing both crews to lower their lifeboats. As they pulled away from the fatally stricken ship, the survivors spied the supposedly doomed *Frigorifique* through the thick mists. Her screw was still turning as one of her funnels belched thick black smoke.

Rendlesham Forest Encounter

The pine trees of Rendlesham Forest in Suffolk, England, separate a Royal Air Force Base at Bentwaters from its American counterpart at Woodbridge, two miles distant. In the early morning hours of December 27, 1980, according to U.S. deputy base commander Lieutenant Colonel Charles I. Halt, Woodbridge security patrolmen spied unusual lights outside the base's back gate.

Thinking that an aircraft might have gone down in the forest, they asked permission to investigate. Three patrolmen soon reported a strange glowing object in the forest. They claimed it was metallic in appearance and triangular in shape, approximately two to three meters across the base and two meters high. It illuminated the entire forest with a white light.

"The object itself had a pulsing red light on top and a bank of blue lights underneath," Halt reported in his signed statement. It was either hovering or on legs. As the security force approached the object, it maneuvered through the trees and disappeared. At this time the animals on a nearby farm went into a frenzy. The object was briefly sighted approximately an hour later near the back gate.

"The next day," Halt continued, "three depressions one and a half inches deep and seven inches in diameter were found where the object had been sighted on the ground. The following night the area was checked for radiation. Beta/gamma readings of 0.1 milliroentgens were recorded, with peak readings in the three depressions.

"Later in the night a red sunlike light was seen through the trees," Halt's bizarre statement read. "It moved about and pulsed. At one point it appeared to throw off glowing particles and then broke into five separate white objects and then disappeared. Immediately thereafter, three starlike objects were noticed in the sky, two objects to the north and one to the south, all of which were about ten degrees off the horizon. The objects moved rapidly in sharp, angular movements and displayed red, green, and blue lights."

When queried about the Rendlesham Forest incident, the British Ministry of Defense denied any knowledge. Later, a copy of Halt's signed statement was acquired in the United States through the Freedom of Information Act. A voice recording made by Halt was also obtained.

Authorities from both governments have subsequently declined to comment further, except to say that their "defense security was never in danger." Skeptics have claimed that the whole incident was caused by the revolving beam of a nearby lighthouse!

1897 Airship Flap

Human conquest of the skies supposedly began on a December's day in 1903, when two bicycle mechanics, the brothers Orville and Wilbur Wright, first flew their flimsy biplane a few scant yards above the sand dunes at Kitty Hawk. But seven years before the brief but monumental flight, in November 1896, *something* apparently manmade was seen in the skies over San Francisco. By April of the following year, when reports peaked, the Great Airship of 1897 had been sighted on both coasts and throughout the heartland of the nation, from Chicago to Texas.

Hardly a community was spared. Yet the ubiquitous 1897 airship has never been satisfactorily explained. Historians of "official" aviation dismiss it as beneath contempt. But the moldering pages of the newspapers of the day headlined the mystery airship in terms surprisingly reminiscent of latter-day UFOs. Even folklorists and sociologists are hard pressed to explain the prevalence of the reports.

Typically, the sightings fell into two categories: Some people described only nocturnal lights and beams of bright illumination. Others reported a magnificent flying machine crewed by an odd assortment of individuals. The ship was often reported stranded in the countryside, usually in need of simple repairs, before continuing on its way.

There was so much speculation about the airship's origins that famous inventors like Thomas Alva Edison regularly called press conferences to deny the contrivance was theirs. Other, less honorable inventors did claim the airship as their own, though they were never able to produce a working model on demand. By the fall of 1897, however, airship reports dropped off dramatically and by the turn of the century they were virtually gone.

Nevertheless, students of anomalous phenomena continue to debate the significance of the Great Airship to this day. Charles Fort, America's greatest cataloguer of the odd and unusual, suggested that the flying machine was simply an idea whose time had come. Others believe that the Great Airship of 1897 somehow spurred the subsequent advances in aviation technology. The Wright brothers may not have been innocent innovators, these pundits argue, but rather the unwitting tools of an unconscious evolutionary urge. This outward impulse, some even suggest, is mirrored in the prevalence of today's UFO reports.

Scandinavian Ghost Rockets

In the aftermath of World War II, before the modern era of ufology had really begun, people from Norway to Finland were terrified by ghostly, rocketlike objects in the sky.

The first sightings, made over northern Finland near the Arctic Circle on February 26, 1946, were initially described as meteors. However, it soon became apparent that meteor activity could hardly account for the hundreds of hurtling daylight objects that were variously compared to a football, cigar, bullet, or silver torpedo.

Such silhouettes, in fact, seemed more in keeping with the Nazi V-1 and V-2 rockets that rained death and destruction on London and other wartime targets. But the German guided-missile bases on the European mainland had either been captured or bombed into submission. Besides, their maximum range was barely a fourth of that required to reach northern Finland, Norway and Sweden, where the ghost rocket reports proliferated. Even if the Soviets had captured a contingent of working V-2s, as the Swedes and others feared, why would they waste them over the Scandinavian countries for no apparent purpose?

What is known is that the Scandinavians themselves took the ghost rockets seriously. Proscriptions against publishing such reports in public, so as not to aid "the power making the experiments," were first taken by Sweden on July 17, 1946. Norway followed suit two days later, and Denmark enacted similar strictures on August 16. The Swedish news blackout came in the wake of a single 24-hour period, during which 250 individuals across the country reported a streaking, silvery, teardrop-shaped object high in the heavens. The following day, the Defense Staff named a committee of both civilian and military specialists to look into the matter. Altogether, more than a thousand reports were collected.

Meanwhile, the ghost rockets had attracted international attention. On August 20, 1946, an RCA vice-president and former general, David Sarnoff, landed at Stockholm's Bromma Airport. He was joined the same day by Douglas Rader, a former colonel in the RAF, and American war hero James Doolittle. On August 21, the distinguished trio met with Sweden's top Air Force brass.

What transpired remains shrouded in secrecy. Doolittle, who served on several U.S. intelligence operations after the war, declined to publicly discuss the Swedish mission. Sarnoff supposedly reported directly to President Truman on his return to the United States. He also told a group of electronic experts he thought the ghost rockets were real and not imaginary.

History has tended to ignore the significance of the Scandinavian mystery missiles because they were never as widely publicized as the flying saucers that followed in their wake. Many curious questions remain. Were the rockets part of a ghostly phenomenon that somehow assumes different shapes in response to the anxieties and preoccupations of a particular culture? Or did the Soviets, or some other power, unbeknown to the world at large, vastly improve the range and performance of Nazi Germany's most advanced weapons? And if that's the case, could the same phantom perpetrators be responsible for today's UFOs?

Wilhelm Reich: UFO Buster

The career of pioneer Freudian analyst Wilhelm Reich was so scarred with controversy that his most controversial work, his battle against invading UFOs, was hardly noticed at all.

Born in Austria in 1897, Reich quickly displayed a temperamental genius for human psychology, becoming a Freudian convert while still at the university. In fact, he might have succeeded the master psychoanalyst had he not out-Freuded Freud, so to speak, with his insistence that free-flowing libido energy, otherwise known as the uninhibited orgasm, was an unmistakable sign of physical and mental health. That philosophy promptly got its author thrown out of the International Psychoanalytic Association as well as the fledgling Communist Party.

Reich retreated to Scandinavia, where he claimed to have discovered the "bion," a microscopic blue cell that was the basic building unit of all living matter, and "orgone," the organizing energy of life itself. Subsequently hounded out of Scandinavia, Reich eventually settled at an estate in Maine that he called Orgonon in honor of his discovery. From here he waged war on UFOs with his "cloudbuster," a device designed to drain negative orgone energy from clouds.

Reich became convinced that UFOs were interplanetary life forms spying on his work, and also that they were accumulators of what he called "deadly orgone" that caused desertification of the planet. He wondered what would happen if he trained the hollow tubes of his cloudbuster on the UFOs. The answer came on the evening of October 10, 1954, as a series of red and yellow

UFOs (beneficial ones, according to Reich, would have been blue) converged over Orgonon. Reich declared that aiming the cloudbuster at the lights caused them to dim in intensity and take evasive action.

Writing in his logbook of the experiment, witnessed by several coworkers, Reich noted that, "Tonight for the first time in the history of man, the war waged from outer space upon this earth . . . was reciprocated . . . with positive results."

But Reich would not live to see the war won. He died in November 1957, while confined to a federal penitentiary for having refused to stop selling "orgone boxes," which he claimed could cure cancer.

King of the World

According to the beliefs of many Mongolians and Tibetans (and attested to by numerous Buddhist monks who claim to have visited it), a vast underground country called Arghati lies beneath the high plateau of Central Asia. From within the tunnels of Arghati, the prophecy goes, will one day emerge the mystical King of the World and his subjects.

Before the king comes forth, sometime around the close of the present millennium, the Buddhist teaching says, "men will increasingly neglect their souls. The greatest corruption will reign on earth. Men will become like bloodthirsty animals, thirsting for the blood of their brothers. . . . The crowns of kings will fall. . . . There will be a terrible war between all the earth's peoples . . . entire nations will die . . . hunger . . . crimes unknown to law . . . formerly unthinkable to the world will be committed."

During this period of lawlessness, the prophecy continues,

families will be dispersed and multitudes will flood the escape routes as the world's "greatest and most beautiful cities . . . perish by fire.

"Within fifty years there will be only three great nations . . . and, within the next fifty years there will be eighteen years of war and cataclysms. . . . Then the people of Agharti will leave their subterranean caverns and will appear on the surface of the earth."

The Men in Black

Perhaps the strangest wrinkle in the already perplexing UFO phenomenon are the semidemonic figures known as MIB, or Men in Black. The first MIB report in modern ufology came from Albert K. Bender, a teenage UFO buff who directed the International Flying Saucer Bureau and published the bureau's news bulletin, *Space Review*. In September 1953, Bender claimed, he was approached by three men clad in black suits, who told him he must abandon his UFO research if he wanted to stay safe. Bender did indeed abandon his career in ufology, but the MIB phenomenon went on. UFO investigator and author John Keel, for instance, has talked to numerous eyewitnesses who claimed to have been confronted by similar MIB entities.

Some unusual aspects of the MIB phenomenon emerged when the reports were studied by folklorist Peter Rojcewicz. For instance, Rojcewicz notes, MIB "often dress in black clothing that may appear soiled and generally unkempt or unrealistically neat and wrinkle-free. On occasion they display a very unusual walking motion, moving about as if their hips were on swivel joints, their torso and legs at odds with one another. Some display a penchant for black Cadillacs or other large, dark sedans.

Some MIB show an unusual growth of hair, suggesting that their hair had grown back unevenly after having recently been shaved.'' Nearly all races and complexions, he says, have been reported, with Asian features predominating.

The motives of MIB remain murky, though they are frequently bent on retrieving UFO data and warning witnesses away from any further involvement with the subject. ''They may show up at the home or workplace,'' says Rojcewicz, ''demanding photographs or negatives of UFOs *before* the witness has even let it be known publicly that he possesses any.'' On several such occasions, the MIB posed as military intelligence officers.

Where MIB come from and where they disappear to after their mischief is accomplished is an enigma. What is known, however, is that their presence further clouds the waters already made murky by the UFO.

Mokele-Mbembe

Most scientists maintain that dinosaurs have been extinct for millions of years. But people in the Cameroons, along the western curve of Africa, continue to report a huge, four-footed creature that bears every resemblance to the brontosaurus itself. In fact, when shown a drawing of a brontosauruslike dinosaur and asked to name it, the local inhabitants inevitably refer to it as *mokele-mbembe*.

The earliest authenticated accounts of mokele-mbembe were collected by Captain Freiherr von Stein zu Lausnitz in 1913. According to his report, the elephant-sized animal was brownish-gray in color, with smooth skin and a long, flexible neck. This unusual behemoth was said to live in underwater caves washed out by the river, and that any canoe that dared approach was doomed. On at least one occasion, however, a band of pygmies allegedly killed one of the creatures and feasted on its carcass. Those who actually ate the flesh were said to have sickened and died.

In recent years, Westerners such as University of Chicago biologist Roy Mackal have mounted four expeditions to the relatively isolated lakes and rivers of the Cameroons in search of the elusive beast. Although no specimen has been captured, unidentified animals resembling the native accounts have been seen, photographed, and even recorded on videotape.

Unfortunately, the local political situation and turgid terrain is hardly conducive to "drop in" explorations. Most Western observers agree that if a dinosaur *wanted* to hide out, it could hardly have chosen a better locale. But perhaps one day soon even these impediments will be overcome and the world will learn whether it harbors a surviving remnant of its fantastically remote past.

Miracle Man Sai Baba

The modern tendency, hardly well-founded, is to dismiss religious miracles as a thing of the past. That way they can be safely disregarded as the product of a more gullible age.

But disciples of numerous religious leaders continue to bear witness to a panoply of paranormal events that hark back to the prophets and messiahs of other ages. Most accomplished of these contemporary divines is India's Sai Baba, a yogi who claims to be a reincarnation of his namesake, Sai Baba of Shirdi, who died in 1918, eight years before his own birth in provincial Puttaparti.

The second Sai Baba had a relatively normal life until the age of fourteen, when he suffered a debilitating seizure, during which he periodically broke into song and recited poetic passages of Vedantic philosophy. Emerging from the trancelike illness, he suddenly announced to his surprised parents that he was an avatar, or divine reincarnation, of the celebrated holy man who had died almost a decade before his own birth.

Other yogis from the mysterious East have claimed to have mastered a psychic trick or two in the course of their public careers. Sai Baba, by contrast, demonstrates miracles in a businesslike way as most of us would balance a checkbook or write a letter.

Among the feats of faith Sai Baba is alleged to have accomplished are teleportation, levitation, psychokinesis, and the manifestation of material objects—he seems to have a distinct preference for rose petals—out of thin air. He has also supposedly resurrected the dead and multiplied a store of food a hundred times.

Fish Falls

Back in the 1800s, the French Academy of Sciences declared that meteors do not exist. The peasants who claimed they saw stones falling from the sky, said the experts, were simply imagining the whole thing. Cuvier, the French scientist who was the founder of comparative anatomy and vertebrate paleontology, categorically stated that stones "cannot fall from the sky because there *are* no stones in the sky."

Science responds in similar fashion today to widespread reports of falling fish. Since there aren't fish overhead, runs the orthodox objection, how can they possibly come splashing down? If such stories are true, the fish must have been plucked out of water by a whirlwind, transported distances great and small, and then deposited in someone's backyard.

The fish, nevertheless, do fall. The city of Singapore, for instance, was rocked by an earthquake on February 16, 1861, and for the following six days rain poured in buckets. After the sun came out on the twenty-second, French naturalist Francois de Castlenau looked out his window to see "a large number of Malays and Chinese filling baskets with fishes which they picked up in the pools of water that covered the ground." When asked where the fish had come from, they simply pointed overhead. The fall, involving a species of local catfish, covered an area of fifty acres.

Almost a century later, on October 23, 1947, marine biologist D. A. Bajkov was eating breakfast with his wife at a Marksville, Louisiana, cafe when it started to rain. Before long fish filled the streets outside. Bajkov identified them as "sunfish, goggle-eyed minnows, and black bass up to nine inches long." They were also found on rooftops, stone cold dead, but still fit to eat.

Nor are fish the only animate matter to have fallen from the sky. Those chronicling this sort of anomaly have also reported deluges of birds, toads, yellow mice, snakes, blood, and even chunks of raw meat, suggesting that the heavens may harbor more varieties of food than the manna that reportedly fell down on the Israelites.

How Long Did Dinosaurs Survive?

According to prevailing scientific opinion, dinosaurs died out 65 million years ago, never to be seen again. But comparatively modern artifacts from five widely separated sites all bear eerie likenesses of animals that can only be described as dinosaurlike. Are they hoaxes or racial memories of living creatures, perhaps buried in the collective subconscious of ancient artisans? Or did the dinosaurs themselves survive significantly longer than once thought?

The first indication that dinosaurs may have been a relatively recent phenomenon emerged in 1920, when ranch hands digging on the property of William M. Chalmers near Granby, Colorado, discovered a granite statuette weighing sixty-six pounds and standing fourteen inches high. The stone, found at a depth of six feet, portrays a stylized human with what purports to be a Chinese inscription dating to approximately 1000 B.C. More intriguing are two inscribed animals on the sides and back that appear to be a brontosaurus and a mammoth. Although clear pictures were made of the object from several angles, the Granby Stone itself has long since vanished. Even the site where it was found has disappeared, submerged by the waters of the Granby reservoir.

An unusual piece of evidence came to light in 1925, when University of Arizona archaeologists working in a lime kiln outside of Tucson unearthed a short, heavy broadsword inscribed with a brontosaurus. Other artifacts found at the site bore both Hebrew lettering and a form of Latin used between A.D. 560 and 900. Even though many of the Tucson artifacts were unearthed by professionals, controversy continues to rage over their authenticity. Common sense, however, suggests that the last thing any hoaxter hoping to be taken seriously would inscribe on a sword blade would be an extinct dinosaur.

Another curious collection of indeterminate artifacts can be found in the church of María Auxiliadora in Cuenca, Ecuador, under the protection of Father Carlo Crespi. The pieces, mostly plaques, number in the hundreds and have been brought in by the Jivaro Indians from outlying jungle caves. Some have been fashioned from gold; others are obviously modern fakes, made out of olive oil cans. A bewildering variety of forms and styles are present, including dinosaur portraits and motifs that appear to be Assyrian and Egyptian in origin. Ancient Phoenician, Libyan, and Celt-Iberian inscriptions have also been identified.

While mastodons are not to be included in the dinosaur era, they are generally supposed to have become extinct before man developed any recognizable civilization. But an interesting find of a mastodon's skeleton was made in Blue Lick Springs in Kentucky at a dig that had reached twelve feet below the surface, and as the excavating team dug deeper, looking for more bones, they came across a set-stone pavement, three feet *under* where they had found the mastodon.

Finally, an Ica, Peru, museum owned by Dr. Javier Cabrera presently houses almost twenty thousand riverbed stones, all intricately inscribed with curlicued pictographs portraying several dinosaur species and other long extinct animals. Again, the brontosaurus seems to be an artistic favorite. The Ica stones, moreover, are characterized by an artistry casual hoaxters would find hard, if not impossible, to emulate. Precise anatomical details abound. And the sheer numbers raise the question of why anyone would go to such trouble for little or no reward. More importantly, similar stones have been dug out of pre-Columbian graves nearby.

The Levelland Egg

A series of sightings reported in the small Texas Panhandle town of Levelland on the night of November 2, 1957, qualify as one of the strongest cases in UFO annals.

First to call in was a "terrified" farmhand named Pedro Saucedo. Saucedo and a friend had been driving on Route 116, four miles west of Levelland, at about 10:30 P.M. when "lightning" flashed off to one side. "We didn't think much about it," Saucedo said later, "but then it rose up out of the field and started toward us, picking up speed. When it got nearer, the lights of my truck went out and the motor died. I jumped out and hit the deck as the thing passed directly over the truck with a great sound and a rush of wind. It sounded like thunder, and my truck rocked from the blast. I felt a lot of heat."

What Saucedo called "it" was a torpedo-shaped object approximately two hundred feet long. Patrolman A. J. Fowler, who handled his call, thought Saucedo was drunk and dismissed it. But less than an hour later, "it" was back. This time the caller was Jim Wheeler. He, too, had been on Route 116 when he came upon a two-hundred-foot, egg-shaped UFO blocking the highway. As Wheeler approached the object, his headlights and engine died.

Before morning's end, five other motorists in the immediate vicinity of Levelland would report a similar experience: a large glowing egglike object straddling the highway or squatting nearby, and a failure to their vehicle's electrical system, which returned to normal when the UFO departed.

The most amazing thing about the legendary Levelland sightings, however, is the fact that the Air Force's Project Blue Book, following a cursory examination, "solved" them by attributing the phenomenon to ball lightning!

Nina Kulagina and Psychokinesis

Nina Kulagina is probably the leading psychic in the U.S.S.R. She is best known for her psychokinetic skills, which she reportedly uses to move objects mentally from one spot to the next. Indeed, films smuggled out to the West show the famous psychic using hand or eye motions to deflect a variety of things: Matchsticks, compasses, small boxes, cigarettes, and plexiglass tubes were all grist for her psychic mill.

The best of these films was taken by Zdenek Rejdak, a Prague Military Institute researcher who visited the U.S.S.R. in 1968 specifically to study Kulagina and test her PK. "After we sat down around the table," Rejdak explains, "I required Mrs. Kulagina to leave the position at which she had decided to sit, and to sit at the opposite side of the table. The first test was to endeavor to turn a compass needle first to the right and then to the left. Mrs. Kulagina held her hands approximately five to ten centimeters over the compass, and after an interval of concentration, the compass needle turned more than ten times. Thereafter, the entire compass turned on the table, then a matchbox, some separate matches, and a group of about twenty matches at once."

When the display was over, Dr. Rejdak placed a gold ring on the table and, he said, Kulagina had little difficulty moving it as well. Finally the Czech scientist said, he watched her use PK to move some glassware and some plates.

Despite the seemingly effortless nature of these powers, Rejdak reported that Kulagina's PK seemed guided by several standard principles. For instance, it was easier for her to move cylindrical objects and more difficult to move angular ones. Objects with which she was unfamiliar tended to move *away* from her. And when she exerted herself to make objects move, they tended to move in exact coincidence with her body, sometimes continuing to move even when she had stopped.

Beginning in the late 1960s, a few Western researchers visited the Soviet Union to study Kulagina for themselves. Dr. J. C. Pratt and Champe Ransom from the University of Virginia were the first, and their observations corroborated Rejdak's. In his book, *ESP Research Today*, for instance, the late Dr. Pratt recounted how he watched Kulagina "practice" her PK from his position behind a slightly opened door.

"I could see Kulagina through the open door," he recalled. "She was sitting on the far side of a small round table facing me and the matchbox and compass were lying in front of her on the table. After a time I noticed that while she held her hands stretched out toward the matchbox, it moved several inches across the table in her direction. She put the box back near the center of the table and it moved again in the same way."

Because of the publicity Soviet parapsychology received in the late 1960s, Kulagina was soon placed off-limits to Western researchers, but this dictate was relaxed around 1972. Today, Kulagina still gives occasional demonstrations to foreign parapsychologists, and her name was mentioned in many a Western newspaper when she was called in to help doctors deal with Khrushchev's ailing health.

The Highway of Remembrance

Déjà vu translates literally from the French as "already seen." It manifests itself in the form of an intense feeling of familiarity with a situation or place, even though the person has never experienced it before. Many experts say such incidents could be caused by small seizures in the brain, but some cases stretch beyond psychology, suggesting that the paranormal is at work.

A fascinating case reported by parapsychologist D. Scott Rogo serves as a case in point. In 1985, a New Jersey woman wrote to tell him about a trip she had taken along the New Jersey Turnpike. The landscape was strangely familiar, and the woman finally turned to her traveling companion and said, "You know, I have never been here before, but I believe about a mile or so down the road is a house I used to live in.

"Approximately three miles or so passed," the woman related "and I told my friend that around the bend we would come to a small town set very close to the turnpike. I told her that the houses would be white-frame, two-story homes, rather close together. I felt I had lived there when I was six years old or so, and that I used to sit with my granny on the front porch. The memories overwhelmed me, and I could remember sitting on the swing on the front porch as my grandmother buttoned up my high-topped shoes."

When the woman got to town, she recognized the house immediately, even though the front porch swing was gone. She also recalled walking two blocks down the street to a drugstore with a high marble counter, white, and ordering lemonade. Driving down the street, the women found the building, boarded up and run-down, but still there.

As the two friends continued driving out of town, the woman had her next experience of déjà vu. "In about three blocks there will be a small hill, rolling, and a cemetery is *there*, and that is where they buried me." The cemetery *was* there, but the woman's friend, by now totally panicked, refused to stop and search for the grave.

Suicide Hotel

Can a person "tune in" to past events? Yes, according to psychic Joan Grant, who was convinced by an experience she had in 1929.

Vacationing with her husband on the Continent, Grant had spent the night in a Brussels hotel room. For some inexplicable reason, the room made her uneasy, but since no other accommodations were available, she remained. Her husband thought her fears were nonsensical and soon left to do some errands.

Grant finally decided that taking a hot bath would calm her nerves, but when that didn't help, she read and then went to bed. That's when the shock came. For while lying on the bed, she experienced a frightful vision: A young man seemed to run from the bathroom and hurl himself out the window. She expected to hear the thud of this body striking the ground, but it never came. The perplexed psychic tried to pray, but later on she experienced the vision again.

It was then that Grant concluded her uncomfortable feelings about the room stemmed from an event in the past. A suicide victim, she reasoned, had once rented the room, and was now communicating his discomfort to her. She also decided she could free the suicide's spirit, or whatever was haunting the room, by merging with it. Her greatest fear, however, was that she would merge with the suicide too completely and would plunge out the window herself.

Taking a chance, she went to the window and said, "Your fear has entered into me and you are free." She repeated this message several times before she felt the room suddenly become clear.

When her husband returned later that evening, Grant was annoyed. "You monster," she said. "Going off like that and deliberately leaving your wife to deal with a suicide. No thanks to you that I didn't fall out the window and break my neck."

"What's the matter?" he replied. "What happened?"

"This room's been haunted," Mrs. Grant informed him. "I told you something was wrong with it. A fellow kept running out of the bathroom and jumping out the window. I had to shift level and release him and I practically went over the edge myself."

The next day, Mr. Grant checked out the story with the hotel manager. It turned out that a suicide *had* actually occurred in the room only five days earlier, when the occupant jumped from the window.

Death Flight at Godman

Captain Thomas Mantell, a highly experienced Air Force pilot, died in a controversial plane crash on January 7, 1948. According to the official report, the plane continued upward until a loss of power caused it to level out, then dip to one side and dive in a fatal spiral. Mantell himself, officials said, lost consciousness due to oxygen starvation and never revived.

In truth, Mantell's death flight began when the tower at Godman Field in Kentucky sighted a large, bright, disc-shaped object in the sky. The tower crew decided the object was not a weather balloon and, unable to identify it, finally sent Flight Commander Mantell, along with a group of planes, to see what was going on. Mantell climbed to 15,000 feet, at which point the other planes turned back because a higher altitude required different oxygen equipment. But Mantell went on. Finally he issued his last known radio contact: "It looks metallic and it's tremendous in size. It's above me and I'm gaining on it." Sections of Mantell's plane were later recovered permeated with hundreds of small holes.

Despite these facts, Air Force officials denied the possibility of a UFO, and later determined that Mantell saw either the planet Venus or one of a series of large Navy weather balloons supposedly in the vicinity at that time.

Ufologists, however, were quick to respond: The sun would have been too bright to allow people standing on the ground to see Venus that clearly. Indeed, the sightings were simply too widespread for all to have seen Venus, or even Venus and a balloon.

Air Force officials finally countered that witnesses saw Venus and *two* balloons, seemingly attached together to form one massive UFO. But they could never explain the rumors surrounding Mantell's body: It was apparently removed by the police and immediately enclosed in a coffin, convincing some investigators that Mantell had been covered with strange wounds or that no body was ever found at all.

Tears of Joy

Newspapers frequently report on cases of paintings or statues that show either tears or blood flowing. These cases usually come from members of the Roman Catholic faith, where belief in the miraculous abounds. Sometimes, however, such reports come from Protestant sources as well.

Just such a case was reported by the Reverend William Rauscher, rector of Christ Episcopal Church in Woodbury, New Jersey, who was attending seminary school in 1975. Rauscher was visiting the room of his friend, Bob Lewis, when the conversation turned to Bob's grandmother. The first to introduce young Lewis to the joys of religion, she had cried for joy when she learned he was embarking on a religious career. But she died before seeing her grandson graduate from the seminary.

While relating this tale, Lewis noticed that a picture of the elderly woman, kept on his dresser, was crying. "The photograph of Bob's grandmother was soaking wet, dripping, with a small pool of water spreading onto the dresser from it," Rauscher explains. "Examining the picture, we found that it was wet *inside* the glass. That was genuinely puzzling. The back of the picture, made of dyed imitation velvet, had streaked and faded.

"Removed from its frame, the photograph didn't dry quickly. And when it did, the area around the face remained puffed, as though the water had originated there and run downward, from the eyes."

In short, Rauscher could never find a normal explanation for the incident. And as for Bob Lewis, he graduated from the seminary content in knowing that his beloved grandmother had again wept for joy.

The Ganzfield Effect

Some experts believe that everyone is psychic. The problem, they point out, is tapping this sixth sense in the secret vaults of the mind.

One of the most successful procedures to help people learn to use ESP is the Ganzfield technique, in which the volunteer subject is seated in a sealed, soundproof booth and told to relax while halved Ping-Pong balls are taped over his eyes. Since the translucent spheres diffuse the light, the subject sees nothing but an undifferentiated red visual field. Headphones placed over his ears emit a gentle hissing sound, and the subject is now cut off from most sources of sensory input.

Now the experimenter, sitting in a separate room, looks at randomly selected pictures and tries to send them to the subject via ESP. When the experiment is over thirty-five minutes or so later, the subject is then asked to separate copies of the target pictures from several dummies.

In Ganzfield's experiments, first reported by Charles Honorton of the Maimonides Medical Center's division of parapsychology and psychophysics in 1973, close to half the subjects chose the correct target. When the target theme for one session was "Birds of the World," for instance, the subject reported "a large hawk's head" and "the sense of sleek feathers."

You can't get much more telepathic than that.

Since the Maimonides workers first reported their success, the Ganzfield Effect has been replicated by several other parapsychology laboratories. It remains one of the field's most reliable tools for ESP testing to this day.

The Strange Visit of Mary Roff

In the long-debated issue of reincarnation, one of the earliest cases on record is also the most startling. It is the story of Mary Lurancy Vennum, who as a thirteen-year-old in 1877 suffered some epileptic fits with strange results.

The first evidence of Vennum's reincarnation emerged following a seizure that rendered her unconscious for five days. When she woke up, she told her parents she had visited heaven and talked to a brother and sister who had died. Mary Vennum had no brothers or sisters; and to her parents she seemed destined to wind up not in heaven but in an asylum, particularly after she started speaking in the voices of a strange woman and man.

But Asa Roff, a friend of the family, intervened. Roff's daughter had died sixteen years earlier during an epileptic seizure, and he knew of a doctor who could help. Dr. E. W. Stevens arrived to find Mary Vennum in a trance, taking on the character of the man and then the woman. Stevens quickly hypnotized the girl, who told him she had been taken over by evil spirits. When the doctor suggested *another* spirit from beyond was needed to help her sort out the personalities, Mary herself offered a suggestion: She proposed summoning Mary Roff, Asa Roff's deceased daughter. The startled Asa vigorously agreed.

Whatever psychological disorders the girl may have been suffering from, the science of psychology can hardly offer an explanation for what followed. The next day, Mary Vennum seemed to become Mary Roff, and when Mrs. Roff and a daughter visited, she called the sister by name, though they had never met, and hugged them both and cried. She went back home with the Roffs and seemed to recognize everything and everyone in the neighborhood, constantly recalling incidents from Mary Roff's childhood. Questioning her at length, Stevens himself was convinced that the girl knew all about the life of Mary Roff.

After a short time, the girl told the Roff family that she could only stay a few months. Later she announced the exact day she was departing, and finally said goodbye. After that, she returned to the Vennum home, where Mr. and Mrs. Vennum were happy to find Mary Lurancy Vennum back for good—and cured of her epilepsy in the bargain.

Catching Shoplifters With ESP

If you have a penchant for petty theft, don't try it at the Shoppers Drug Mart in Canada. Instead of using an elaborate security system, the chain employs a psychic to spot shoplifters, and officials there claim he's worth every cent.

In fact, Reginald McHugh, psychic watchdog, has had a long and distinguished career. One day, while waiting to speak with reporters from Mediavision, a film company making a documentary about him, McHugh suddenly became excited. Even though he was sitting in a windowless room toward the back of the store, he exclaimed, "Wait. I feel vibes. Soon a dark woman in a long orange dress will come in and steal a blue box with yellow stripes on it." The psychic immediately relayed his impressions to the store detective.

Ten minutes later, in walked an East Indian lady wearing an orange sari. The store detective watched her slip a small box into her purse and promptly apprehended her when she tried to leave. The blue and yellow box contained throat lozenges.

The film crew was disappointed that they hadn't caught the episode on film, so they came better prepared the next day. This time McHugh wore a microphone under his collar and correctly predicted and pointed out several shoplifters.

"Shoplifting takes place so quickly," says associate producer Tony Bond, "that unless you know who's going to do it, there's no way to film it. It would be an absolute fluke, with all the aisles and displays, if you were to catch someone in the act. And we did that several times."

Psychic Plant Growth

It was the craze of the sixties: Talk to your plants and help them grow. Now, it seems, there was a method to the madness. Scientific evidence gathered by McGill University morphologist Bernard Grad shows that some people *can* use psychic power to help plants thrive.

To perform his experiment, Grad planted barley seeds in several separate plots, where they were watered with a salt solution to stunt their growth. The catch was that some of the beakers containing the solution were "treated" by Hungarian-born psychic Oskar Estebany, who held them and embued them with his healing powers. Needless to say, the plots watered with the specially treated solution gave richer yields than those given the straight saline.

Grad soon replicated the experiment, but this time used two mental patients suffering from depression for his healers. He wanted to see if a person's mood could influence plant growth. The patients were instructed merely to hold the beakers of water before the plants were fed. The yield of their plots was later compared to those of a lab assistant, who had taken part in the original work with Estebany. The results were partially consistent with the earlier research. The lab worker's plots grew better than that of one of the mental patients. But the other subject's plots grew rather well. Dr. Grad was confused by the results, until he discovered that taking part in the experiment had so excited the patient that she had been roused from her depression.

Therapeutic Touch

Therapeutic touch is the most recent name for what was previously called the "laying-on of hands." The practitioner runs his or her hands over the patient, trying to infuse or redistribute energy throughout the body. People receiving therapeutic touch report feeling better and often find their pain gone. But is there any objective evidence that it really works? Yes, according to a report published by Dr. Janet Quinn in 1984.

To determine whether therapists were actually transmitting energy, Quinn first had them enter a state of inwardly focused consciousness, supposedly necessary before the treatment can work. Then she had them administer treatment by moving their hands above the patients' bodies. Each patient rated his or her level of anxiety both before and after receiving the treatment. Just as predicted, the patients reported a significant reduction in their anxiety after receiving therapeutic touch.

Quinn also tried to rule out the placebo effect, which some skeptics believe can explain the effectiveness of therapeutic touch. To do that, she made sure that *some* patients received "mock" therapy, administered by nurses not skilled in the technique. These practitioners were told how to mimic therapeutic touch, but didn't know how to enter the special state of consciousness that helps it work. Those subjects receiving the bogus treatment reported no effects at all. Quinn also videotaped the nurses performing both the real and the fake procedure, and showed the tapes to judges who were asked to differentiate between the two groups. The judges couldn't tell the difference, indicating that the patients couldn't have either.

The Ghost of Washington Irving

Would the author of one of the most famous American ghost stories ever return from the dead to play a prank? Washington Irving, author of *The Legend of Sleepy Hollow*, was a witty man who liked to have fun, sometimes at the expense of others. Shortly after Irving's death, one of the author's old friends, a Dr. J. G. Cogswell, was working in the library when he saw a man shelve a book and disappear. Cogswell felt certain the man was Irving—until he saw another ghostly figure, the image of a second deceased friend, return a book as well.

That was not the end of it. Irving's nephew, Pierre, reportedly saw the ghost of his uncle in the Irving home in Tarrytown, New York. There, Pierre and his two daughters said they clearly saw the famed author walk through the parlor and into the library, where he used to do his work.

While alive, Irving professed no belief in ghosts. The headless horseman of his writing, after all, was really a mortal dressed to scare away a rival. It's likely his nephew shared that belief—until Irving himself proved them both wrong.

Floating Fakir

Transcendental meditation gained great notoriety in the 1970s, when leaders of the movement claimed that practitioners could levitate. But despite all the assertions, not a single meditator was ever seen to float above the ground.

This doesn't mean, however, that the powers of the mind can't help a person defy gravity. Eyewitness reports of human levitations dot the history of cultures both East and West. One of the most impressive of these eyewitness reports was made in the 1860s by Louis Jacolliot, a French judge who traveled extensively in the East. According to Jacolliot, his interest in yoga was piqued when he befriended a fakir named Covindasamy in 1866. The two men began conducting psychic experiments together, and one day before lunch Covindasamy decided to give his friend a startling demonstration.

The yogi was walking toward the door to Jacolliot's veranda, the judge wrote in his book, *Occult Science in India and Among the Ancients*, when he obviously had second thoughts. "The fakir stopped in the doorway from the terrace into the backstairs, and folding his arms, he was lifted—or so it seemed to me—gradually without visible support, about one foot above the ground. I could determine the exact height, thanks to a landing marker upon which I fixed my eyes during the short time the phenomenon lasted. Behind the fakir hung a silk curtain with red, golden, and white stripes of equal breadth, and I noticed that the fakir's feet were as high as the sixth stripe. When I saw the rising begin, I took my watch out."

According to Jacolliot, the fakir remained suspended for about ten minutes; for five of those minutes, he appeared not to move at all.

Psychic Stream

Some experts believe that we receive psychic impressions continually during the day, even if these messages never enter into waking consciousness. This idea was merely a theory until the 1960s, when New Jersey electrical engineer E. Douglas Dean decided to demonstrate it.

Drawing upon some earlier research done in Czechoslovakia, Dean used two subjects for his experiments. The first subject, the "receiver," was placed alone in a room, his finger hooked up to a plethysmograph, a device that monitors blood flow in the body. Meanwhile, in a different room, the "sender" went to work. He or she would study a series of cards, each one either blank or labeled with a random name, a name emotionally significant to the sender, or a name significant to the receiver. Dean hoped that when the sender became aroused by seeing an emotionally significant name, the subject would also respond. Such a reaction would show up on the plethysmograph chart, which would show a sudden increase in little dips.

The experiment was successful, but not in the way the experimenter had expected. What happened was that the subject's blood flow responded when the sender looked at names significant to his experimental partner. It seemed as though the subject's unconscious mind was constantly vigilant during the experiment, looking out for any messages that might be important. While subjects were not consciously aware when the ESP signals were received, their bodies subtly responded to them.

Child Finder

A woman desperate to find her missing children will do almost anything. Take New Yorker Joanne Tomchik, who lost her children, aged three and five, when they were kidnapped by her former husband in 1972.

Frantic, Tomchik enlisted the help of police and even hired private detectives. But one year and six thousand dollars in fees later, there was still no clue as to the whereabouts of her husband or children.

Then she heard a radio broadcast about ESP and decided to enlist the aid of a psychic. The group involved in the broadcast referred her to Mrs. Millie Cotant, who focused on photographs of the Tomchik children and finally came up with a vision. She saw a trailer and a light-blue pickup truck with Carolina plates.

That was enough for Mrs. Tomchik. She notified the police in both North and South Carolina, furnishing them with photos of her children and their father. One month later, in Wilson, North Carolina, Andrew Tomchik was located, living with the children in a trailer park. He had been using a light-blue pickup truck. Tomchik was found guilty of violating his visitation rights, and Mrs. Tomchik was happily reunited with her children.

Papal Prophecies

One of the Middle Ages' more obscure prophets was Saint Malachy, an Irish monk who became Archbishop of Armagh. He died in 1148, but his prophecies, found in note form, were collected and published by Vatican officials in or about 1595.

Saint Malachy's prophecies were couched in the form of a papal register, or list, projected from the twelfth century forward, with a comment about each of the new popes or the character of his reign, many of which have proven surprisingly apt. The register ends with "Peter the Roman," at a time calculated as roughly the end of this century, or the coming of the millennium.

Between Peter and who appears to be Pope Pius XI will be six other Vatican rulers. During Peter's reign, "the city of the Seven Hills will be destroyed, and the Awful Judge will judge his people."

The prophetic history of the papacy has often been referred to among Catholic theologians. Knowledge of it may have even contributed to the vision reported by Pope Pius in 1909. Emerging from a trance, he said, "What I see is terrifying. Will it be myself . . . or my successor . . . the pope will quit Rome and after leaving the Vatican he will have to walk over the dead bodies of his priests."

Time, of course, will tell whether Saint Malachy's terrifying prophecies come to pass.

Bodily Elongation

The most prolific performer of modern miracles was unquestionably the nineteenth-century spirit medium, Daniel Douglas Home (1833–86), who once floated out a second-story window and back again in broad daylight, in full view of witnesses.

Among Home's stable of miraculous secular feats were the ability to levitate heavy objects, converse with spirits of the long departed, and wash his face in burning embers without suffering apparent harm. The physically frail Scotsman could also elongate his body dramatically, adding as much as six inches to his height.

On one occasion this feat was witnessed by no less a personage than Lord Adare, son of the third Earl of Dunraven. Standing between the Lord and a Mr. Jencken, Home entered into the familiar trance state in which the majority of his miracles were accomplished. "The guardian spirit is very tall and strong," he intoned. Without notice, Home suddenly sprouted an additional six inches, his head rising above those of the two dumbfounded men who stood to either side.

To their inquiries, Home responded, "Daniel will show you how it is," and unbuttoned his coat. (He always referred to himself in third person while in a trance.) The elongation appears to have taken place from the waist upwards, Lord Adare noting that four inches of new flesh now showed between Home's waistcoat and the waistband of his trousers.

Home shrunk back to his original size, then said, "Daniel will grow tall again." And to Lord Adare's obvious amazement, he did.

Dressed in slippers, Home stalked the room, stamping his feet to show they were planted firmly on the floor, and slowly returning to his normal height. As with most of his startling feats, Home could apparently perform the height "trick" almost at will.

Mystery on Mitchell Flat

Ghost lights that haunt the same locale year after year are hardly an isolated phenomenon. At least thirty-five such sites are known in the U.S. and Canada alone. But few ghost lights can match the lore and lure of those that are said to hover over Mitchell Flat, outside the present-day town of Marfa in west Texas.

Reports of dancing globes of luminosity above the desert floor here date back at least to the time of the Mescalero Apache. One of the first white settlers in the area, Robert Ellison, saw them as early as 1883, and thought they were Indian campfires. More recently, James Dean, while filming *Giant* in Marfa in the 1950s, kept a telescope perched on a barbed-wire fence in hopes of spotting the lights.

Nowadays, when conditions are right, the lights can be seen like glowing Mexican jumping beans from a vantage point on Highway 90, about eight miles east of town. Usually they dance in the distance, midway between the highway and the Chinati Mountains, but on rare occasions they venture close enough for accurate observation.

Charles Cude, a San Antonio funeral director, was parked at the roadside pullover one night when he saw two lights that "looked like an automobile racing across, going from east to west." At the same time that Cude realized there weren't any roads out there, one of the lights suddenly shot straight up.

A few moments later, another light shot between Cude's car and the one adjacent, disappearing across the desert floor. Cude said the light appeared to be between eighteen and twenty-four inches in diameter. Its surface reminded him of pictures of the earth taken from outer space, a glowing globe covered with swirling clouds.

The False (or Real) UFOs in the Hudson Valley

The largest mass-sighting incident in UFO history began on New Year's Eve 1982, inundating the Hudson Valley in New York, and particularly Westchester and Putnam counties. By the summer of 1987, more than five thousand people had seen (and in many cases photographed and videotaped) a huge, triangular-shaped UFO outlined in lights that became known as the "Hudson Valley Boomerang."

Most of the sightings fell within the years 1983 and 1984. Motorists on the Taconic Parkway would frequently pull their cars to the side of the road staring up at a gigantic, slow-moving, silent object that many described in terms of football fields rather than feet. One stunned witness said it was as large as an aircraft carrier. Another compared it to a "flying city."

In spite of the number of authentic photographs, and reliable witnesses that included pilots, engineers, and corporate executives, skeptics rashly declared the case "solved." The culprits were supposedly a group of private pilots who, in direct violation of FAA regulations, gathered together in the evenings to scare the living daylights out of local residents. The "Martians," as they called themselves, reportedly flew their Cessnas in tight, night formations to give the illusion of a large, lighted object maneuvering overhead.

The only problem with the skeptical "solution" was that several witnesses filmed both the "Martians" and the UFO in flight, and the difference was easily distinguishable. Other witnesses said the Cessnas could plainly be heard, whereas the UFO was eerily quiet. Moreover, the huge, illuminated boomerang *hovered* over the local nuclear power plant, an acrobatic achievement that civilian Cessnas, no matter how accomplished their pilots, have yet to manage.

Finally, if the skeptics feel they've really solved the case of the Hudson Valley UFO, they are morally obligated to turn the offenders over to the authorities for proper punishment. Otherwise, we're forced to conclude that giant, unidentified flying objects lie outside the present jurisdiction of the Federal Aviation Administration.

Psychophysics and Silver Futures

Can psychic powers help predict the movement of the commodities market? That's the question recently asked by psychologist and psychic Keith Harary and physicist Russell Targ. To conduct their experiment, the researchers focused on the silver market, which is notoriously unstable and fluctuates rapidly from day to day. Several investors were willing to bet sizable sums of money on Harary's predictions.

In order to smooth the experiment and keep Harary from feeling too strained while making his predictions, the prognostications were made in a second-hand way. Every Thursday beginning September 16, 1982, Targ asked Harary to describe the object—chosen from a group of objects—that he would see the following Monday. Each of the four objects designated a particular flux in the silver market, from up a lot to down a lot.

After the psychic had given his responses, Targ would look over the target pool and decide which object Harary had described. The corresponding flux in the silver market would then be communicated to investors, who would use the information to either buy or sell.

The experiment was a striking success. Seven consecutive transactions were made based on the seven correct predictions, and the investors made $120,000 on the gamble.

Shirley MacLaine Conquers Stage Fright

In an up-and-down acting career that suddenly began to rocket, Shirley MacLaine has become a major star, a multitalented one who sings and dances as well as acts. She even won an Oscar for her performance in the hit movie, *Terms of Endearment*, but then, she knew she would. While preparing for the movie, she says, she envisioned the future events as they occurred. The movie was a hit, she won the Oscar, and then wrote a book about her psychic experiences entitled *Out on a Limb*.

Throughout her long career, MacLaine said, she had suffered from stage fright, not uncommon for actors. But she found a cure. It came after visiting an acupuncturist in the New Mexican desert. After undergoing treatment, MacLaine, like many of his clients, recalled past lives. In fact, she said, one life had been lived as an eighteenth-century court jester beheaded after one particular performance before the king. She said that in her recall experience, she could actually see the jester's head rolling on the floor.

"No wonder I had stage fright," she noted. The vision helped her work through the problem, she noted, and contributed to her future success.

Haunted TV

Many gifted psychics claim they can project images onto sealed film. But there are a few who say they can actually transmit pictures to the screen of a TV.

One of the most unusual such cases was reported by the Travis family of Blue Point, New York. The three Travis children were up early one morning watching television when they saw a face appear on the screen, obscuring the program they were trying to watch. Mrs. Travis didn't believe the story when it was reported to her, but she stopped dead in her tracks when she saw it for herself. The face seemed to be female, and it looked like a profile in silhouette. Even when the set was turned off, the silhouette remained clearly visible.

News of the "haunted" TV spread quickly throughout Blue Point. And for the next two days, dozens of people, including news reporters, photographers and TV repairmen, flocked to the house. Everyone had a theory as to how the face came to be there. Some of the witnesses, for instance, thought the profile was an electronic residue of singer Francy Lane, who had appeared on TV the day before. But this suggestion and others never panned out.

The picture finally faded fifty-one hours later, as mysteriously as it had materialized, though several photographs remain to prove the image was actually there.

Hazelnuts From the Sky

Alfred Wilson Osborne and his wife like to tell the tale of a day in March 1977 when they were showered with objects from the sky.

Osborne, a newspaper chess correspondent from Bristol, England, says he and his wife were on their way back home from church on a Sunday morning when they were barraged by several hundred hazelnuts plummeting to the ground. Over the next few minutes, the nuts banged and pinged on passing cars, the parked cars of a nearby car dealer, and passersby.

The incident was reported in the Bristol paper with no explanation. It was a nearly cloudless day, there were no nut trees on the road where the event occurred, and the objects clearly seemed to be falling from the sky.

Osborne was amazed at what he saw, but said the most amazing thing of all was that the hazelnuts, not in season until September or October, were fresh and ripe. "I have thought that it might be a vortex that sucked them up," he said, "but I don't know where you suck up hazelnuts in March."

Is the *Dutchman* Still Flying?

Of all the tales of the sea, none is ghostlier than that of *The Flying Dutchman*. The legend is based on an actual vessel, captained by a skilled but boastful seaman named Hendrik Vanderdecken, a Dutch East Indian who set sail from Amsterdam to Batavia, then a port in Dutch East India, in 1680. Though he was commissioned by a trading company to sail the company's boat and bring back a full load of cargo, Vanderdecken was certain he would bring back enough of his *own* loot to make himself rich as well.

When Vanderdecken's ship was battered by a tropical storm, legend has it, he tried every maneuver he knew to advance the ship. The safe course would have been to wait out the storm, but prodded by a challenge from the devil in a dream one night, he decided to ignore the Lord's warnings and try to steer the ship around the Cape. It soon foundered, and the crew died. For his penance, it is said, Vanderdecken was cursed to sail his ship until Judgment Day.

An exciting and romantic legend it is, but witness after witness swears it is more. In 1835 the captain and crew of a British ship saw a phantom ship approaching through a heavy storm with all sails set, which suddenly disappeared as it came dangerously close. In 1881, sailors on the British ship H.M.S. *Bacchante*, said a crew member fell from the rigging to his death the day after another midshipman saw the ghostly vision.

A more recent and highly acclaimed sighting of the *Dutchman* reportedly took place in March 1939, on Glencairn Beach in

South Africa. The day following the sighting, a newspaper carried the story of dozens of bathers watching the ship, discussing details of the vision, and noting that it was full-sailed and moving steadily, despite the lack of any wind at the time.

Some scientists explained the group sighting as a mirage. But witnesses protested that it would have been difficult for them to envision a seventeenth-century sailing vessel in such detail, since most had never even seen one.

The Staircase Ghosts

The National Maritime Museum, located in Greenwich, England, is toured by thousands of visitors each year. Many preserve their memories with photographs.

That's what the Reverend R. W. Hardy had in mind when he and his wife, touring the facility in 1966, tried to photograph one of the museum's most popular exhibits—the Tulip Staircase, originally built for Queen Anne of Denmark. Hardy waited until the rest of his tour group passed upstairs so he could get a clear shot of the staircase's metal bannister, featuring tulip designs sculpted into the ironwork.

Hardy, his wife, and officials at the museum all declared that the staircase was empty when the photo was taken. Yet when Hardy returned to his native Canada and had the film developed, two figures appeared on the stairs. Shrouded in white, they were clearly not normal humans, but ghostly apparitions. Both appeared to be walking up the stairs, one hand on the bannister, and taking no notice of the camera. A large ring was discernible on the hand of one of them.

The Reverend Hardy did not believe in ghosts, but seeking an explanation, he eventually contacted the London Ghost Club.

The club had Hardy's negatives analyzed by Kodak, where it was found the film had not been tampered with in any way. Club members also interviewed the Hardys at great length and determined they were honest and in no way trying to perpetrate a fraud or a hoax.

Eager to pursue this event, the organization soon sponsored an overnight ghost watch at the staircase, employing cameras, electronic sensors, temperature gauges, and devices to measure wind and atmospheric conditions. The investigators soon recorded a number of strange sounds, which they identified as footsteps and weeping, but collected no images on film. The apparitions, the club members concluded, were ghosts that appeared only during the daytime; the identity of the figures in the photo, they added, could not be determined.

D. D. Home: Fakir or Faker?

Daniel Douglas Home, an American who died in 1886, kept the company of princes and kings. His claim to fame? He could put himself in a trance, becoming immune to fire or intense heat. Not only could he pick up red-hot coals, but he could transfer his immunity at will to spectators, handing the coals to them with no harm done.

Sir William Crookes, then director of the British Society for Psychical Research, witnessed his feats and reported that Home took a hot coal as "big as an orange" and held it with both hands. Then he blew on the coal until it got white hot and a flame flickered above it around the man's fingers. Crookes inspected Home's hands before and after, but could find no evidence of any kind of ointment or other treatment. And he was amazed to find Home's hands soft and delicate, "like a woman's."

Lord Adare of Ireland, a frequent companion of Home's and the author of a book on his life, wrote that he once saw him put his entire face into a fire and shake it back and forth. Home also put a scalding hot coal in Adare's hand; Adare claimed he held the coal for several moments, and, he added, it barely felt warm.

Home professed other spiritual powers as well. He held countless séances and was said to be able to make objects move. Once, before three witnesses, he allegedly floated out of a second-floor window and then floated back in. Closer scrutiny showed a number of flaws in the story, including the possibility of a hidden rope or even the blackmailing of Lord Adare by threats of uncovering Adare's homosexuality.

No one, however, has ever explained Home's immunity to fire, which was witnessed by countless others time and again.

The Ghosts of Flight 401

Next to the ghosts in the White House, one of the most acclaimed and popular ghost stories of recent times is known as the Ghosts of Flight 401. Bob Loft was captain of Eastern Airlines Flight 401 the day it took off from New York to Miami on Friday, December 29, 1972. That night, the plane crashed in the Everglades, and more than 100 were killed, including Loft and Dan Repo, the flight engineer. An investigation was launched and the cause of the crash was officially listed as a combination of equipment failure and pilot error. After the investigation, salvageable parts were collected for use on other Eastern planes.

Soon after, the rumors began: Pilots and flight crews on various Eastern flights reportedly saw the ghosts of Loft and Repo, who seemed to appear most often aboard Plane Number 318. In early incidents, some flight attendants found the lower galley where food was prepared to be abnormally cold. Others had the strong feeling of someone else in the room with them when no one was there. Then, a flight engineer arrived to make his preflight inspection and saw a man in an Eastern second officer's uniform. He immediately recognized his old acquaintance, Dan Repo, who told him not to worry about the inspection because he had already taken care of it. On yet another flight, the ghost of Captain Loft was seen by a pilot and two flight attendants. Occasionally Repo or unidentified flight attendants would be seen through the glass panel on the elevator from the lower galley—and then vanish before the door opened.

An informal investigation into the stories was hampered both by an unwillingness of employees to talk, and by a reported series of missing log sheets from the plane. But investigators did eventually learn one striking fact: Many parts salvaged from Flight 401 were later used on Plane Number 318.

Photographing the Yeti

March 6, 1986, was the date when Bigfoot hunters finally got the "hard" evidence for which they had been patiently waiting. While traveling in the Himalayas, an explorer caught the yeti—Tibet's counterpart of our indigenous Bigfoot—with his camera.

Anthony Wooldridge, a British traveler, was mountain climbing near Nepal in order to study village life when he spotted the creature. He was jogging in the snow by some trees when he chanced upon some tracks. "I wondered what was sharing the wood with me," he said, "but could think of no satisfactory explanation. I took two quick photographs of the tracks and pressed on knowing that time was precious if I was to reach my destination before the snow became too soft. Perhaps half an hour later, as I emerged above the tree line, there was a sudden bang followed by protracted rumbling."

The explorer was continuing up the slopes to better evaluate the risk when he spied the Abominable Snowman by some shrubbery. "Standing behind the shrubs," explains Wooldridge, "was a large, erect shape up to two meters tall." Convinced that whatever it was it would disappear quickly, Wooldridge took several photographs. It didn't take long, he said, "to the realization that the only animal remotely resembling the one in front of me was the yeti."

Wooldridge later submitted the photos to the International Society for Cryptozoology, which investigates reports of strange or unknown animals. Since that time, his best photograph has been published in *BBC Wildlife*, causing more than a little controversy. *BBC Wildlife* first sent the photograph to Dr. Robert D. Martin, a physical anthropologist at University College, University of London. Martin noted that the creature *could* have been a Hanuman langur, though langurs are generally smaller than the creature in the photograph, and they have tails. Similar observations have been puzzling anthropologist John Napier, a well-known Bigfoot skeptic who also examined the photograph. The possibility that Wooldridge really did photograph a previously unknown life form, says Dr. Napier, "is remarkable but quite logical."

Remembrance of a Former Life and Death

Hypnotists often take adult subjects back to childhood. Many mesmerists have also taken the regression further, using hypnotism to help subjects trace former lives.

English hypnotist Henry Blythe, for instance, began experimenting with a woman named Naomi Henry, from Exeter. Under hypnosis, Henry claimed she was an eighteenth-century Irish farm woman named Mary Cohen. Cohen described her entire life, including her youth, her stressful marriage to a violent farmer, and even her death.

Blythe's subject described her last moment, a point past pain, when suddenly she became silent. Blythe watched in panic as the color left the woman's face. Soon she had stopped breathing and he could find no pulse. "You are safe," he kept repeating. Finally, after several seconds, her pulse returned and she began breathing again. Slowly, she returned to normal.

Everyone was relieved, and Blythe later reported that Henry had told him of another life as an English girl in the early 1900s.

The Unhappy Times of Black Gold

A famous thoroughbred named Black Gold won many a dollar for bettors, owners, and jockeys, but a trail of misfortune followed the colt from its first day of life. Born "under the light" of a comet, the horse was branded a bad omen by owner H. M. Hoots, who caught pneumonia that very night and then died.

Black Gold himself nonetheless became a winner, overcoming the pain of a weak left foreleg to be an entrant in the 1924 Kentucky Derby. The horse won at ten-to-one odds, but the bookies made off with the betting money and no one got paid. Some time later, J. D. Mooney, Black Gold's jockey, gained so much weight that he was dismissed, and the trainer was also fired for allowing the horse to overwork his bad leg. The stable agent, Waldo Freeman, thought he had beaten the curse when he won bets in three big races, but he died of a heart attack before the day was over. Perhaps the worst fate hit Black Gold himself when he was put out to stud late in 1924. He was found to be sterile.

The Unlucky Sevens of Captain McLoed

Captain Hugh McDonald McLoed became a captain when he was nineteen years old, but it was the sinister number "7" that seemed to figure prominently in his life. And well it should, for he was the seventh son of a seventh son.

Hailing from a sailing family, McLoed had two brothers who were also captains. In fact, on December 7, 1909, his siblings set sail as captain and first mate on the steamer *Marquette & Bessemer No. 2*, bound for Port Stanley, Ontario. But the steamer never made it. The ship and its entire crew disappeared. Four months later, on April 7, Hugh was notified that his brother, John, had been found, his body encased in ice in the Niagara River. On October 7, 1910, his other brother's body was washed up onto shore at Long Point.

Four years later on April 7, 1914, Captain McLoed, then skipper of a whaleback steamer named the *John Ericsson*, was towing a barge down Lake Huron. The fog was so thick he couldn't see the ship being towed—the *Alexander Holly*—at all. But he finally caught sight of the *Holly*'s flag flying at half-mast. He slowed his ship down and pulled in the tow line, only to learn that the barge's captain had been washed overboard—the day before.

It should be no surprise that McLoed finally retired from his command on December 6, 1941, at the same time the Japanese were bombing Pearl Harbor, on December 7, across the International Date Line.

Curse of King Tut's Tomb

Though the great pyramids of Egypt stood intact and untouched for centuries, by the early 1920s many of the structures and tombs of the pharaohs had been plundered by looting archaeologists and treasure-seekers.

One tomb, however, remained intact: that of the now famous Tutankhamen, or "King Tut." Legend had it that the tomb was guarded by a curse dooming anyone who entered to death. But that didn't stop George E.S.M. Herbert, fifth Earl of Carnarvon, who first went to Egypt hoping that the dry climate would ease his troubled breathing.

Though Herbert had no background in archaeology, he had the money to sponsor expeditions. And before long, he and archaeologist Howard Carter had set out to find the fabled tomb.

After several digs over many years, they finally found some fragments of pieces bearing the name of Tutankhamen. And the pieces led them to the gold-laden, treasure-filled room housing the long-sought Tutankhamen.

A party of twenty stood witness as Carter made his way into that room on February 17, 1923, but Lord Carnarvon hardly lived to relish the find. He died in April in the Hotel Continental in Cairo, after suddenly contracting an undiagnosed high fever that racked his body off and on for twelve days. Within minutes of his death, there was a power failure in Cairo. And Carnarvon's dog, at home in London, died that same day.

Before the year was out, twelve others out of the original party of twenty were dead. But others would die, too. George Jay

Gould, son of financier Jay Gould and a friend of Carnarvon's, came to Egypt after his friend's death to see the site for himself. He died of bubonic plague within twenty-four hours of visiting the tomb.

By 1929, sixteen others who somehow came in contact with the mummy had died as well. Victims included radiologist Archibald Reid, who had prepared the Tutankhamen remains for x-raying; the wife of Lord Carnarvon; and Richard Bethell, his personal secretary. Even Bethell's father died, taking his life by his own hand.

The mystique of this famous mummy, renowned in grade-B horror films, was probably a large factor in the overwhelming success of the United States tour of the Treasures of King Tutankhamen. But as the tens of thousands who saw the mummy can attest, the curse seems ended, at least for now.

But the others who entered the tomb certainly had occasion to remember, while they lived, the hieroglyphics written on the seal at the entrance: "Death will come on swift wings to he who violates the tomb of the Pharaoh."

Miracle at Remiremont

Remiremont, a small French town close to the German border, contained a statue of the Virgin Mary called *Notre Dame du Trésor*. Presented to Remiremont in the eighth century, the statue had long been considered the town's protector and every year since 1682 it had been paraded through the streets during a special ceremony in its honor.

But in 1907 the statue became the center of a heated dispute: When the Pope gave the ceremony his official sanction, anti-Catholic forces within the town gave vent to violent protest. City officials were so intimidated by the threats that the ceremony was canceled and no public procession took place for the first time in centuries.

It seemed like divine retribution when a fierce and sudden hailstorm struck Remiremont on May 16, shortly after the procession was to have been held. Some of the stones were the size of tomatoes and didn't break upon hitting the ground. Others, according to reports, were actually impressed with the likeness of the *Notre Dame du Trésor*.

A detailed description of the stones was even placed on record by the Abbe Gueniot, a local priest: "I saw very distinctly on the front of the hailstones, which were slightly convex in the center, although the edges were somewhat worn, the bust of a woman, with a robe that was turned up at the bottom, like a priest's cope," he wrote. "The outline of the images was slightly hollow, but very boldly drawn."

The figure found on the stones, however, represented only one miraculous outcome of the storm. Those special hailstones, townsfolk reported, fell at the same time that other, normal ones plunged to the ground. But they seemed to fall slowly, as though floating to earth, and did no damage to anything at all.

The Case of Renata

Czech psychiatrist Stanislov Grof, an expert on hallucinogens, currently works at America's famous Esalen Institute in Big Sur. But before he left his homeland, he treated a self-destructive young housewife named Renata.

Grof asked his patient to recall her painful past with the help of LSD, and before long, she began to report scenes from seventeenth-century Prague. She correctly described the architecture, dress, and weaponry of the period. She had vivid memories of Bohemia's invasion by the Austrian Empire of the Hapsburgs. And she even described the beheading of a young nobleman by the Hapsburgs.

Grof tried to understand the visions with every therapeutic tool at his disposal, but could find no psychological explanation at all. He left for the United States before the case could be resolved. But two years later he received a letter from his former patient. It turned out that Renata had encountered her estranged father, whom she hadn't seen since early childhood. During their talks, she learned that her father had traced their family line back to the seventeenth century—to a nobleman beheaded by the Hapsburgs during their occupation of what is now Czechoslovakia.

Just how Renata came to "recall" this information remains a mystery, since her father apparently made these discoveries after leaving his family. Renata believes her impressions emerged from some form of "inherited" memory. Grof himself contends that Renata's memories stem from a past life in Prague.

Gypsy Curse

For years, legend has it, the Epsom Derby was plagued by a curse, courtesy of a gypsy woman named Gypsy Lee. One year, it seems, the gypsy had predicted that a horse named Blew Gown would win the derby, and she wrote her prediction down on a piece of paper for all to see. One of the owners at the track, however, haughtily pointed out that the horse was named Blue Gown, not spelled with a "w" at all. Bristling at the thought of looking foolish, Gypsy Lee issued a curse: No horse with a "w" in its name would win the Epsom Derby, she decreed, as long as she lived. And none ever did. But when Gypsy died in 1934, her mourning family bet all they could on Windsor Lad, and the horse won, paying seven-to-one.

Rasputin's Murder Foretold

"Count" Louis Harmon was best known by his stage name of Cheiro. A celebrated clairvoyant and palm reader, he was widely courted by royalty and other notables earlier this century for his amazingly accurate readings.

In 1905, for example, in the course of a meeting with the controversial Mad Monk of Russia, Cheiro warned Rasputin of the fate that awaited him. "I foresee for you a violent end within the palace," he said. "You will be menaced by poison, by knife, and by bullet. Finally, I see the icy waters of the Neva closing above you."

Rasputin's subsequent checkered career as spiritual guide for Tsar Nicholas II and his family certainly earned him enemies in Russia's royal court. Still, he was not suspicious when Prince Felix Yusupov invited him to his palace for dinner the night of December 29, 1916, promising him an assignation with a lady of the court who wished to meet him. Refusing wine and tea, Rasputin munched instead on pieces of cake the prince had laced with cyanide. Yusupov was startled to see the monk consume several pieces without ill effect.

The prince then drew a pistol and shot Rasputin in the back. While he was leaning over the body, Rasputin's eyes flew open and a desperate struggle ensued. Other plotters came to the prince's rescue, a conspirator named Purishkevich pumping two more bullets into Rasputin's body. Yusupov then battered the fallen "monk" with a steel bar.

Prince and helpers tied Rasputin's arms and carried his seemingly lifeless body down to the Neva. Breaking a hole in the ice, they pushed his body into the river, but Rasputin came to life again. His last act was to make the sign of the cross with one hand. Then he slipped beneath the icy waters, fulfilling Cheiro's prophecy and one of his own.

Before his murder Rasputin had warned the royal family: "If I am killed by common assassins you have nothing to fear. But if I am murdered by nobles, and if they shed my blood, their hands will remain soiled. Brothers will kill brothers and there will be no nobles in the country."

Within the year the Bolsheviks mounted the Russian Revolution. On July 16, 1917, the Tsar and his family were murdered at Ekaterinburg. And the nobles found that to remain in Russia was highly dangerous to one's health.

Lightning Balls

At five minutes after midnight, Eastern Airlines Flight 539 was over New York City, bound for Washington, D.C. The night was moonless and dark, with thunderstorms roaming the eastern seaboard. Suddenly the plane was enveloped by an electrical discharge.

Passenger Roger Jennison, a professor of electronics from Kent University, was even more startled to see "a glowing sphere a little more than twenty centimeters in diameter emerge from the pilot's cabin and pass down the aisle of the aircraft." Jennison described the light ball as blue-white in color and seemingly solid. It moved at about the same pace as a person would walk, at a height of about seventy-five centimeters off the floor.

Fortunately, no one was injured in the incident, and the plane managed to land safely at its destination. Such balls of light *have* been known to explode on occasion, frequently with devastating results.

Scientists call the elusive phenomenon "ball lightning," but that hardly explains it since lightning itself still holds so many mysteries for physicists. One curious theory, however, was put forward by researchers M. D. Altschuler, L. House, and E. Hildner of the National Center for Atmospheric Research at Boulder, Colorado. The trio theorized that thunderstorms might act like giant natural particle accelerators capable of emitting protons charged with enormous energy. When the charged protons collide with atomic nuclei in the atmosphere, a mini-nuclear reaction generates highly charged atoms of oxygen and fluorine. In turn, these decaying atoms would emit both positrons and gamma rays—plenty of energy, in other words, to power ball lightning.

If the theory is correct, it means that close encounter victims of ball lightning may have another problem to worry about: namely, a lethal dose of radiation.

Seven Times Seven

When the late Arthur Koestler published *The Roots of Coincidence*, a study of curious synchronicities in time and place, he was bombarded by letters from people who had had similar experiences.

The most consistently coincidental of all probably came from Anthony S. Clancy of Dublin, Ireland, who was born on the seventh day of the seventh month of the seventh year of the century, which also happened to be the seventh day of the week. "I was the seventh child of a seventh child," he wrote, "and I have seven brothers; that makes seven sevens."

Actually, it makes eight sevens if one counts the number of letters in his first name, but to continue: On his twenty-seventh birthday, according to Clancy, he went to the track. The seventh numbered horse in the seventh race was named Seventh Heaven, and was handicapped seven stone. The odds against Seventh Heaven were seven-to-one, but Clancy bet seven shillings anyway.

Seventh Heaven finished seventh.

Vice Versa

Allan Falby was a motorcycle captain with the El Paso, Texas, County Highway Patrol in the 1930s when a collision with a speeding truck almost ended his career. His life was slowly seeping out a severed artery in his leg when a passerby, Alfred Smith, stopped to render aid. Smith tied off the bleeding leg and Falby survived, although it was several months before he was fully recovered and able to resume his duties.

Five years later it was Falby who arrived at the scene of another accident in the area. A man had crashed his car into a tree and was bleeding profusely from a severed artery in his right leg. Before the ambulance arrived Falby was able to tie off a tourniquet and save the man's life. Only then did he realize that the victim was his own savior of five years before—Alfred Smith.

Falby took the incident in professional stride. "It all goes to prove," he said, "that one good tourniquet deserves another."

Fireflies

The Victorians, known for their sense of adventure, often encountered things in their world travels that still remain unexplained. In 1895, for example, while exploring the Niger Protectorate and Gabon region of Africa, Mary Kingsley camped on Lake Ncovi between the Ogowe and Rembwe rivers.

In her book, *Travels in West Africa*, Kingsley told how she set out alone in her canoe one night to take a bath. "Down through the forest on the lake bank opposite," she wrote, "came a violet ball the size of a small orange. When it reached the sand beach it hovered along it to and fro close to the ground."

Within a matter of minutes the violet ball of light was joined by a similarly colored companion that approached from behind one of the islets. The two small globes of light then proceeded to play a game of tag, darting at and circling around one another.

Kingsley beached her boat nearby, but one of the lights vanished in the bushes and the other set out across the lake. Following in her canoe, Kingsley was amazed when the violet apparition suddenly sank beneath the surface of the lake. "I could see it glowing," she said, "until it vanished in the depths."

The intrepid Kingsley thought the phenomenon might be a rare species of luminous insect. But the natives she interviewed referred to it as an *aku*, or devil. Whether devil or insect or even swamp gas, the phenomenon remains unexplained.

The Man Wouldn't Hang

Standing on the steps of the scaffold erected for his execution, John Lee was asked by the hangman if he had any last words. "No," he said. "Drop away."

The date was February 23, 1885, and Lee was about to hang for the murder of his employer, Emma Ann Keyes of Exeter, England, who had been found with her throat cut and head battered with a hatchet. Now justice was about to be served. The hangman slipped a sack over Lee's head and tightened the noose around his neck. Then he gave the signal to drop the trapdoor. Nothing happened.

The noose was removed from Lee's neck, and the trapdoor mechanism examined for defects. Nothing wrong could be found, so the prisoner was put in place again. Again the order was given, and again the trapdoor failed to release. This time the edges of the door were planed to assure a loose fit. But for a third and finally a fourth time, the trapdoor refused to drop.

Baffled, the sheriff returned Lee to his cell. His case quickly made the headlines and even the House of Commons joined in the debate about what to do with "the man they couldn't hang." Eventually, Lee's sentence was commuted to life in prison. After twenty-two years behind bars, the luckiest man alive was released on parole in December 1907.

Lee lived at least another thirty-five years, and is thought to have died in London about 1943. Although his miraculous escape from the hangman's noose was frequently resurrected by reporters of the odd and unusual, no satisfactory explanation for the faulty trapdoor was ever found.

The Learjet to Jeddah?

Most mysteries fall into clear-cut categories, whether it is UFOs, lake monsters, Bigfoot, or puckish poltergeists. On occasion, however, something so strange and bizarre occurs that it establishes a new category all its own. This certainly seems to be the case with the disappearance—and discovery—of a Learjet that was lost over the Egyptian Desert southwest of Cairo.

The jet was presumed missing on August 11, 1979, when it left Athens, bound for Jeddah, but failed to arrive. Aboard were the jet's owner, Lebanese shipbuilder Ali El-din al-Bahri, Swedish oil expert Peter Seime, Theresa Drake, and two pilots. The plane was tracked on several radars, and had an estimated four hours flying time left in its tanks when it was last contacted by Cairo air controllers. No distress call was heard.

But the Lear never arrived at Jeddah. Egyptian and Saudi Arabian air forces both mounted an extensive search along the plane's flight path, but no wreckage was spotted. Al-Bahri's family spent an additional $1.5 million hiring private searchers who roamed as far afield as Kenya. Still, no Learjet was found.

In February 1987, however, a team of archaeologists stumbled across the lost plane, 270 miles southwest of Cairo. The fuselage was intact, and there was no sign of fire, though one wing was a mile from the main site. Bedouins had apparently found the jet a couple of years earlier and stripped its interior.

At first glance there were no human remains aboard. Closer inspection, however, revealed crushed, almost powdered, human bones piled on the aircraft's floor. The largest, said Theresa Drake's father, Tom, was "no bigger than a thumb."

Professor Michael Day, an osteologist at London's Saint Thomas Hospital, thought the bones should have been almost intact. "In eight years they would certainly not have begun to disintegrate. Even wild animals would not have left such tiny fragments," Day said.

Australia's Yowie

The Himalayas have their yeti. And in Australia, shaggy apelike creatures are known as yowie. In fact, according to local naturalist Rex Gilroy, the Blue Mountain area west of Sydney is home to more than 3,000 historical sightings of such creatures.

In December 1979, Leo and Patricia George ventured into the region, located in eastern Australia, in search of a quiet picnic spot. Their Sunday soiree was suddenly shattered when they came across the carcass of a mutilated kangaroo. Moreover, said the couple, the apparent perpetrator of the mutilation was only a scant forty feet away. They described a creature covered with hair, and "at least ten feet tall," that stopped to stare back at them before finally lumbering off into the brush.

The picnic was quickly canceled, but Gilroy still has plans to mount an expedition of his own in search of the legendary beast.

Plague of Defense Deaths

Between March and June 1987, the British press reverberated with a series of seemingly unrelated deaths that struck individual scientists involved in the defense industry. There were ten incidents in all, including eight suspicious suicides, a disappearance, and one case in which the victim survived a sixty-foot fall. Five of the victims were employees of Marconi, an electronics company with many government defense contracts, and several others had ties to programs involving the Stingray torpedo and nuclear submarine countermeasures.

The first incident actually occurred on August 5, 1986, when a Stingray software specialist jumped to his death from the Clifton suspension bridge in Bristol. Vimal Dajibhai was only twenty-four, and had no apparent motive for driving from London to Bristol to commit suicide. Press reports said that small puncture marks were found on his buttocks.

On October 28, 1986, another Marconi employee, Ashad Sharif, twenty-six, reportedly killed himself on Siston Commons, Bristol, by tying a rope to a tree, looping it around his neck, and driving off. He, too, had driven up from London. On January 8, 1987, a friend of Dajibhai's, working for the Ministry of Defense on a sonar project, disappeared while on an outing at a Derbyshire reservoir.

Four days earlier, a Marconi computer consultant, Richard Pugh, had been found with a plastic bag over his head. The same month a Royal Armaments computer consultant died of carbon monoxide poisoning. Carbon monoxide also took the life of Peter Peapell, forty-six, on February 22, 1987. Peapell had been a specialist in Soviet beryllium technology, a metal crucial to nuclear reactors.

On March 30, 1987, David Sands committed suicide by loading cans of gasoline into his sports car and driving it at high speed into an abandoned restaurant. Wife and colleagues reported that Sands had been "acting strangely" prior to his successful suicide.

On April 24 of the same year, Mark Wisner, a twenty-five-year-old Royal Air Force software designer, was also found dead with a plastic bag wrapped over his head. He was wearing a woman's corset and boots at the time of his death. Another defense-related scientist, Victor Moore, is said to have killed himself with a drug overdose. Robert Greenhaigh, forty-six, a Marconi employee, survived a sixty-foot leap from a Maidenhead railway bridge when he landed in soft grass. Greenhaigh had been a friend of alleged double agent Dennis Skinner, with whom he worked for fifteen years. Skinner was said to have been pushed from a Moscow flat to his death in 1983.

Such a string of suicides and defense-industry related deaths seems to stretch the definition of coincidence. Now that man has brought hostilities into the heavens, via Star Wars, perhaps the heavens have decided to fight back.

The Min Min Lights

For more than a century a ghostly luminous phenomenon has haunted the remote outback east of Boulia, in southwest Queensland, Australia. The lights are named after a combination post office and pub called Min Min, which has long since crumbled to dust. But the lights continue to perplex the casual and curious alike.

One of the first written accounts, published in March 1941, tells of a stockman who was traveling between Boulia and Warenda Station one cloudy night. About 10 P.M., as he passed the old cemetery left over from Min Min's wilder days, he spied a strange glow emanating from the middle of the graveyard. The light swelled to the size of a watermelon, hovered momentarily above the tombstones, then moved off in the direction of Boulia. According to the stockman, the light followed him all the way into town.

Earlier reports subsequently surfaced, however. In *Walkabout*, Henry Lamond recounted his own childhood experience with the Min Min lights in 1912. At first he thought it was headlights of an approaching automobile. "Cars," he said, "though they were not common, were not rare." But it quickly became evident that this was no normal light. "It remained in one bulbous ball," Lamond noted, "instead of dividing into two headlights as it should have done. And it floated too high for any car. There was something eerie about it."

The light floated gradually toward Lamond, who was on horseback, until it passed by him, about 200 yards away. "Suddenly," he said, "it just faded and died away. It did not go out with a snap. Its vanishing was more like the gradual fading of the wires in an electric bulb."

The Min Min light—whatever it is—still startles people who travel along on lonely stretches of road in the Australian outback.

Ghost Lights

The Welsh called them "corpse candles," and associated the ghostly globules of dancing light with impending death. They have also been called ghost lights, jack-o'-lanterns, and will-o'-the-wisps.

In his book, *British Goblins*, Wirt Sikes, a former U.S. consul to Wales, collected several eyewitness accounts of such mystery lights, including one in which the passengers of a coach between Llandilo and Carmathen saw three pale lights as they crossed a river bridge at Golden Grove. Three men drowned at the same spot a few days later, when their small boat capsized.

John Aubrey, author of *Miscellanies*, recounted the tale of a woman who said she saw five lights hovering in the newly plastered room of the house in which she worked. A fire was lit to dry the walls, she said, and five other workers subsequently died from fumes.

Other firsthand stories of ghost lights can be found in William Corliss's encyclopedic collection, *Lightning, Auroras and Nocturnal Lights*. One particularly haunting tale comes from a Lincoln, England, man who was riding horseback in the spring of 1913. In the course of his outing, he said, "a jack-o'-lantern caught my attention, proceeding in the same direction as I was traveling. Its motion was irregular, sometimes near the surface, and then suddenly, rising to the height of five or six feet.

"I followed very cautiously for some distance, being determined, if possible, to obtain a near view of my luminous guide. As the night was rather dark, I had everything favorable for observation.

"At length it rested just at an angle in the road. I dismounted in hope of capturing it. But by this time I was disappointed. For, on my near approach, whether from the noise I made, or some other cause, it suddenly rose from its resting place, about two feet from the ground, cleared a high bank, and pursued its course in a direct line over the adjoining fields.

"The broad and deep dikes rendered pursuit fruitless. But my eyes followed its almost butterfly motion till the glimmering taper was lost in the distance."

The Sheep With the Golden Teeth

George Veripoulos, a Greek Orthodox priest living in Athens, was in for a surprise in 1985 when he sat down to eat a dish of kefalaki—boiled sheep head. He was just about to enjoy his repast, given to him by his sister, when he noticed something strange. The sheep's bottom teeth were filled with gold.

The priest took the head to a jeweler, who confirmed that the teeth were filled with gold worth about $4,500. The priest next reported the strange find to his brother-in-law, Nicos Kotsovos, who immediately checked the rest of the flock—all four hundred sheep. None of them had similar teeth. A local veterinarian was consulted, but he, too, remained baffled by the golden teeth. Finally even the Greek Ministry of Agriculture was called in to the bizarre case. A veterinarian/spokesman for the ministry later told reporters, "There is also gold in the jawbone. How do you explain that? I can't. I'm completely baffled."

Everyone else was baffled, too. But in Athens, the local farmers have begun checking their sheep's mouths very carefully.

This Is Where We Came In

After the first atomic bomb was tested in Alamogordo in 1945, the site of the explosion was found to be covered with a floor of fused green glass, sand transformed into glass by the blast.

Several years after the end of World War II, scientists happened to be digging in the vicinity of Babylon, the once great metropolis of Mesopotamia and presumed site of the Tower of Babel. For the purpose of ascertaining how far down the layers of ruins and artifacts extended, archaeologists dug an experimental mine shaft straight down to catalog their discoveries by epochs.

They dug below the era of great ancient ruins, and through an earlier city buried under layers of flood loess. Then farther down, they found villages indicating an agrarian culture. Still farther down, they discovered settlements of a hunting and herding culture with even more primitive artifacts. The excavation came to an end when, underneath the preceding layers, a solid floor of fused glass was encountered.

About the Author

CHARLES BERLITZ was born in New York City. He is a graduate of Yale University and a grandson of Maximillian Berlitz, founder of the Berlitz Language Schools. He speaks twenty-five languages with varying degrees of fluency and is considered one of the fifteen most eminent linguists in the world. His interest in archaeology and underwater exploration led to his writing *The Bermuda Triangle*, *Atlantis: The Eighth Continent* and *The Lost Ship of Noah*. Mr. Berlitz was awarded the Dag Hammarskjöld International Prize for Nonfiction. He lives in Florida.